CIVILIZATION

Hinduism, Buddhism & Vedic Religion

CIVILIZATION

Hinduism, Buddhism & Vedic Religion

Dr Chandrika Singh
Dr Suraj Singh Sisodiya

Manas Publications
(We Convert Fighters into Writers)
New Delhi - 110 002 (INDIA)

MANAS PUBLICATIONS
(We Convert Fighters into Writers)
(Publishers, Library Suppliers, Importers & Exporters)
4402/5-A, Ansari Road (Opp. HDFC Bank)
Darya Ganj, New Delhi - 110 002 (India)
Phones: Off.: 011-23260783, 23265523, Res.: 011-23842660
E-mail: manaspublications@gmail.com
manaspublications@yahoo.com
Website: www.manaspublications.in

ISBN 978-81-7049-544-4

₹ 995.00

Designed at
Manas Publications

Printed in India at
R.K. Print Service, Delhi
and published by Mrs Suman Lata for
Manas Publications, 4402/5-A,
Ansari Road (Opp HDFC Bank),
Darya Ganj, New Delhi - 110002 (INDIA)

Preface

Vedas means knowledge and knowledge is immortal. It is scientifically accepted universal fact that knowledge is the basic source of creation of the universe. The facts mentioned in the Vedas and the associated literature are permanent, eternal and unchangeable. Vedic knowledge is eternal and ultimate truth of the universe, law of universe, and understanding of creatures. Hindu civilization that is also known as Sanatana Dharma is closely as well as reciprocally related to Indian ancient Vedas is as old as Vedic religious philosophy. The Vedas which are four in number came into existence not in a particular period of time. It is impossible to trace out the origin of the Vedas. The *Vedic Hymns* which are the product of great Indian Meditators' mind are called Rishis and Munis. To understand the Vedas and grasp their actual philosophical as well as religious aspects, later on, some more literature, such as the *Vedantas* including the *Brahmanas*, *Aranyakas*, *Upanishads*, *Puranas*, *Gita*, *Ramayana*, *Mahabharata* etc, were developed by a number of great ancient Indian thinkers, authors, meditators and poets who played a vital role to expand and explain Vedic knowledge. These Vedic Scriptures left everlasting influence upon the Indo-Aryans and paved the fertile ground for growth and expansion of Hindu civilization. Vedic literature was developed in India by Aryan scholars and thinkers who migrated from Central Asia towards West South Indian subcontinent and where they permanently settled occupying different terrains and tracks of North-West India. The Aryans gradually adopted established Vedic way of life and this way Vedic religion became their source of philosophy, religion, morality, ethics and thinking as well as living.

As Hindu's philosophical religion is the product of Vedic philosophy, Hindu civilization cannot be understood properly without understanding of the Vedas and Vedanta. Each and every aspect of Hindu's culture and civilization is rooted in Vedic Philosophy.

The Hindu's way of thinking and living is Vedic. As Vedic is original, real and universal truth, Hindus as per their literary resources maintain all their aspects of human knowledge. It is not only true but universal, humanitarian, morally adoptable, religiously useful and philosophically highest. That way the Indian knowledge related to the entire universe, civilization, morality etc, is highly useful to one side and greatly inspirational to another side. The teachings of the *Vedas* by holy and spiritual personalities from the time immemorial, are still brightening like the Sun and the Moon in the Universe of knowledge and philosophy. Hindu civilization comprises unchangeable Godly truth, universal reality, moral values, universal brotherhood and humanitarian thinking. Like-mindedness, kindness and love for all living creatures, hatred for inhumanity, cruelty, theft and inclination as well as involvement in truthful life, sacrifice, simplicity and service to needy creatures, protection of environment etc, are the features of Vedic religion and Hindu civilization.

The authors have applied all possible efforts to make the book more resourceful, authentic and informative about Vedic values and Hindu civilization. Relevant material have been collected from different reliable as well as authentic sources, and facts have been scientifically examined, analysed and explained. However, satisfaction of the readers would be a great reward for the authors.

Dr Chandrika Singh
Dr Suraj Singh Sisodiya

Acknowledgements

While researching the present work we came across several scholars and authorities who helped us to sharpen our angle and correct our attitude. We express our heartfelt gratitude to each of them. First of all, we would like to express our gratitude to Almighty God who, being invisible, provided us with the wisdom and understanding to write such an authentic book. We are thankful to many friends in the academic field, who on reading our article titled 'Religion in the Grip of Misconception' published in the *University Newsletter*, encouraged us to present a book explaining the meaning and scope of religion, discussing various resources of religion. We are very much obliged to Prof Arun Kumar, Professor of Ancient Indian History, Magadh University, Bodhgaya. Prof Kumar spared a lot of his precious time to sit with us and discuss historical facts, related to religious philosophies of India. We are grateful to Prof Ram Sakal Singh, Professor of Political Science, Magadh University, Bodhgaya, for his cooperation in researching material to complete the book. We are thankful to Prof Mithlesh Kumar, Professor of Economics, Nagaland Central University, Lumami, who kept up our courage as well as our morale, which enabled us to go ahead and present the book. We would also like to thank personalities like Prof Prabhakar Chaudhry, Professor of Mathematics, Prof Deo Nandan Prasad, Professor of Chemistry and Prof Shashi Bhusan Prasad, Professor of Physics, all from Magadh University, Bodhgaya. They, while participating in discussions related to Aryan religion and the concept of God, contributed their views which helped us to develop the concept, related to scientific understanding and critical analysis of facts and figures. Lastly, we express our gratitude to Manas Publications and all those authorities and persons who assisted us to write the book and give it a final shape.

Dr Chandrika Singh
Dr Suraj Singh Sisodia

Contents

1

Introduction

India has been a land of metaphysical prosperity, philosophical insight, religious as well as ritual performances and a place for divine incarnation. A number of renowned rishis, maharishis, munis, seers, saints, philosophers, thinkers, social reformers and poets of eminence have been born in India whose contributions in the field of religion, philosophy, astrology, science and fundamental social values, from time to time, have attracted great philosophers and thinkers of the world. Vedantic philosophy reflected in various Vedantic literature established global reputation. In course of time, the vast treasure of knowledge popularly known as Vedantic Darshan became the lifeline of Hindus. No doubt, Hinduism, in course of time, tilted towards Brahminical cult of ritualism, ultimately paved the way for the growth of blind religious faith and superstitions. A notable fact of Hinduism is that it never remained inimical to other religions. That is why religions like Buddhism, Jainism, Islamism, Sikhism, Christianity, etc, availed the supportive circumstances to grow and prosper in India. India is known as Deva Bhumi (land of gods) because divine personalities like Lord Rama, Sri Krishna, Mahavira, Gautam Buddha, etc, were born here who taught the world the lessons of humanity, morality, way of life, and means of achieving happiness and eternal bliss in life.

The Indo-Aryans, who migrated to India from Central Asia, making India their permanent abode, were sensitive, inquisitive and foresighted. In India, highest philosophy of Vedanta related to transcendentalism which saw the emergence of Absolute Truth is still the root of eternal Hindu Dharma. Various religious scriptures like the *Vedas*, *Srutis*, *Smritis*, *Brahmanas*, *Puranas*, *Upanishads*,. *Bhagavad Gita*, *Ramayana*, *Mahabharata*, etc, were emanated from the philosophy of Vedanta. The philosophy of Vedanta, in nutshell, talks the Absolute Reality that is eternal, omnipotent, omnipresent, all pervasive, all powerful and the final abode of origin and demolition of everything in the creation of the mundane world of ours.

Vedanta basically is related to the concept of God, soul and humanity at large. The creation (world), according to Vedantic philosophy is nothing but a reflection of the supreme energy of the all-pervasive Absolute *Brahman*. When we talk of the soul we mean the soul which is an integral particle of God that is immortal, illuminative, energetic, stable, as pure as God and which is the base as well as the primary cause of creation. It is neither born nor does it die because it is eternal.

Vedic religion and Hindu civilization is old and ancient, but with the arrival of the British in India and with the establishment of their rule over the country, further investigations into India's past began. Orientalists or Ideologists took deep interest in discovering India's ancient history. As a result, several European scholars like Max Muller, Mill, etc, learnt the Sanskrit language, the language in which the Vedas and related scriptures were produced. They made the Vedas and other Vedic literature as their main area of study, and their focus of study remained mostly confined to understanding India's ancient religious scriptures and investigations into the social and economic aspects of ancient Indian civilizations.

These European scholars had arrived in India to participate in the administration of the East India Company. As administrators of India, they required a specialized knowledge about past and present India which inevitably led them to study the literature in Sanskrit and Persian. The study of Sanskrit language and literature not only gave shape to the discipline of comparative philology, but also became the source material for the reconstruction of ancient Indian society. Vedic Sanskrit, the language of Vedic literature in particular, was used extensively in the reconstruction of both Indian and Indo-European society. It was these foreign authors who, having the knowledge of Sanskrit, interpreted ancient Indian society without having proper knowledge and understanding of India and her people. It was these scholars who developed the theory of the Aryan race. While developing the theory in this regard their attitude and angle both did not remain impartial and free from the views of racial superiority. They were biased about European racial superiority. They were not at all ready to accept Indo-Aryans as a superior race despite rich philosophical literature of ancient India.

Historical Background of Indo-Aryans

A pertinent question which sought satisfactory answers to decide who the Indo-Aryans were, and what root did they belong to. In that respect another question may be raised here as to who are the Hindus. Are they descendants of the Indo-Aryans? To answer such questions the need was felt to investigate into the ancient history of the Aryans who, in due course of time, came to be known as Hindus. HS Spencer hypothesized that Aryans originally lived in the North Polar Region and that they were compelled to leave their original habitat due to onset of the Ice Age and to migrate southward around 10,000 BC. He writes, "Even those migrating Aryans had by then developed such a high state of civilization and culture that they were able to face and conquer the other races in course of time to establish their sway over the whole of Asia and Europe." The Aryans believed and adored deities representing the various aspects of natural phenomena, no doubt, but above all, they subscribed to a system of religious meditation which may be described as 'stellar worship.'

The study of India's ancient literature makes it absolutely obvious that the Indo-Aryans were intelligent, industrious, smart and powerful race from the very beginning. They established their own social system, political order, cultural ethos, economic organizations and religious ways. The history of Hinduism is, in a way, the history of Aryanism. When they entered into the territory of north-western India, crossing the mountainous regions, they faced the indigenous people who were treated by them as uncivilized. Dasgupta says that "The Aryans were savage to the aborigines, the children of the soil, when they were not ready to be their bonded slaves." The Aryans tried to maintain their superiority. They were proud of having documented history, religion, science, literature, language, social as well as apolitical philosophies, etc. It were the aborigines who came to be known as non-Aryans, and later on some of them availed the status of Shudras.

It appears that the *Rigveda*, being the most ancient literature, served as the basic source of information regarding origin of society and civilization, both in India and in the European countries. The village community of Vedic history was looked upon as the earliest survival of a common past. Observing the Hindus' base of rural society, James Mill is of the view that ancient Indian society was static, retrogressive and conducive to economic backwardness. But Hegel dismissed ancient Indian civilizations as being static, despotic in its orientation, and outside the mainstream of relevant world history. With the advancement of native writers and thinkers, the concept and understanding about past India began to change. Several Indian nationalist scholars went deep into the past history of India and established that the literature and views produced by scholars of ancient India were far-far ahead of the world literature produced at the time. Max Muller, too, accepted that the Sanskrit literature of India was the most superior among the literature produced in other languages of the world.

The discovery and excavation of the cities of the Indus civilization has pushed back the beginning of Indian history to the third millennium BC. The cities of the Indus pre-date the Vedic culture by at least a millennium and the diffusion of Sanskrit as a part of the Vedic culture is believed to have begun at the end of the same millennium. The Indus cities epitomize a Copper-Bronze Age urban civilization based on commerce, both within the northwestern area of the Indian subcontinent as well as West Asia. The earliest of the Vedic text, *Rigveda*, reflects pastoral, cattle keeping people unfamiliar with urban life. The decline of the Indus civilization is not because of Aryans' invasion over the cities, but due to various reasons such as extensive ecological changes. The repeated flooding of the Indus, the rise of the water-table and salinity of the land under civilization, the change in the course of the Saraswati river with a consequent encroaching of the desert and major sea-level changes affecting the ports along the west coast, seem more convincing explanations for the decline of the Indus cities. So, the earlier hiatus between the Indus civilization and the Vedic culture is no longer acceptable, and the Indus Civilization has now to be seen as the bedrock of early Indian culture.

The Vedic period had been a highly advanced period, not only economically, but also philosophically. It served as the richest treasury of knowledge providing coming India a strong base of civilization. Ramachandra Ghosh correctly writes that, "To the Vedas must be attached an undying interest and an ever increasing value not only for their greatest antiquity, but also for the immense flood of light which they throw on the primitive state of Indo-Aryan society, Indo-Aryan speech, and general mythology." The Vedas are the primeval sources of Indo-Aryans' theological, philosophical, moral, ethical, social, religious and political understanding. They abound in the knowledge of theology, philosophy, astronomy, geometry, etc. In the words of Ramachandra, "In process of time, the Vedic religion, whatever it was, has become, through the corruptions and prejudices, of a most revolving type of a heterogeneous medley of theology, philosophy and science." The age in which the Vedas and their appendages were produced, has exercised the blandest influence upon all succeeding periods of Indian history. Every later branch of literature is closely connected with the Vedic traditions because the traditions had become an intrinsic part of the people. The religious and moral ideas what the Hindus have today, have been derived from the Vedic traditions. The rishis of Indo-Aryans of ancient India were great people of vision, idealism, intelligence, wisdom, insight, foresightedness and morality. While exploring the nature of the physical world, they landed in the world of transcendentalism where they visualised the Supreme Power and its manifesting divinity. What they produced is all godly, both in thought and behaviour. The *Rigveda* consists, with few exceptions, of detached prayers dedicated to divinities. The Vedas, in point of time and even in a point of literary development, are the oldest of books and the earliest repository of Aryan faith.

Hymns of the Vedas contain moral ideas and spiritual hopes and aspirations. Morality, divinity, spirituality, humanity, non-violence and universal brotherhood are the richest values of India, even today, because they all emerged from the womb of the sacred Vedas. Today, India abounds in international morality, universal brotherhood, mass-scale humanity and the highest spirituality due to its historical background that is abundantly available in Vedic literature. Thus, it were the ancient ancestors who laid the foundation of India's moral and philosophical base upon which the strong and attractive mansion of India's cultural as well as religious epitome has been built.

The hymns of the Vedas which are full of prayers of various gods and goddesses indicate that the ancient Indian rishis had discovered divine forces that have manifested in the world of ours and also in the entire universe. Prayers and admirations have been made to various natural as well as supernatural powers with the expectation to obtain blessings and goodness. It is in these ways the vastness and supremacy of the deities have been described. It shows that they were fully convinced of natural as well as supernatural forces and they expected blessings from them by offering sacrifices and doing prayers.

The Indo-Aryans discovered or recognized the presence of the divine in the brighter aspects of nature, and therefore, they called the blue sky, the fertile earth, the genial fire, the bright day and the golden dawn as their deities. Their interest was less in physics, but more in metaphysics. To them the former was the result of the latter. In the words of Ramachandra, "The flaming orb of the mighty brilliant Sun, the rattling thunderstorm, the flatting lightening, the rolling thunders, the fitful whisperings of the forest trees, the furious blasts, rain, mist and hail awaken bright fancies in the mind of the thoughtful and poetic man. These, indeed, are the powers that thrilled and awed our ancestors; and made a tremendous impression upon their desponding mind." The early Aryans, either Indo- or others, were too much curious about natural phenomena, and they tried to penetrate into the ultimate cause of such phenomena. Such curiosity did not made them into scientists, but philosophers because they penetrated into the abstract not into concrete. This led them in search and research of reality spread over several centuries.

It may be said that the Vedas and their appendages that developed during the ancient period of Indian civilization is the base of India's Hindu civilization and culture. They contain the philosophy that is related to both transcendental as well as mundane worlds. They present a vast picture of the transcendental world that is not manifested; and that is the primal source of all kinds of manifestations including living and non-living things. The God that we talk of is the divine concept both manifested and not manifested. In Vedas that concept is *Brahman* which is the ultimate sources of creation from Brahma down to grass. The not manifested (*Avyakta*) is the sleeping condition of Brahma who is asleep. Out of that, all manifestations (*Vyakta*) are manifested when Brahma awakes. The *Avyakta* is also called *Akshara*, the Imperishable, which is the highest place of God; and one who reaches there never returns to the mundane world. All living creatures, right from Brahma to the smallest living being, is nothing but a reflection or manifestation of the *Brahman*. The mundane world is the material world, which is completely wrapped in *Maya* (illusion), is the product of *Prakriti*; and the living beings of this world, though they are an integral part of the Absolute God, are ignorant of their real nature with the result that they have been wandering after material prosperities that are subject to transitory existence. Falling in the lap of *Maya*, which include fastening elements like desire, greed, lust, wrath, etc, all the living beings of the mundane world are subjects of bondage living through various troubles and pains like birth, death, oldness, diseases, scarcity, etc.

The Vedas teach people how to be liberated from such bondage of *Maya* and return back to the immortal place, reaching which no one returns to the mundane world. This is called salvation. In other words, the Vedas describe not only the nature of *Brahman*, but also presents ways to mankind for revival and liberation. *Karmakandas* prescribed in the Vedas are the means to please various gods and goddesses to satisfy the longings of man. While practising *karmakandas* a man comes to realize the divine significance and ultimately he inclines towards the power of ultimate resource. His desires are satisfied gradually by performing sacrifices and his knowledge as well as wisdom develop to such an extent, that he gradually lands into the land of God, where there is neither ignorance nor bondage. He learns from the Vedas and its appendages like Srutis, Smritis, Puranas and Upanishads, etc, the glories of God that makes Him pure and capable of grasping divine knowledge that results in devotion to God. He realizes his true nature (soul) and establishes a close link with God and His blessings. At such a stage of his spiritual development his illusions disappear; and he develops the qualities that takes him to the divine land, a place that is immortal, perfect, pure, free from all types of pains like birth, death, etc. This is a place that stands above the land of destruction. Here, there is neither *Maya* nor ignorance. If there is anything, that is divine, rays of non-manifested *Brahman* that never ends. It is *Sanatana* (without beginning and end), full of divine bliss, illuminated without Sun and Moon, and beyond the approach of *Maya*. Thus, the Vedas and their appendages help one to realize his soul and its nature and its relationship with God; and adopt the devices to emancipate oneself from the bondage of *Maya* and ignorance. Vedas present the nature of God and explain the advent of the creation of the world, its qualities and nature and also relationships between the spiritual and the material worlds.

Critics of the Hindu religion are of the view, that it supports polytheism which is an attack upon the divine concept of monotheism. Reality is, that the critics fail to grasp the reality of Hindu religious philosophy. It is all because the critics lack complete knowledge of Hindu religious philosophy enshrined in religious scriptures and *Dharma Shastras*. Hindu religious philosophy propounds the concept of Absolute God. The Hindu religious scripts, while talking about metaphysics, talk of an absolute non-manifested God (*Brahma*), who is absolutely alone, having no shape, but all pervading. The doctrine of polytheism was developed in search of that universally pervading God while explaining and interpreting different aspects of the manifested God which is known as polytheism. Other religious scriptures talk of the concept of monotheistic God where there is no place at all for existence of any subordinate or inferior God. Their angle as well as approach is limited to the God only who is called *Nirguna-Nirakara* (devoid of any attributes and shape). Vedas and its appendages talk of *Nirguna-Nirakara* God along with *Saguna-Sakara* God also. Other religions like Islam and Christianity describe about a non-manifested single God, no doubt, but they do not talk about the attributes of God that pervade after His manifestation while the latter explains in detail various divine attributes and powers of God after His manifestation. Such God is popularly known as *Saguna-Sakara* (divine manifestation with qualities and shape). Christianity and Islam present the concept of single shapeless God. According to these religions, it is God who created everything. But they do not describe how God created everything. It is Hinduism that presents details about creation of the universe and the expansion of divine forces.

Except Sanatana Dharma of Hindus, no religion or religious philosophy presents an account as to how the world was created and what are the powers that are enshrined in creation, and who upholds the cosmic order. The Sanatana Dharma explicitly explains the advent of creation and working of its systems. It is the Hindu religious scriptures that evidently present the nature and features of God, His absoluteness, pervasiveness, supremacy, independence, eternity, etc. The Vedas begin with monotheism, and in support and explanation of Vedic monotheism, the Indian rishis began to visualise polytheism. Various gods are nothing, but reflections of the Ultimate Supreme God, in the creation having different assignments to support, and uphold the creation. They are manifested aspects of God. That is why they appear like gods possessing various qualities and powers. The Indian rishis, sages, munis and philosophers discovered and recognised the energy of God which is present in each atom of the universe. The questions that puzzled them were what is the universe? How does it exist? How did it come into existence? Who is the creator of the universe? In trying to find an answer to these questions they invented not only the Vedas and their appendages, but also discovered the Community of gods and their performances that are nothing, but expanded forms of God. Thus, it is evident that the theory of polytheism is not different from the theory of monism.

The rishis of the Indo-Aryans penetrated into the mysteries and the complexities of the innumerable systems of the universe, and discovered the Sole and Ultimate Power (God) from whom every creation emanates, in whom every creation resides and prospers; and lastly every creation dissolves into the unfathomable ocean of eternity. They found that God stands above everything in the manifested world, where there is timelessness. Their concept went beyond *mahashunya* (absolute nothingness), where no religion of the world could reach. This is the unique feature of Indian philosophy. They also discovered that from that Ultimate Source of Power appears intelligence, wisdom, non-illusion, patience, self-restraint, calmness, pleasure, pain, birth, death, fear, and security. He is the beholder of equanimity, contentment, austerity, beneficence, fame, shame, etc. Everything evolves from Him. They recognised Him as the Supreme *Brahman*, the Supreme Light, Purifier Eternal, Divine *Purusha*, the Primal God, Unborn, and Omnipresent. They found Him as the Ultimate source of all glories, both heavenly and otherwise. Different gods are nothing but extensions of God's power and expansion of God's divine glories.

All cosmic manifestations, moving and unmoving, are manifested by different activities of the Supreme Godhead. The energy we witness in the universe, including the Sun and the Moon, is manifested attributes of God. Except God no one is independent. All depend upon Him. He is the source of everything.

The names given to various gods by different rishis at different times gradually came to signify distinct divinities. The rishis invented names after names to grasp and comprehend God. Though their aim and objective were to identify with the Ultimate Power, yet they discovered the origin and growth of deities who came to be known by various names like Agni, Surya, Rudra, Vayu, Indra, Vasu and Savita, etc. Since their goal was to discover the first cause of creation of the universe, the deities which they visualised were taken, sometimes, as the first cause or ultimate power. So, they prayed to them with hymns. To them, sometimes, Agni present in nature was the first cause, and sometimes they felt that Indra in the form of rain and water was the primal God. In that course the researchers went on and on towards the search of their final goal and discovered various powers whom they named differently. This is evident from the names of gods mentioned in the Vedas. Though gods of the *Rigveda* remain the same in the other Vedas, their rankings and powers went on changing. For instance, Rudra of the *Rigveda* becomes Shankara of the *Yajurveda*. This is all due to the broadening concept of the Aryan rishis. The names which were given were not as important as the concept hidden behind these names. And in such names there must have been, as it were, some presentiments of monotheism. In the words of Ramachandra,

> "they were evidently meant to express the Beyond, the Invisible behind the Visible, and The Infinite within the Finite, the Supernatural above the Natural, the Divine, the Omnipresent and the Omnipotent."

2

Historical Background of Indo-Aryans

The history of ancient India, especially the history related to Rigvedic and post-Rigvedic period, is controversial in several aspects because no relevant authentic written documents are available. The information what one gets about the Vedic history of India, is available from the ancient religious scriptures of India like the Vedas, Upanishads, Smritis, Srutis, etc. Buddhist and Jain religious literature also throws light in discovering ancient Indian history. However, in all these religious scriptures the facts are scattered and the languages are difficult, making it complicated to deduce actual meanings.

Investigations into Indian history began with the work of Orientalists or Indologists. It was the European scholars who took deep interest to research, interpret and write about ancient Indian history, especially during the period of the British rule in India. They devoted much time and wisdom to understand the ancient language of India and examine the nature of ancient rules as well as the socio-economic, political and social structure of ancient India. It is surprising to note that several European authors, who never visited India, have presented ancient Indian history, claiming supremacy of their thoughts and opinions. What they wrote about ancient India was based on their personal imagination and ideal calculations. The majority of such Indologists like Jones, Colebrook and Wilson, were employed by the East India Company in various administrative capacities. As administrators, they were required to have specialized knowledge of traditional Indian laws, politics, societies and religion, which inevitably led them to study and analyse the literature in Sanskrit and Persian. Thus, scholarly and administrative knowledge coalesced in the writings about ancient Indian history by these writers. The Western authors who took deep interest in ancient Indian history were mostly Christians by faith, and to them, no religion of the world was superior to Christianity. Some of them regarded Vedic religion and thoughts as special treatment, but denied to accept Vedantism as a superior religion of a civilization.

The term Indologists came to include those who had purely academic interest in India and who were actually curious about India and the Indian past. In the words of Romila Thapar, "The study of Sanskrit language and literature not only gave shape to the discipline of comparative philology, but also became the source material for the reconstruction of ancient Indian society. Vedic Sanskrit, the language of Vedic literature in particular, was used extensively in the reconstruction of both India and Indo-European society, since the linguistic connection between the two had been established."[1] It helped them to understand the beginning of civilization on the earth.

These European scholars, having interest in the history of ancient India on the basis of Sanskrit language, interpreted ancient Indian history "with little or no personal experience of the Indian reality."[2] One of the most influential scholars in his time was Max Muller, whose comprehensive and appreciative description of contemporary Indian village communities would hardly have led anyone to suspect that he had never visited India. His contribution to the understanding of the ancient Indian language of Sanskrit was so attractive and convincing that no room was left for the contemporary Indian scholars and thinkers, not to believe in his interpretations of ancient Indian history. Mill was another Indologist who wrote about ancient Indian history with the marked objective to justify Colonial rule in India.

The interpretations of Indian history by these scholars carried the imagery and preconceptions, not only of the sources, but also of those interpreting them. They interpreted the theory of the Aryan race logically, no doubt, but whimsically. The word 'arya', which occurs in both the Iranian Avestan and Vedic Sanskrit texts, was given a racial connotation, as referring to the race of Aryans. They were described as physically different from the indigenous population and their cultural distinctiveness was apparent from the fact that they spoke an Indo-European language. It was held that large number of Aryans, described as a branch of the Indo-European race and language group, invaded Northern India in the second millennium BC. They conquered the indigenous people and established the Vedic Aryan culture which became the foundation of Indian culture.[3] The identifying language and race was seen to be a fallacy, even during the lifetime of Muller. The later Indian nationalist writers, while writing ancient Indian history, rejected such views and presented a different theory about the origin of the Aryans and their subsequent arrival in India.[4]

The European scholars of the nineteenth century wrote early Indian history, applying their respective hypotheses to substantiate a general standard of growth of history, both in Asia and Europe. It is surprising to note that, they used Vedic literature as the base of their source material. They developed two theories – Aryan race and Despotic Orientation. The former was believed to be based on the most up-to-date philological evidence. The theory of Oriental Despotism was opposed on several grounds. The nationalist historical writings took up the theme, among other things, the importance of religion in Indian society. The bipolarity of the spiritual content of Indian culture and the materialist basis of Western culture was seen as an essential and inherent difference. This was in part a reaction to the earlier view, that religion was such a central factor in traditional Indian society, which obstructed progress.

Investigations into the Indian past began with the work of the Orientalists or Indologists, mainly European scholars who had made India, and particularly Indian languages, their area of study. These European scholars had arrived in India to participate in the administration of the East India Company. As administrators, they were required to have specialized knowledge about past and present India which inevitably led them to study the literature in Sanskrit and Persian. The study of Sanskrit language and literature not only gave shape, to the discipline of comparative philology, but also became the source material for the reconstruction of ancient Indian society. Vedic Sanskrit, the language of Vedic literature in particular, was used extensively in the reconstruction of both Indian and Indo-European society. It was these foreign authors, who having the knowledge of Sanskrit, interpreted ancient Indian society without having proper knowledge and understanding of India and its people. It was these scholars who developed the theory of the Aryan race.

The word Arya, which occurs in both the Iranian Avestan and Vedic Sanskrit texts was given a racial connotation as referring to the race of Aryans. They came to the conclusion that the race of Aryans whose early home was in Central Asia migrated in two groups. One group who reached the European Continent was called the Indo-European race and another was the Indo-Aryan race that settled permanently in north-western part of India. The Indo-Aryan group invaded India in second millennium BC.

It is curious that the Aryans were interpreted in racial terms since in the texts, it refers merely to honoured persons of high status and in Vedic contexts, this would refer to one who spoke Sanskrit and observed caste regulations and rituals. The racial connotation may have been due to the counter-posing *Drya* with Dasa, in the *Rigveda*. It was argued that the Dasa is described as physically dissimilar to *Drya*. It was the group of *Drya* which gradually evolved into three upper racial groups – Brahmin, Kshatriya and Vaishya, while the Dasa remained the lowest.

The Aryan race theory is based on the work in recent years from three different disciplines – archaeology, linguistic and social anthropology. The discovery and excavation of the cities of the Indus civilization has pushed back the beginning of Indian history to the third millennium BC, and the Indus civilization has replaced the Vedic Aryan culture as foundational to Indian history. The cities of the Indus pre-date the Vedic culture by at least a millennium and the diffusion of Sanskrit as a part of the Vedic culture is believed to have begun at the end of the same millennium. The Indus cities epitomize a copper-bronze age urban civilization, based on commerce, both within the north-western area of the subcontinent as well as West Asia. The earliest of the Vedic texts, the *Rigveda*, reflex pastoral, cattle-keeping people, unfamiliar with urban life.

The Vedic society has been described as tribal. The term tribal refers to a community of people claiming descent from a common ancestor. In its application it has been used to cover a variety of social and economic forms. The more recently preferred term, lineage, narrows the focus. Lineage does emphasis succession and descent with the implication that these are decisive in determining social status and control over economic resources. It also helps differentiate between chiefships, where lineage dominates, and kinship, which, as a different category, evokes a larger number of impersonal sanctions. The concept of *vansha* (succession of inheritance) carries a meaning similar to lineage and is central to Vedic society with its emphasis on succession even as a simulated lineage. The *vansha* is used to mean lineage or descent group among the *rajanyas*. Kshatriyas lineage also became intrinsic to the structure of each *varna*, defined by permitted rules of marriage and kinship and by ranking in order of status, the control over resources being implicit. In this sense the emergence of the four *varnas* is closely allied to the notions of a lineage based society.

The Aryans should have been interpreted in racial terms. The Aryans, having good physic and fairer skin colour, were persons of high status who spoke Sanskrit and observed caste regulations and rituals. The racial connotation has been due to the counter-posting of *Drya* with Dasa in the *Rigveda*, and it has been argued that the Dasa is described as physically dissimilar to *Drya*.[5] This was interpreted as two racial types with the *Drya* evolving later into three upper castes – Brahmin, Kshatriya and Vaishya, with the Dasa remaining the lowest. Dasa, in fact, included the Shudra caste. The racial identity of both the *Drya* and Dasa was preserved by forbidding inter-caste marriages. The pre-eminence of the *Drya* was explained as successful conquest of the *Dryas* over the Dasas. The term *varna*, etymologically associated with colour and occurring as a technical term referring to *varna* or the caste organization of society, was used as yet another argument to support the Aryan theory of race. It was believed, to have a scientific explanation for the caste system, namely, the four main castes representing major racial groups, the racial identity was preserved by forbidding inter-caste marriages and making birth the sole criterion for caste status. The distinction between Aryans and Non-Aryans, and the polarity of Aryans and Dravidians, as suggested by European scholars, for the Indian scenario, echoes to a degree which can hardly be regarded as coincidental. However, in the European context, the Aryan–Non-Aryan distinction and the Aryan-Semitic dichotomy is based on language and race. The suggested social bifurcation is also remarkably similar, the upper castes were the Aryans and the lower castes were the non-Aryans.

A pertinent question may be raised here as, who the Hindus are and what is their root. To answer the questions one must look into the ancient history of the Aryans, who, in due course of time, came to be known as Hindus. Here, a short description is given about the history of Aryans. HS Spencer hypothesized that the Aryans originally lived in the North Polar Regions and that they were compelled to leave their original habitat due to the onset of the Ice Age; and to migrate Southward around 10,000 BC.[6] He further writes, "Even those migrating Aryans had by then developed such a high state of civilization and culture that, they were able to face and conquer the other races in course of time to establish their sway over the whole of Asia and Europe."[7] The Aryans believed and adored deities, representing various aspects of natural phenomena, no doubt, but above all, they subscribed to a system of religious meditation which may be described as 'stellar worship'.[8] Thus, it is evident that Aryans were intelligent, industrious, smart and powerful race. They established their own social system, political order, cultural ethos, economic organizations and religious ways. The history of Hinduism is, in fact, the history of Aryanism. When they entered into the territory of India, they faced the indigenous people whom they called *Dasyu*, who were uncivilized and uncultured. Dasgupta writes, "The Aryans were savage to the black aborigines, the children of the soil, when they were not ready to be their bonded slaves."[9] The Aryans were fair-skinned while the *Dasyus* were dark. The Aryans maintained their superiority. They were proud of having documented history, religion, science, literature, language, social as well as political philosophies, etc.

Havel took Indo-Aryans as a 'dominant and masterful race', having tall physical figures and fair skin.[10] The Indo-Aryans called the *Dasyus* (Dasas) *Mleccha* and neglected them. According to Sengupta, the Aryans were a virile and hearty race, "a fair-skinned, tall, stalwart, people" who "despised the snub-nosed, dark-skinned phallus worship people."[11] According to Goetz, "They (Aryans) were a branch of related group of nomadic and semi-nomadic peoples originally inhibiting the steeple country of Southern Russia and Central Asia. Other branches of these peoples penetrated into Europe bringing with them Indo-European language groups which are now spoken there."[12]

It appears that the *Rigveda*, being the most ancient literature, served as the basic source of information, regarding origin of society and civilization, both in India and in the European countries. The village community of Vedic history was looked upon as the earliest survival of a common past.[13] James Mill, however, believed that ancient Indian society was static, retrogressive and conducive to economic backwardness. Further intellectual support for this view of the pre-modern history of India was found in writings of the more eminent Western philosophers of history of nineteenth century. For instance, Hegel remarked on the absence of dialectical change in Indian history and consequently dismissed the ancient

Indian civilization as being static, despotic in its orientation, and outside the mainstream of relevant world history.[14]

In early Rigvedic period economic structure was based on the absence of private ownership. The early life of the Aryans was typically tribal and before settling permanently, they travelled from one place to another like vagabonds. The structure was in the form of a pyramid, with the king at the apex, and self-sufficient, isolated village communities at the base. The surplus was collected from the cultivators by the bureaucracy, and the process of re-distribution led to a substantial portion being appropriated by the king and the court.

The Indian nationalist views that appeared in the twentieth century, during the freedom struggle of India, presented different viewpoints regarding the ancient history of India as presented by the Western thinkers. They (Indian writers) accepted the theory of Aryan race, no doubt, but they rejected the theory of Despotism. They accepted the view that there were four *varnas* (castes) based on qualities of a person and there existed barriers to inter-caste marriages. According to Thapar, "Nationalist historical writings took up the theme, among other things, of the importance of religion to Indian society. The bipolarity of the spiritual content of Indian culture and the materialist basis of Western culture seemed as an essential and inherent difference. This was in part a reaction to the earlier view, that religion was such a central factor in traditional Indian society that it obstructed progress – the latter being defined as social and economic change."[15]

The discovery and excavation of the cities of the Indus civilization has pushed back the beginning of Indian history to the third millennium BC. The cities of the Indus pre-date the Vedic culture by at least a millennium and the diffusion of Sanskrit, as a part of the Vedic culture is believed to have begun at the end of the same millennium.[16] The Indus cities epitomize a copper-bronze age urban civilization, based on commerce, both within the north-western area of the Indian subcontinent as well as West Asia. The earliest of the Vedic text, the *Rigveda*, reflects pastoral, cattle keeping people, unfamiliar with urban life. If the Aryans had conquered north-western India and destroyed the cities, some archaeological evidence of the conquest should have been forthcoming. The decline of the Indus cities is generally attributed to extensive ecological changes. The repeated flooding of the Indus, the rise of the water-table and salinity of the land under the civilization, the change in the course of the Saraswati river with a consequent encroaching of the desert and major sea-level changes, affecting the ports along the west coast, seem more convincing explanations for the decline of the Indus cities.[17]

Palaeo-botanical views represent a change in climatic conditions from humid to dry.[18] The Indus civilization survived into the second and first millennium cultures in spite of the decline of the cities. The earlier hiatus between the Indus civilization and the Vedic culture is no longer acceptable, and the Indus civilization should now be seen as the bedrock of early Indian culture.

Ancient history of India began from 2500 BC with the Indus Valley Civilization and survived till 1759 BC. By the end of 1800 BC, two great cities of the Civilization, namely Harappa and Mohenjo-daro, met the fate of destruction. Various reasons have been estimated to be the causes of destruction of the Indus civilization. However, the most valid and convincing reason is regarded to be foreign invasions, and it were the Aryans who, migrated from Central Asia to this part of India, destroyed the old Indian civilization. But there may be other reasons to be instrumental in destruction of the Indus Valley Civilization. It could have been floods on a large-scale, earthquake, breaking out of fire, drought, epidemics, etc.

It is significant that some of the Proto-Dravidian words borrowed in Sanskrit refer to agricultural processes. It is learnt from archaeological evidence that plough agriculture was practised by the Indus settlements, and from the Rigvedic hymns it is apparent that pastoralism and not agriculture was the more prestigious profession among the early Aryan speakers. Anthropological study of early Indian society, reveals the truth that the valid distinction between *varna* as caste in the sense of ritual status, and *jati* as caste in the sense of actual status is again, to help the social historian. The most useful contribution, however, has been the study of the formation of castes, which has made it apparent that caste society does not require the precondition of different racial entities, nor the conquest of one by the other. It does require the existence of hereditary groups, determining marriage relations, where groups are arranged in a hierarchical order and perform services for one another. The hierarchy is dependent on occupation, certain beliefs of purity and pollution, and on continued settlement in a particular geographical location. The formation of a new caste has, therefore, to be seen in terms of the historical change in a particular region. As the economic structure of a region changed, yielding various professions, various castes or sub-castes emerged. Thus, a tribe incorporated into peasant society could be converted into a caste.[19] According to Romila Thapar, "Religious sects, frequently protesting against the caste hierarchy, often ended up as a caste themselves. Possibilities of social mobility and variations in status were linked to the historical context of time and place."[20] The discovery of iron and use of tools made of iron served to a great extent to change the economic structure first and then the social structure. With the growth of agriculture, road communications, coinage and weight system, trade and commerce developed which required different groups of people to carry on the works. It all helped in expansion of various castes based on different professions.

By the time of the Maurya empire land had become private property which could be sold or purchased. Descriptions mentioned in the *Dharma Shastras* and in several inscriptions of the period confirm the fact that agriculture had become an established profession. There was provision for grants and transfer of land. In areas where the land granted was already under cultivation, the persons from whom the land was acquired and the person to whom the land was transferred were mentioned together with the location of the piece of land, the authority of the officials under whom the transfer was completed and the consent of the village within whose jurisdiction the land lay were also mentioned. The documents of the *Dharma Shastras* and the available inscriptions present the history of economic structure and religious accounts of the period. Many of these records provide information on the rise of families of relatively obscure origin to high social status, usually through the channels of land ownership and administrative office. Those who became powerful had genealogies fabricated for themselves, bestowing on the family Kshatriya status and, if required, links with royal lineage as well. Such period of historical change demanded new professions, professions which finally evolved into castes. For instance, administrative complexities relating to grants of land on large-scale needed professional scribes. A new caste called Kayastha who worked to maintain the land records came into existence.

The religious impact of Indus civilization as well as early Aryan civilization is found even today. These two civilizations of ancient India, in fact provided the base for the growth of religious, economic and political history of India. Worshipping of goddess Kali, Lakshmi and Saraswati began from the Indus Valley Civilization. The rituals, which related to preserving the longevity of husbands involved worshipping and offering prayers to trees and plants like Pipal, banyan, Tulsi, etc, began during this period. Even worshipping of snakes took place. People of ancient India developed the art of making various kinds of ornaments for ladies. The belief in the origin of ghosts and the art to protect people from their wrath and evil action also developed during that period. People began to worship animals like rat, buffalo, peacock, lion, elephant, bull, etc, whom people treated as transports of various gods and goddesses.

The ancient accounts mentioned above provide evidence of the categories of ownership of land, and refer to waste land. It was all because of extension of agricultural land. Use of iron helped farmers to invent various types of implements and instruments which helped them to clear jungles and cultivate new land. New villages appeared where the Sanskrit culture was introduced and local traditions gradually merged into the former culture. The interplay of these two levels of belief systems was a necessary process in the delineation of Indian society.

A changing economic structure needed the centralised bureaucracy to adjust the interests of the people and administer them. The size and area of kingdoms began to expand during the Maurya period due to emergence of powerful rulers and their conquests. The importance given to the centralised bureaucracy, even in the Gupta period model, was perhaps a reflection, among other things of the nineteenth century administrator as the pivot of the imperial system[21] because the bureaucratic system of early India was rarely centralised, except in the infrequent periods of empires.

During the early Rigvedic period people had not yet settled at a particular place and their chief means of livelihood was hunting and keeping animals. They were hunters and herdsmen. Agriculture was either unknown to them or impossible to do in absence of instruments, etc. But during the post-Rigvedic period they learnt the art of making iron which helped them to invent various types of instruments that were used for cultivation and clearing the forests. Now the Aryans settled permanently, making cultivation as their chief profession. Before the discovery of iron, copper was the chief metal known to them. When they discovered iron, they prepared various types of weapons of war like sword, spear, shield, etc, which enabled them to conquer their enemies. The wars that occurred between the Aryans and the non-Aryans enabled the former to dispel out or enslave the latter.

People of the early Vedic period were simple and vagabonds. Their needs were limited. But during the later Vedic period the life of the people became complicated due to the growth of agriculture along with the increasing needs of their lives. This resulted in growth and development of trade and commerce, creating a new class of traders and businessmen. Belief prevailed among the people that they originated from different organs of the *Virata Purusha*. They were categorized under four *varnas* – Brahmins from the mouth of the *Virata Purush*, Kshatriyas from his arms, Vaishyas from his stomach and Shudras from his legs – with marked objectives. The Brahmins were supposed to perform religious functions having Vedic knowledge; Kshatriyas were supposed to protect the life of the people from their enemies; Vaishyas to earn wealth and support the subject and Shudras to serve the other three *varnas*. Thus, the four *varnas* came into being creating a social structure and marking their differences through their jobs.

The changing economic structure required a bureaucracy comprising of various ranks for administration and for implementing the rules prescribed by the rulers. The bureaucracy system of early India was not centralized. Recruitment was impersonal, and most levels of administration were filled by local people. It was at the more localized levels that the effective centres of power were located. In periods of empire, the surplus did find its way into the hands of the royal courts. But during the many centuries of kingdoms, the income from revenue was distributed among a large number of elite groups, which in part explains the regional variations and distribution in art styles, where the pattern was not a distant emperor but the local king. The tendency towards local decentralization was accentuated from the Gupta period (600 AD), when grants of revenue and later grants of land became the mechanism of remuneration.

The span of Indian history was seen as one long stretch of empire with an occasional change of dynasty. Yet in fact, empires were of short duration and very infrequent. There was only one empire in the early period, the Maurya empire, lasting from the end of the fourth to the early second century BC, which would even approximately qualify as an imperial system. It was not until the historical writings of the twentieth century that some concession was made to change and the imperial golden ages were interspersed with the dark ages of smaller kingdoms.[22]

The reign of the Maurya dynasty founded by Chandragupta continued for a longer period. Two kings, Bindusara and Ashoka, added more charm to the Maurya empire. Bindusara was the son of Chandragupta. He probably reigned from 300 BC to 273 BC. Like his father he was brave and dashing. He seems to have retained undiminished the empire of his father. Tradition credits him with the suppression of a revolt in Taxila. Whether he added any new conquest to his empire is not recorded. His empire must have embraced not only the greater part of northern India but also a considerable portion of the

Deccan, probably as far south as the Chitradurg district of Mysore. The kingdom of Kalinga, embracing the major part of Puri, Ganjam and some adjoining tracts, is known, however, to have been independent. Like his father he was a good diplomat, and he maintained a good relationship with the Hellenic empire.

During the early period of the Magadha empire, Shudras acquired supreme power in the lower Ganges valley. The state of things in the lower valley of the Indus was different. Great political power was exercised by the Brahmins. The *varna* system was still firm with some relaxations. Monarchy system that existed as a base of rule was hereditary. With the growth of kingdoms and incorporation of new territory, the office of the viceroy and provincial governor became more and more important. Among other State functionaries, the Purohit (priest), belonging to the class of Brahmin, who became officials of importance, was the most important feature of administrative development of the period under review which also saw the rise of a class of high officials called *mahamatya*. They all came from the class of Brahmins and Kshatriyas. Shudras were still suppressed and a neglected class. After the Maurya empire such ranks of officials began to decline. These officials dealt with various subjects such as general affairs, justice, army, etc. In the administration of justice, the king continued to play an important part. It was his duty to give decisions in accordance with the special laws of the districts, castes, and families. There was no equality before law or rule of law. There was a different set of laws for people of higher castes while for the lower castes there was discrimination in legal affairs.

The significance of land for agriculture was realised even before the advent of the Maurya empire. However, during the Maurya empire agriculture developed because more and more land was brought under cultivation. Since the area of the empire expanded, people had more land for agriculture. The kings helped the people to cultivate greater areas of land because agriculture had become the basic source of revenue for the state. In the eastern parts of India greater part of land was occupied by Brahmins and Kshatriyas. Those who possessed vast tracts of agricultural land were called *grihapatis*. They produced enough food grains.

The theory of divinity of the king based on religious beliefs provided the king or the emperor with absolute political strength. They became religious and political authorities. To quote Thapar once more, "The attribution of this quality of divinity to kingship was probably the result of earlier studies on kingship and divinity in the ancient Near East. The interrelation between divinity and political authority was never absolute in ancient India. Divinity was easily bestowed, not only on kings, but on a variety of objects, both animate and inanimate. Far from emphasizing divinity, the kings of the Maurya empire were patrons of the heterodox sects, which denied the existence of any god and ignored the notion of divinity. Initially, divinity appealed due to the rise of monarchy as a political form, in the first millennium BC."[23] Thapar is of the view that the rise of obscure families to kingships came into being due to the changing economic structure which coincided with the theory of divinity of kingship. The fabricated genealogies that appeared at the time argued that divinity was a form of social validation and its significance was largely that of a metaphor. Appearance of Buddhism as well Jainism challenged the rigidity of caste superiority, enabling many inferior castes to achieve ascendancy in both economic and political fields. Buddhists had been challenging the notion of gods especially established by Brahminism.

The early Indian historical traditions, which are now receiving the attention of historians, are being analysed in terms of ideological content, does reflect a distinct image of the past, and whose concerns were different from those of modern interpretations of the past.[24] The unit of history is not the empire, but the *janapada*, the territory settled by tribes, which later evolved into a state, generally a kingdom. References are made to emperors as universal rulers, the *samrat* and the *chakravartin*, but these are at the abstract level. Reality revolves around the kings of smaller kingdoms. The genealogical sections of tradition explain the settlement of tribes, and with the emergence of states, the association of dynasties.[25]

To protect people and defend the kingdom, an army was maintained. A typical army of this period usually consisted of four elements – infantry, cavalry, chariots and elephants. To these, the later epic adds the navy, labourers, spies, and local guides. Usually brave persons were recruited into the army. Kshatriyas were given preference because they were good fighters. The Indian infantry, clad in cotton garments, usually carried long bows and iron-tipped cane arrows. Some were armed with spears. They also carried two handed swords and a buckler of undressed ox-hide. The cavalry usually had the same equipment as the infantry. The chariots were drawn by horses or wild asses. According to Greek writers, that in the art of wars, Indians were far superior to other people of Asia. Their failure to offer a successful resistance to foreign invaders was often due to inferiority in cavalry. Weak rulers had sometimes to appease their conquerors by paying heavy tributes.

To maintain a big army, kings required financial resources and collection of revenue from the people was the chief source of financial resources. The oldest source of revenue was the *bali*, a contribution mentioned as early as the Vedic hymns. The reaped corn became the most important source of revenue in the later years. The village headmen were authorized to collect corns from the farmers for kings.

With the Aryan expansion, over practically the whole of India, came a wide diversity of social conditions. Customs not approved in the Gangetic Doab were admitted as good usage in North India. Women in South India enjoyed certain privileges which were denied to women in Central India. The wife, in the South, was allowed to eat in the company of her husband, and restrictions on the marriage of cognates were not as strict in the South as in the North. Widow marriage and Levirate had not fallen into disuse even in the Ganges valley. Burning widows was not sanctioned by the orthodox law-givers. But the practice of *Sati*, especially among the higher classes, could not have been unknown in the north-west. In the epics, one hears of the self-immolation of a princess born in the Madra country in the Punjab. The picture of women in the Greek accounts, Buddhist discourses or epics does not always agree with that portrayed in the formal codes of law. The women of the Dharma Sutras were helpless beings, and they were always dependent on their male relations and were classed with properties of minors or sealed deposits. According to the *Ramayana* and the *Mahabharata*, women belonging to royal families had the freedom to choose their husbands through the celebration of *swayamvara*. Women of lower classes, especially of the Shudras, had no sanctity. Upper class people could hardly marry a woman from the lower classes. There was no practice of *Sati*-system among the lower classes.

The common people mostly lived in villages, in humble dwellings made of thatch which were sometimes mud-plastered for fear of fire. Kings resided in fortified towns (*purs*) or cities (*nagaris*) provided with lofty walls, strong ramparts, watch-towers and gates. The cities contained pleasure parks, street lighted with torches and watered, assembly halls, dancing halls, gambling houses, courts of justice, with booths for traders and work-places of artisans. However, there were not many big cities. The royal residence, as mentioned in the *Brahminical Sutras*, was a modest structure, probably built of wood. There is also mention of buildings of seven storeys. In early times, the superstructure, at least of all dwellings, was either of wood or brick. However, some buildings were made of stones. Singing and dancing were very much popular. Both, men and women used to take part in singing and dancing. Kings were fond of such arts and employed artists to entertain them.

Social distinction, as the years rolled down, became rigid. The epic philosophers had declared that the whole of this universe was divine, having emanated from Brahma. Everyone was created equally by the Supreme Spirit. The only toughness was the *varna* system. But as the new civilization grew and the caste system was designed according to professions of the people, such epic declarations began to disappear and the caste system based on superiority and inferiority became tough and rigid. The rural population included, besides the village agriculturists, a considerable body of ranchmen who tended cattle. They avoided towns and villages and lived in cattle-ranches. Some of the cowboys roamed about, with their cattle, in forests and on the mountain slopes. The herdsmen were frequently employed to guard the royal cattle and to take the flocks of the village folks to the common grazing fields away from the cultivated parts of land.

People involved with handicrafts constituted a large part of the population, both in rural and urban areas. The number of crafts was large and included works in stone and ivory and fresco painters. In some of the industries a considerable degree of specialization was reached. There were also, to a large extent, localized and limited to particular families and castes, for there was a general tendency among artisans for the sons to follow the paternal calling. Eighteen of the more important crafts were organized into guilds. Each guild was presided over by a *Pramukha* (foreman). There were also a *Mahasreshthin* (supreme chief). Above all the guild officials stood the *Bhandagarika*, who combined the post of State Treasurer with supreme headship over all the guilds.

During the Gupta period, Vedic Dharma availed the golden opportunity to get revived. All social institutions came under the influence of the *Dharma Shastra*. Both Buddhist and Jain Dharma began to decline due to the growth of Hinduism. Brahminism once more became strong. The *varna* system, based on four classes, was still in the practice. Foreign invaders like Saka, Kushana and Huna, etc, who had established their hold over Indian territories, gradually merged into Hindu religion and joined the class of Kshatriyas. Those who were yet uncivilized and uncultured remained under the class of Shudras. Besides the four Vedic *varnas* – Brahman, Kshatriya, Vaishya and Shudra – there emerged a number of new castes and sub-castes following their different professions. Social conditions of all *varnas* and castes remained under the direct influence of *Manu Smriti* which guided them. Chinese travellers and pilgrims have also mentioned about the existence of *varna* system. The great poet Kalidasa, who himself was a Brahmin, was a strict supporter of the four *varna* system. Fa-Hien noted that the Brahmin *varna* was supreme and they followed a life of purity and simplicity. They were honoured by the Kshatriya rulers, who treated Brahmins as the most pious people, having complete knowledge of the Vedas and the *Dharma Shastra*. Kshatriyas were rulers and they ruled India for several centuries. Their basic duties were to rule over people, to protect them from foreign aggression and maintain law and order in the society. The class of Vaishyas was related to business and commerce for economic benefits. They used to exchange commodities. The fourth class were the Shudras who were labourers. They worked in the agricultural fields and served the superior castes.

During the post-Gupta period a number of new states emerged. In fact, there was multiplicity of state formation, particularly in areas hitherto regarded as peripheral or marginal and often characterized by a lineage society. Many of these new states emerged as a consequence of the changes in agrarian relations in the earlier established status, when the system of making grants of land became in force. The changes required new processes of authority, law and revenue collection in areas which earlier were either outside the state system or on the edge of it. The change was not limited to the political arena but also introduced new forms of wider social mobility. There was a growth of sectarian religious groups, some of which professed a doctrinal cult, others which attempted to systematize more earthly cults of fertility and magic. Both Buddhists and Jains had shown a sense of centring their sects in avowedly historical events which imparted a certain historicity and added to the intellectual strength of their institutions.

During the Maurya period the state had control over agriculture, industry and trade, but during the Gupta period the state began to lose their absolute hold over them. Some trades and commerce came under the control of individual owners. Some new towns appeared that became the centre of commercial activities. Due to economic growth and growth of individual property rights a system of feudalism developed. Under this system, which developed from 500 AD onwards, two factors appeared – decentralization of power and localization of administration.

The Gupta period is known as the golden period in the history of ancient India. It is all because the country marked development in every aspect of human life and society. Besides economic development, the rulers of the Gupta period applied all the possible efforts to develop art, culture, religion, painting, medicine, etc. Due to advent of Buddhism and Jainism and their protest of Hinduism and Brahminism, the development of Sanskrit culture based on Vedic literature had been badly affected. But during the Gupta and post-Gupta period special attention was paid to the growth of Vedic literature and Sanskrit civilization. Sanskrit had remained the language of Brahmanas only. But during this period, Sanskrit availed, once more, a golden opportunity to expand its influence. Authors like Kalidasa wrote various Sanskrit dramas that became very popular. The Gupta rulers were very fond of Sanskrit and arts. They honoured poets and scholars. Samudra Gupta himself was a great scholar. Shudraka was a great dramatist of the period. Vishakhadatta wrote the famous drama, *Mudrarakshasa*. The *Panchatantra* by Vishnu Sharma, a collection of a number of good fables, presented individual as well as social morality. Besides literature, instructive stories were also written during the Gupta period. Moreover, besides development of literature and arts, progress was marked in the field of mathematics, geometry, astrology, medicine, science of metrologies, etc, the astrologers of India, belonging to the Gupta period, discovered various planets. Aryabhatta, the Indian mathematician of the Gupta period established the truth that the Earth is round and it moves around the Sun on its axis. Lunar and solar eclipses are the result of the movement of the Earth and its moon around the Sun. Varahamihira, the famous astrologer wrote two books – *Brihat Samhita* and *Pancha Siddhanta*, during this period. The astrologer Brahmagupta wrote his famous book *Brahma Siddhanta* in 600 AD. Dhanvantari, the most famous scholar of *Ayurveda* was present during this period. Banabhatta wrote his famous book *Ashtanga* during the rule of the Gupta and post-Gupta kings.

Thus, it is quite obvious that the Gupta period was, in fact, a golden period of ancient India. There was no aspect of life where attention was not paid for development. The rulers supported and honoured scholars and encouraged them to create new historical literature. The influence of Buddhism and Jainism began to decline during the Gupta and post-Gupta periods due to return of the Hindus to their old knowledge and civilization. Protests against Buddhism and Jainism was such that these two new Dharmas did not find ground for further development.

After the death of Harsha, his empire faced the problem of disintegration. After him there was no powerful king to keep the people united and provide a strong leadership and able administration. There was no authority to suppress rebellions. Attempts were made by princes like Yasovarman, and probably Indra Raja as well to restore the fallen fabric of imperialism and restore the pride of Kanauj which was there during the reign of Harsha. The history of the Upper Gangetic valley from the end of 646 to 836 is one of internal strife and of external invasions which ended when the royal throne of Harsha passed into the hands of the Pratiharas.

It is significant that in the Gupta years, which almost synchronises with Harsha's death, Dharasena IV, the son of Dhruvabhata, assumed the imperial titles of *Paramabhattaraka*, *Maharajadhiraja*, *Parameswara* and *Chakravartin*. However, he could not prove himself as per his titles with the result that the history of India after the death of Harsha resulted in disintegration and divisions of territories, anarchy, disorder and internal conflicts. All these factors encouraged the foreigners of Eastern Asia to invade India and plunder its enormous wealth and glorious fame.

The period from AD 300 to 700 is marked by the revival of Brahminism which had lost its significance and popularity due to the growth and development of Buddhism and Jainism. Brahminism was attacked by new religious sects for its extreme emphasis on practice of ritualism and *karmakanda* where blind superstitious faith prevailed and sacrifices of animals got prominence. With its revival, Brahminism once more assumed ascendency with certain relaxations. During this period many foreigners merged into Sanskrit culture and inter-marriage between settled foreigners and Hindus took place which ultimately resulted in slackness in caste rigidity. However, the position of Brahmins in society remained supreme. They were found busy with studies and teaching. There were some Brahmins who adopted professions like cultivation and trade. Kshatriyas were mostly engaged in wars. Under the category of Vaishyas many new castes and groups like farmers, traders, animal keepers, carpenter, blacksmith, goldsmith, weaver, baniyas, etc, appeared. Their economic conditions improved due to their engagement in various jobs and professions. The attitude of the people began to change towards Shudras. The significance of their services was recognized. There are various examples of inter-caste marriages. For instance, the Wakatak Brahmin king Rudrasen was married to the daughter of Chandragupta II. Some Brahmins of Ikshvaku dynasty began to marry the women of the Saka dynasty. Hunas also married into Brahmin families.

After the fall of the Gupta empire, things began to change fast in India. From AD 700 to 1200 great revolutionary changes were marked in the Indian society. Some old castes either disappeared or came on the verge of disappearance. From all the four *varnas* several new castes appeared. Due to Muslims' aggression on the country, the caste rigidity once more became significant. The tradition of early child marriage began. Brahmins still enjoyed supreme status and their chief profession was to obtain knowledge and teach people. Respect and honour of Brahmins increased due to the practice of priesthood that gained popularity everywhere. Some of the educated Brahmins were given a place in the administration as well. They were divided into several groups or clans such as Dikshit, Shukla, Tripathi, Dwivedi, Agnihotri, etc. Among the Kshatriyas, too, various sects like Chauhan, Pratihar, Parmar, Garhwal, Chandel, Kachwaha, Rathor, etc, came into existence. Most of the Vaishyas, giving up the profession of cultivation, engaged in trade and commerce because these professions were more profitable. They became rich and their prestige in the society increased. Improvement was also marked in the social and economic conditions of the Shudras. Many of them engaged in agriculture. The traditional attitude of people belonging to higher status changed towards the Shudras. However, among various Shudra castes the attitude of higher and lower status remained in practice.

In the *Rigveda* the word *varna* has been mentioned at several places and it talks of two colours – white and black. The people of black colour, in course of time came to be known as Shudras. The *Rigveda* talks that in the society the class that stands above is aristocratic; the class interested in power and dignity is Kshatriya; the class that is found busy with earning wealth is Vaishya; and the lowest people, who are incapable of doing anything worth except service are Shudras. (*Rigveda*, 1, 113, 16). The *Yajurveda* talks that all these four *varnas* appeared from different organs of Brahmin. (*Yajurveda*, 31, 10-1). Besides the *Vedas*, other ancient religious scriptures like the Smritis, Srutis, Upanishads, *Mahabharata* and *Ramayana*, etc, also present the view that four *varnas* existed in ancient India. The institution of *varna* was so strong that everyone had to abide by the traditions established by the system. All four *varnas* had their respective Dharmas and they all were bound to follow that. Since the *varna* and caste system existed among early Indo-Aryans, it would be convenient to have cursory views about the origin and nature of Indo-Aryans and their arrival in the Indian peninsula.

All these words like *varna*, Brahmin, Kshatriya, Vaishya, Shudra, Jati, Kula, etc, are all related to Hindu society the origin of which can be traced to the rise and growth of Brahminism or Brahmin Dharma. Hinduism has been a Brahmin dominated religion which gathered itself in a somewhat paternalistic pattern where a variety of sects drawing on a range of Buddhists, Jains, Vaishnavas, Shaivas and Shaktas gradually came into existence. The texts and the traditions were viewed as inspirational, initially orally preserved, with multiple manifestations of deities. Hinduism was projected largely in terms of its philosophical ideas, iconology and rituals. Brahmanism and Sramanism are two basic religions which differ totally in their approach and texts. They are organizationally separate and had different sets of beliefs and rituals and often disagreed on social norms. This distinction was recognized from the edicts of the Mauryan king Ashoka as well as by those who visited India and left accounts of what they had observed. Megasthenes, Fa-Hien, Hiuen Tsang and Alberuni were foreign travellers who closely observed the ancient Indian society as well as religions and left their accounts. Patanjali refers to the hostilities which existed between Brahminism and Sramanism. Early Brahminism demarcates the twice-born upper caste from the rest. The twice-born has to observe the precepts of Sruti of the Vedas and of Smriti (the auxiliary texts to the Vedas) and particular ally, the *Dharma Shastras*. The *Dharma Shastras* were all about conforming to the separate social observances and ritual functions of each caste. The actual nature of belief in deity was left ambiguous and theism was not a requirement. The sacrificial rituals developed and supported by the Brahmins formed the base of social and religious behaviours of the people. Sanskrit as a highly developed language remained vague for the common people due to its tough grammatical composition and difficult pronunciation. Thus, it became the sole linguistic property of the Brahmins of the time who mastered the language. The focus of worship was the sacrificial ritual. Brahminism came closest to having "a subcontinental identity largely through its ritual functions and use of common language, Sanskrit, even though it was prevalent among only a smaller section of people."

The word 'caste' is an offshoot of the word '*varna*' with the rolling down of years and ensuing changes in the economic structure of the society, *varna* developed into various castes following various professions and maintaining the system of blood inheritance. However, there were some castes in India even before the arrival of the Aryans. People of these castes generally lived in forests and mountains. For instance, Shabers, Kiratas, and Bhils were castes of people who had been living in Indian forests and mountains from time immemorial. Over time the number of castes increased in India due to the influx and subsequent settlement of foreigners. The invaders who came into India from time to time, settled in the country adopting the existing *varna* and caste system. These peoples were Yavanas, Sakas, Parthians, Kushanas, Hunas, etc. Except the Yavanas, other foreign groups, who settled in India were people of low quality and they did not possess a developed culture or civilization of their own. Hence, they adopted easily the Indian culture and civilization expanding the number of Hindus. According to some scholars some Rajput castes like Pratihara, Parmar, Chauhan, Chalukya, Guhil, Rathor, etc, originally belonged to similar foreign groups. They were assigned the title of Rajput because they were brave and expert in warfare. Besides that,

Lichchavis, Mauryas, Sakas, etc, were tribal communities who maintained *Janapadas*. Powerful Indian emperors annexed the *Janapadas* to their empires and brought them under mainstream Indian administration.

Thus, the close study of *varna* and caste system reveals the fact that the growth and development of caste in India has been a continuous process. In each period it had its special significance. In the beginning, the process and regulations of castes were simple, but it became rigid and difficult as the years passed. During the Rigvedic period there was no prohibition on common food or on marriage among different *varnas* except Shudras. People were unaware of separation. During later Rigvedic period things began to change due to marked changes in the socio-economic structure of the society. Now different *varnas* and castes got divided strictly and each followed their different course of life. Their rights and duties also differed. The system of *varna* and caste became so restricted that no one could dare to deviate from the prescribed circumference of duties and status. The Brahmins, as stated above, assumed the supreme social status while the Shudras were divided among a number of castes all of whom remained below the social stratum. Kshatriyas, being the protector of Dharma and people, obtained the status of rulers and warriors. Day-by-day the condition of the Shudras deteriorated. They became the subject of hatred and negligence. Among them the condition of *Mlecchas* and Chandalas became the worst because people of upper stratum did not like even to see and talk to them.

As legitimizers of political authority, the Brahmins, in the first millennium AD, were given grants of land by the Maurya and Gupta rulers which enabled them to become major landowners. The institutions which emerged out of these grants became centres of control over rural resources as well as of Brahminical learning and practice. It was probably the high social and economic status of the Brahmin caste which encouraged the modern idea that Brahminism and Hinduism were synonymous. On the other hand, Brahminism had to come down from their social hierarchy and make a compromise with local cults which was the result of the process of acculturation between Brahminic 'high culture' and the 'low culture' of local cults. The perspective was generally limited to that of Sanskritization of the local culture. The Brahmins accepted the deities of low culture because the cult of *bhakti* exclusively pleaded unity of mankind and equality of all religions. Local cults associated with the new social groups led to the emergence of the more popular Puranic religion. Vedic deities were subordinated or ousted. Vishnu and Shiva came to be worshipped as the pre-eminent deities. The thrust of Puranic religion was in the assimilative and accommodating processes. A multitude of new cults, sects and castes were worked into the social and religious hierarchy. Religious observance often coincided with caste identities.

By the early second millennium AD devotional cult-referred by the generic label *bhakti* had come to form a major new religious expression. They drew on the Puranic tradition of Shaivism and Vaishnavism but were also in varying degrees inheritors of the Sramanic religions. Their emphasis on complete loyalty to the deities has been seen as a parallel to feudal loyalties. The *bhakti* cult caused a departure of indigenous religion to emerging new religion. These religions were god-centred rather than man-centred. The rituals of sacrifices had been substituted by the worship of an icon. The argument that everyone is equal in the eyes of deities and castes were not barriers for worshipping. Conscious efforts were applied to broaden the scope of Hindu society by absorbing people of all sects, but the limitations of location, caste and language, acted as deterrents to a single, homogenous Hindu community.

At this juncture the multiplicity of cults and sects was bound to reflect multiplicity of beliefs. The worship of icons was unthought-of in Vedic religion but the idol became a significant feature of Puranic religion. The consciousness of similarity of rituals and belief in different geographical regions was not always evident. The *bhakti* cults were confined to particular regions and were frequently unaware of their precursors or contemporaries elsewhere. Rama and Krishna were accepted as incarnations of Lord Vishnu, and the identification of their *janmabhumi* (birth place) emerged as centres of religion and became important only by the middle of the second millennium AD.

During the early period of Indian history the rulers came from the circle of Kshatriyas who were assisted by the Brahmins in various affairs such as *yajnas* or sacrifices, etc. Kshatriyas considered themselves to be brave and heroes, while the Brahmins claimed to be spiritual and masters of Vedic knowledge and rituals. These two communities remained attached to each other for long and cooperated with each other. But as the years rolled down and the economic structure of the society changed progressively, the administrative system expanded, inviting more people to participate. The kingdoms expanded into empires and kings became emperors, ruling over large territories. The system of monarchy appeared where power was occupied by the powerful dynasties. The major dynasties recorded in the Puranas up to the mid-first millennium AD start with descendants of recognized Kshatriya lineages, but by the mid-first millennium BC it began to refer to families of non-Kshatriya origin. Others, judging by their names, were Brahmins, such as the

Shungas and the Kanvas. The lesser dynasties dating to the early centuries AD are stated to be Vartya-dvija, Shudra and *Mleccha*, and this is explained as resulting from the inevitable degeneration of all norms in Kaliyuga. Vartyas means servants of the previous ones. These servants, while occupying key ranks in the administrative hierarchy, occupied the throne by overthrowing weak kings. To establish a dynasty what were needed more were not the established norms, but the force and administrative control. Although, in theory the crown was preserved for the Kshatriyas, but in practice powerful persons, belonging to any *varna*, having the courage and bravery, occupied the throne. Thus, claims to a territory were established through the strength of arms.

The encroachment of foreign rulers in the post-Maurya period led to some indigenous families having to recede into the background. Claims to power and to actual status were conceded to the Indo-Greeks – the Sakas, Parthians and Kushanas, but claims to *varna* status was denied to them and they continued to be called Vartya-Kshatriyas (degenerate), having no indigenous land base in the subcontinent nor being able to claim kingship links with any earlier established lineage. Although dynastic status was not confirmed to any *varna*, those who succeeded to kingship from the mid-first millennium AD onwards, often observed the formality of claiming Kshatriya status. So, Kshatriya as a term became the symbol of a powerful ruler who could maintain unity, strength and protect his subjects.

Notes and References

1. Thapar, Romila, 2009 (12th impression), *Interpreting Early India*, Oxford University Press, New Delhi, p 2.
2. Ibid, p 3.

3. Leopold, J, "British Applications of the Aryan Theory of Race to India", 1850-70, *The English Historical Review*, 1874, pp 578-603.
4. For various interpretations of the term Arya, see Bailey, HW, "Iranian Arya and Daha", *Transaction of the Philological Society*, London, 1959, pp 71-91.
5. *Rigveda*, I, 130, 8; 1, 101; 10, 65, 11.
6. Spencer, HS, 1965, *The Aryan Ecliptic Cycle*, Poona, pp 15-16.
7. Ibid, pp 15-16 and 28-40.
8. Ibid, p 18.
9. Dasgupta, "The Myth of India's Unity", in the *Statesman*, Calcutta, August 15, 1990.
10. Havel, 1975, *The History of Aryan Race in India*, New Delhi, pp 3-4 and 32.
11. Sengupta, P, 1974, *The Story of Women in India*, New Delhi, pp 26-27.
12. 'Hindus', in *Encyclopaedia of Britannica*, Vol 8, pp 888.
13. Muller, Max, 1883, *India: What Can it Teach Us?*, London, p 101ff.
14. Hegel, F, 1974, *Lectures on the Philosophy of History*, London.
15. Romila Thapar, 2009 (12th impression), *Interpreting Early India*, Oxford University Press, op cit, p 8.
16. Allchin, R, 1955, *The Birth of Indian Civilisation*, Harmondsworth.
17. Lambrick, HT, 1967, "The Indus flood-plain and the Indus Civilization", *Geographical Journal*, 133, pp 483-95. Also see, Raikes, RL, "The end of the ancient cities of the Indus", *American Anthropologist* 1964 66(2), pp 284-99.
18. Singh, G, "The Indus Valley Culture", *Archeology and Physical Anthropology in Oceans*, 1971 6(2), pp 177-89.
19. Bose, NK, 1953, "The Hindu Method of Tribal Absorption," in *Cultural Anthropology and Other Essays*, Calcutta; Mandelbaum, D, 1970, Society in India, Bombay.
20. Romila Thapar, 2009 (12th impression), *Interpreting Early India*, op cit, p 12
21. Ibid, p 16
22. Ibid.

23. Ibid, pp 16-17.
24. See, Pargiter, FE, 1922, *The Ancient Indian Historical Traditions*, London, Pathak, VS, 1966, *Ancient Historians of India*, London; and Warder, AK, 1972, *An Introduction to Indian Historiography*, Bombay.
25. Romila Thapar, "Genealogy as a source of Social History", in *Ancient Indian Social History: Some Interpretations*, New Delhi, 1976, pp 326-60.

3

Vedas and Vedic Literature

It is an undisputed fact that real history of India begins with the arrival of the Aryas or Aryans who possessed the qualities and knowledge that was yet unknown to people settled in other parts of the globe. While migrating from the Central Asia they first settled in the valley of the river Sindhu (Indus). It is believed that these people migrated towards India from Central Asia in search of a better place and climate. Excavations at several places in the western and northern parts of the Indian subcontinent bear witness that these people who had settled at Harappa and Mohenjo-daro were well-civilized. Ruins of well-built cities and seals surprisingly similar to those discovered at different places of the ancient world have been found in the Indus Valley. The people who evolved this culture were Aryans. Their religion was normally non-iconic where images played no part. In their pantheon the female element was subordinated to the male and deities like Indra, Varuna, Mitras, Surya, Agni and other supernatural beings were given a place of honour, who seem to have been quite unknown to the originators of the Indus culture. According to Majumdar "unfortunately the early literature of the Aryans, called Veda, cannot be dated even approximately, and it is impossible to say with absolute precision in what chronological relation the civilization portrayed in the Vedas stood to the Indus culture of the third millennium BC."[1] Max Muller hesitatingly placed the beginning of the Vedic literature to the latter half of the second millennium BC. Tilak and Jacobi, on the other hand, tried to push the date much further back on astronomical grounds.[2] In the words of Ramachandra Ghosh, "Our Aryan fathers handed to us the scriptural Vedas, which have been canonized as time wore on; and which, notwithstanding many puerilities and repulsive legends, arrest our thoughts and inspire us with keen interest. They looked upon their venerated scriptures as the foundation of their power and prestige. Our heart grows warm when we find the Vedas to be strewn with original and at the same time sober and profound ideas, pure and sublime conceptions, and lofty sentiments which were by no means unworthy of our most distant anscestors."[3]

The Vedas and their various branches which were produced by the ancient Indian great rishis and sages from time to time through deep meditation, served as the strong base of India's Hindu civilization and culture. This chapter investigates into origin of Vedas and their appendages, examines their philosophies and discusses the impact of Vedas on the life and culture of Hindus.

Short Description of the Vedas

India is a vast country where people of different castes and *varnas* have been living together from time immemorial. India with her ancient and illustrious name hoary with hallowed traditions claims a very high antiquity as well as a distinguished rank among the civilized conditions of the ancient world. Vedic period illustrates the picture that throws much light on India's ancient civilizations. Before the Vedic Age the Indus Valley

Civilization was also a highly civilized state of the Indian people who lived in the places like Harappa and Mohenjo-daro. The ruins discovered from the excavations of these areas present ample proof regarding ancient Indian civilizations. However, the Indus Valley Civilization was confined to north-western India and it was an urban type civilization. On the other hand, the Vedic civilization covered a large portion of the country and it served as the base of Indian civilization even today. The word 'Veda' is derived from the Sanskrit word 'vid' which means knowledge. The Vedic history of India is highly developed in the sense that it is related to the highest degree of spiritual knowledge. However, Vedic literature is not recognized as historical facts because it lacked historical proof and its origin is not related to any established historic period. However, it can be definitely said that Vedic literature was developed by the Indo-Aryans some time before the Christian era. Ramachandra has rightly remarked that,

> "in process of time the Vedic religion, whatever it was, has become ... of a most revolving type, of successive ages, a heterogeneous medley of theology, philosophy and science."[4]

Vedanta philosophy of India is the voice of the Indian image, philosophical base and social behaviour. The Vedas are the base of Indian culture, philosophy, religion, ethical views, spiritual visions, ultimate human aims, objectives, dreams and desires. Religious literature of Hindus consists mainly of the Vedas, Brahmanas, Aranyakas, Upanishads, Puranas, *Dharma Shastras* or Smritis, *Grihya Sutra* and *Itihasa*. The Vedas which are four in number are the oldest Sanskrit literature of the world. The *Rigveda* is a collection of hymns, oblation and verses called Samhitas. These sacred hymns and verses are collectively known as the *Rigveda*. The *Yajurveda* is a collection of sacred formulas (Mantras) and sacrificial verses. The *Samaveda* is a collection of melodic recitations and oblation verses, and the *Atharvaveda* is a collection of hymns related to magic, spells, and incantations. Most of the Vedic hymns extol deities who personify natural and cosmic phenomena such as fire, sun, rain, war, and divine authorities. Gayatri is called Vedmata. Gayatri is the Supreme Sublime Goddess, totally abstract in form and prevailing everywhere from natural world to the world of eternity. She is the embodiment of entire knowledge upholding all the Vedas. Next to Vedas are Brahmanas, which give elaborate expositions intended to instruct and guide sacrificial priests. The Brahmanas are concerned with rites and ritual sacrifices; and oblations from the prior part of the Vedas. In other words, Brahmanas are related to ritualism and *karmakanda*. Brahmanas are usually divided into three parts – Brahmana proper, Aranyakas and Upanishads. Most of the Brahmanas have been lost. Of the thirteen that survive, two are attached to *Rigveda – Aitareya* or *Ashvalayana* and *Kaushitaki* or *Sankhyayana*; two to *Yajurveda – Taittiriya* and *Shatapatha*; one to the *Atharvaveda – Gopath*; and eight to the *Samaveda – Panchvinsha* or *Tandya*, *Shadvinsha*, *Mantra*, *Talvakara* or *Jaiminiya*, *Samvidhana*, *Daivata*, *Arshya* and *Vansa*. These Aranyakas contain directions for the rituals of the Brahmins as well as philosophical explanations of the nature of God.

The Vedas are the highly developed ancient literature of the world presented by Aryans. It is the literature that attracted the attention of some of the best scholars of Europe and America. The word 'Veda' is significantly employed to designate those ancient Sanskrit works in which is laid the foundation of Brahminic belief, and these works were originally three in number, i e *Rigveda*, *Samaveda*, and the *Yajurveda*. Frequent mention is made in ancient Sanskrit literature of the Indian scriptures under the name of *trai-vidya* or the triple sciences.[5] The prayers in metre arch called Rik, and those in prose are denominated *Yajur* while those intended to be chanted are Saman.[6] There are altogether four Vedas – *Rigveda* (Veda of hymns), the *Samaveda* (Veda of chants), the *Yajurveda* (Veda of sacrificial formulas) and the *Atharvaveda* (Veda of incantations). The *Rigveda* is evidently composed of heterogeneous materials. The first seven books of this Veda bear a similar character, arranged according to a plan. These books embrace the oldest, the most genuine and the most sacred hymns, and retain, as far as the tradition goes, an integral whole. The eighth and ninth books present quite a different system of internal arrangement. The tenth book which is a kind of appendix to the rest, corresponds with the arrangement of two of the predecessors, and copiously supply with the most distinct evidence of a later origin. In various instances, the tradition is very unreliable with reference to the authorship of the hymns, and even in certain cases it is found to attribute some of them to mythical personages. The flow of knowledge beginning from the Vedas passed through great epics like Brahmanas, Aranyakas, Upanishads etc, and spread across all over India and continues to play an active role to preserve and maintain Indian Hindu religion, culture and civilization.

The ideas, thoughts and philosophies available in the Vedas and Vedantas are values which were discovered over time; and which came into being in unbreakable, constant philosophical as well as religious discoveries. These were discovered by great ancient Indian souls who personified the truth. Vedas are not the creation of one single period of time or one scholar. Rather the Vedas are oceans of knowledge which took many centuries to be completed, and which are the product of great ancient Indian rishis and sages who had devoted their lives to hard penance and deep meditation with the sole objective to know the universe and understand cosmic activities. Their strong curiosity about cosmic affairs and to personify divine forces; and understand their true nature as well as qualities, took them to the pinnacle of the transcendental world. With the help of their deep centralized thinking and meditation these rishis upon reaching the plane of the transcendental world, witnessed through their divine eyes the divine *lila* (activities) where various divine forces (gods, goddesses and demigods, etc) were personified. It was these divine forces, engaged actively in different divine activities of creation, came to be known as various gods and goddesses. The rishis divided these divine forces into three categories – the gods of earth, the gods of space and the gods of beyond space (Goloka or Dhauloka) where the primal God resides. Chief among the earthly gods is Agni who grants wealth, food grains, sons and daughters and worldly prosperity. In space there are gods ruled by Indra who is capable of destroying the enemy (demons or Asuras) and who causes rain on the earth for growth and maintenance of vegetation and crops. The third rank of gods, who stood above these two ranks of gods and goddesses is Lord Vishnu, who along with various other gods like Sabita, Varuna, Aditi, Shradha, Usha, etc, govern the universe as the sole resource of all creation, primal cause of the causes, supervisor as well as controller of all divine forces and destroyer of everything.

Hymns of the *Rigveda* themselves are apparently of different periods spread over several centuries before the Christian era. A few among them being older and a few more recent. Max Muller has termed the most ancient portion of the hymns as *chhandas* and those which are comparatively modern as Mantra.[7] The *Samaveda* is an anthology and purely a derivative production. This Veda was at one time the most comprehensive of the four Vedas. However, it is nothing more than a recast of the Rik, being composed, with some exceptions, of the very same hymns which are in their Rik-form. The *Yajurveda* is in double form – the *Krishna* (black) *Yajur* or the *Taittiriya Samhita* and the *Shukla* (white) *Yajur* or the *Vajasaneyi Samhita*. These in the main have the same matter, but they seem to differ from each other only as regards their details and arrangement. In the *Krishna Yajur*, the formulas for the sacrificial ceremonies are generally accompanied by dogmatic explanations and supplements to rituals while in the *Shukla Yajur* the case is quite different. There they form subjects that are entirely distinct from one another. The *Shukla* embraces the texts that are not found in the *Krishna*. The *Atharvaveda*, though next to the *Rigveda* is the most comprehensive and valuable of the four Vedas. It is almost entirely a *Rigveda*, but it has many points of contact with the *Yajur*, and there is also no room for doubt that its songs rank chronologically with the Brahmanas of the *Rig*, the *Sama* and the *Yajur*.[8] The *Atharva Samhita* is rather a supplement to the *Rigveda* than one of the four Vedas, and has very little coincidence with any of the Vedas in its general character.

Division of Vedic Age

The Vedic Age has been divided by Muller into four distinct periods, namely, the Chhanda period, the Mantra period, the Brahmana period and the Sutra period. The respective styles of compositions of these four periods seem to differ very much from one another. In the Chhanda period the oldest hymns were composed and this period in fact gives a fair picture of the primitive society of the Indo-Aryans at a time when no particular system of religion was prevalent. Even sacrifices were not in vogue. In the Mantra period they came to be held in great estimation and in this period the most recent hymns were composed, and the whole was placed together and arranged into one Samhita. Three other Samhitas were also collected and arranged systematically for a distinct theological or sacrificial purpose. At this time there were priests by profession who had elaborated a most highly complex system of sacrifices. In the Brahmana period, the principal theological and liturgical books bearing this title were composed and marshalled together. Theological speculations were much indulged in. In the Sutra period, the ceremonial precepts of the earlier times were reduced to a systematic form. The works of this period are not written in the enigmatical form of Sutras, but some are in verse and others in prose. The Vedas have their own Brahmanas and Sutras. In the Brahmana and Sutra periods the Sanskrit language must have undergone considerable modifications. The Sutra period extends far into the Buddhist times which fall within the Vedic period.

So far the origin and existence of aforesaid periods is concerned, nothing definite can be said about when the Vedas were written. According to Max Muller, the Chhanda period may have lasted from 1200 to 1000 BC; the Mantra period from 1000 to 800 BC; the Brahmana period from 800 and 600 BC and the Sutra period from 600 to 200 BC. The chronological limits assigned by Max Muller to the four periods of Vedic literature are too narrow rather than too wide. The same conviction has been expressed by Prof Wilson and Dr Whitney as well. To decide the question with absolute certainty as to the dates of these four periods of ancient Sanskrit literature would be impossible because Indian literature is itself almost without known dates owing either to the peculiar organization of the Hindu mind or to the convulsion of Indian society. Uncertainty hangs over these periods and to assign an approximate length to each of these periods is altogether hazardous. However, resting on some general data which have been fully admitted by Indians it may be said that the Vedic period is old not less than five thousands BC.

Vedas and Srutis

Vedic Samhitas, Brahmanas, Aranyakas and Upanishads are collectively known as Srutis which means 'spoken and heard.' It is believed that the Srutis are revelations or the aforesaid Holy Scriptures as have been spoken by God Himself and heard and remembered by the holy-ones (great rishis) in their deep meditation and *samadhi*. That is why the Sruti is taken as the most original, inalienable, unchangeable, imperishable fundamental, transcendental and highly pious words of the Almighty. What is Vedic? Vedic is that which contains the Mantras (holy hymns) directly revealed by God. Since it has been revealed by God Himself, it can never be untrue. In the *Rigveda* there are hymns that speak of various powerful gods and their strengths. *Samaveda* presents beautiful *chhands*, melodious songs in appraisal of gods. *Yajurveda* talks of nature and medicines while the *Atharvaveda* is related to religious perform as well as Mantras and Tantras. After the Vedic period, the period of Sutra comes. Since printing was yet to be discovered, all the Vedas were summarized in very convenient short forms containing profound aphorism (wise saying maxim).

In ancient Sanskrit literature of India the Brahmanas are collective works and there are old and new Brahmanas. But those that have perished are found in diverse manner quoted or referred to. The Brahmanas, in fact, were the productions of the Schools of Brahminic priesthood. They are characterized by dogmatic assertions and by flimsy symbolisms. They contain the oldest rituals, the oldest linguistic expositions, the oldest legendary narratives and the oldest philosophical and mystical speculations, all of which are mixed up with each other. But they seem to differ widely from one another in point of details. It is simply owing to the fact that they belong to one or the other Vedas. With respect to their origin and age they occupy a kind of intermediate position between the transitions from a simple Vedic mode of thought to Brahminical Vagaries.[9] Primary objective of this Brahmana is to show and establish the importance and also the efficacy of the four Vedas. From the Brahmanas sprung those mystical and theosophical writings – the Aranyakas and the Upanishads.

According to *Manu Smriti*, Vedas are divine eyes through which gods, *pitras* (departed souls residing in Pitriloka) and man exist (*Manu Smriti*, 12, 94). As one sees earthly materials with eyes, Vedas enables one to view the transcendental world and cosmic order. Vedas are the primary source of *Dharma Shastras*. Hindu *Dharma Shastras* as well as religious, philosophical and social traditions and behaviours emanate from the Vedas. Vedas talk not only of gods and goddesses, but also present the path to appease them and avail their blessings. It presents logical connotations related to supernatural powers, their abode, their nature as well as various roles in the universe and their status before creation and annihilation. It also talks about the concept of Brahma (eternally self-illuminating divine power) serving as the primary source of all sorts of creations, living and non-living. Vedas and Vedanta are, in fact, the source of various philosophies. The divine conceptual framework of Vedic knowledge teaches people the primary goal of life (salvation), ways of living on the earth, moral philosophy, social as well as psychological behaviour and religious activities.

There are more or less 550 Sutras. Since these Sutras were very vague and complex, the philosophies explained in them were not easy for everyone to understand. It needed further simplification. Hence Bhashyas or commentaries along with sub-commentaries were written by different religious scholars to explain and elucidate the Sutras.

Veda is godly. So, the Vedas are called *apuruseya* meaning not written by man. There are certain evidences to prove that the Vedas are God's creation. (*Rigveda*, 10.90.7; *Yajurveda*, 31.7; and *Atharvaveda*, 10.7.20) According to Indian tradition, the Vedas (knowledge) are eternal (Sanatana), which has neither a beginning nor end. It exists even after complete annihilation of creation. After the new creation of the new universe, it reflects through perceivers who approach the truth and grasp it. According to Vedanta, Vedic knowledge is indestructible and *apuruseya* (not written by human beings). In the beginning of creation it came into manifestation through God Himself. With the creation of the universe Vedic knowledge was revealed by God to the inner-heart of rishis and sages, and through them it percolated and flowed down to others.

The Vedanta has been compared with Plato's idealism. However, Plato does not talk of theology while in the Vedanta a lot has been said about the Supreme governing power of the universe and the ultimate reality. Plato puts emphasis on absolute idealism which is the eternal and ultimate source of all ideas while the Vedanta talks of the Absolute Supreme Power, Universal Self and Creator of the Universe. The *Sankhya* has many things in common with the metaphysics of Pythagoras; the Yoga with the *Zeno*; and the *Nyaya* offers many parallels to the practical philosophy of Aristotle. Of the six systems, the Vedanta is the most orthodox. It propounds the pantheistic doctrine of the Upanishads. According to Vedanta, God is the prevailing spirit; there is no material world as distinct from Him. The world is without a beginning, and everything about it is all *Maya* or illusion. The sole aim of

Vedanta is identifying the human soul with God, and getting salvation from the incessant circle of birth and death. Soul, that is the Self, is an integral part of the Universal Self. Duality is nothing but sheer ignorance that makes man believe in duality. God is eternal, without a beginning or an end. He is immortal, permanent, invisible, omnipotent, omnipresent, all powerful, having the capacity to do anything. The true knowledge of *Brahman* (God) destroys ignorance and produces a belief in non-duality.

System of Vedanta Philosophy

Generally there are six systems of philosophy – Vedanta, Mimamsa, Sankhya, Yoga, Nyaya and Vaisheshika. Vedanta was founded by a great ancient Indian Rishi Vyasa, who is popularly believed to be God's incarnation. He gave proper systematic shape to the Vedas and the Puranas. Jaimini was the founder of the *Mimamsa*. The *Sankhya* philosophy was founded by Kapila while Patanjali is credited to have established the system of Yoga philosophy. Gautam founded the *Nyaya* philosophy and the *Vaisheshika* line of philosophy originated from Kanada. They all were rishis of great wisdom.

Nyaya Darshana

Gautam, who propounded the *Nyaya Darshana* (600 BC), talks about how to get rid of worldly pains. For that, like Gautam Buddha, it is essential to know the root causes of pains and find their remedies in order to permanently come out of the circle of pains and troubles. The *Nyaya Darshana* is founded on scientific logic where there is no chance of any personal view and vendetta. The basic objective of this *Darshana* is to abandon ignorance forever and adopt truth based on scientific knowledge that is obtained through applying various logic and counter-logic. The truth established by this system is scientific because it is based on analytical study and evidences. The *Darshana* presents various ways and means to substantiate truth. It helps one to come out of the world of illusions and doubts. After removing illusions and doubts what is left is only the truth. And it is this truth that is finally acceptable. Hence it is called *Nyaya* because there is no doubt of being misled and falling into darkness. The philosophies related to either the mundane world or the world of transcendental. The world achieved through *Nyaya Darshana* is pure and universal. The truth relating to God or Parameshwar, presented by the *Nyaya Darshana*, is convincing because it is based on tested logic and evidences. God, according to this philosophy, is the Creator, Preserver and the Destroyer of the world of ours. He creates the world not with false items, but with true atoms. God, in subtle form, is present everywhere, watching and controlling the worldly affairs. God is the primal cause of creation. He is great justice who awards punishment and bliss according to the *karmas* of living beings. The truth is that one avails goodness as well as greatness abiding by God's *Nyaya* and depending upon His mercies.

Vaisheshika Darshana

Maharishi Kanada propounded the *Vaisheshika* philosophy. He was a great thinker of ancient India. *Vaisheshika* philosophy puts emphasis on atomic theory. An atom is the smallest particle of a matter that cannot be divided further. Moreover, atoms and their particles are invisible. Everything is made of atoms. Unlike other matter, atoms are eternal and endless. According to Radhakrishnan, atom is round and subtle. There is nothing inside and outside of the atom. Matter like sky, space, time and soul are eternal. They are constantly in existence. Nothing can destroy them. Creation means to create new things by destroying old creative system. When God created another universe after its annihilation, all indestructible matter in the form of atoms began to come into existence on coming in close contact with each other. The external and internal contact of atoms is the result of motion that is in the sky. Thus, according to this atomic theory all activities of the world, right from creation to annihilation, are propelled by atoms which are invisible. It is called *Vaisheshika* because it is better, more logical and perfect than other branches of Indian philosophies especially of the *Sankhya Darshana*.

Both *Vaisheshika* and *Nyaya Darshanas* are similar in several of their objectives. The former like the latter emphasizes on the ways and means to end worldly pain. Both consider that the root cause of worldly trouble is ignorance, and until ignorance is removed, living beings cannot get rid of pain and trouble. *Vaisheshika Darshana* critically analyses subtle *dravya* which is basically devoid of any quality and activity, and it exists independently. *Dravya*, in fact, in subtle form is the root cause of other causes. It is, indeed, the base of all material. *Dravya* is devoid of quality and activity in the beginning. Quality and activity cannot exist independently. Where they live or in which they live is known as matter. There are nine kinds of *dravya* – earth, water, *tej* (effulgence), air, sky, time, space, soul and mind. Among them the first five are called *Panchamahabhuta*. They are characterized by the quality that they can be understood through external contact of five the *jnanendriya* (senses of ear, eye, nose, tongue and touch). The elements like sky, air, earth, water, ether, time, space, soul and mind, etc, emanate from subtle atoms which are unlimited, invisible, non-manifested, having the primal energy through which other materials of the universe reflect and remain active. Both qualities and activities need a base to reside, and it is the atom where they reside and act. Thus, according to Kanada, atoms are such an element that being invisible resides neutrally with all visible elements, causing them to act and qualify. In other words, being formless, devoid of any quality and activity, it is the base of everything and of all activities in the universe. The things are formed coming into its contact and begin to qualify and act. Thus, it cannot be said that the quality and activity of a thing which the thing possesses are not its own, but it gets them upon coming in contact with subtle atoms which is a divine and eternal element.

The earth, water, *tej* (effulgence), air and sky which are called *panchamahabhuta* possess certain qualities. For instance, the earth has quality like smell, water, *rasa*, *tej* (effulgence), *rupa*, air touch and sky ether (*shabda*). When one comes into contact with the external *jnanendriya* (ears, eyes, nose, tongue and touch), he knows or feels them. Time and space are also eternal as well as all pervasive. Soul is eternal, all comprehensive and conscious. *Jnanendriya* is the external agency while the mind is the internal agent of the soul. The material that is formed upon coming in close contact of the atom is destroyable because it is not permanent.

Salvation (*Moksha*) is the vital theme of Indian philosophy. The *Vaisheshika Darshana* also talks of salvation. According to Kanada, the liberated soul in the condition of salvation is completely free from all qualities and activities. Like the clean sky it remains pure and *nirvikara*. There is no motion (*gati*). In the absence of motion and quality the soul abandons all physical contact with body and gets rid of the circle of birth and death forever. Soul is in the circle of birth and death till its consolidated and *prarabdha karmas* are over.

The *Vaisheshika Darshana* while talking about Dharma says that the basic objective of Dharma is to get salvation by understanding the divine elements. According to Kanada, Dharma is not *karmakandas*. Rather it is the knowledge of divinity. He maintains that if duty is performed in the right direction, with pure mind, in support of creation leaving aside the personal material gains, it is pure Dharma, and it brings salvation. In other words, Dharma is the activity of a self-controlled person who acts not for self but for all. When Dharma is performed for personal gains like wealth, prosperity, pleasure, etc, it binds one to worldly pleasures and lust. So, to achieve salvation, Dharma must be performed setting aside all personal longings.

Despite all the merits, the *Vaisheshika Darshana* is criticized for two things. Firstly, it gives much emphasis to God and the unseen world where logic and arguments are meaningless. Secondly, according to this theory, bliss or pleasure remains in existence so long as the soul is in contact with the body. After salvation, where the soul is in the status of pure abstraction, the question of bliss (*ananda*) does not arise. If there is no bliss in the status of salvation, it is like a lifeless stone which has neither feelings nor any form of consciousness.

Sańkhya Darshana

The *Sankhya Darshana* produced by Kapila Muni was evidently produced against the doctrines of the Vedanta. It ignores the existence of God and denies the identity of the individual soul with the universal soul. According to the *Sankhya*, nature is the final cause of creation that is made up of *Sattva, Rajas* and *Tamas*. Nothing exists above nature. If there is anything, it is Absolute *Shunya* (zero), that is, nothingness. These three *gunas* are the attributes of nature that always remain active to cause changes in the universe. Creation takes place by the union of nature and soul. The *Sankhya* is dualistic in its principles while the Vedanta is non-dualistic. Both the systems, *Sankhya* and Yoga, primarily contributed to the development of agnosticism in Asia Minor and to the growth of Sufi philosophy.

The *Sankhya Darshana* puts emphasis on the 'cause-effect' theory. Each effect has its cause. The effect is effectively enshrined in its cause. Basically cause and effect are the same so long as they do not come in manifestation. In manifestation they seem to be different. Nature that is eternal is the root cause of creation of the universe. Nature is the subtle element spreading everywhere. Since nature produces *vikaras*, it is known as *prakriti*. It is the base or root cause of creation of qualities, mind, wisdom, ego, etc. There are two *prakritis* – *para-prakriti* and *apara-prakriti*. The former is absolutely subtle, clean and devoid of any kind of *vikara*, while the latter is impure and temporary. Entire creation, right from Brahma to the each blade of grass manifests from *prakriti* and ultimately merges into it. In other words, creation and annihilation take place in the boundless abode of *prakriti*. During the period of complete annihilation (*Mahapralaya*) all the three qualities of nature (*Sattva, Rajas* and *Tamas*) remain in a status of equilibrium. When the system of equilibrium is broken and the three qualities act independently, separating from each other, creation takes place. Creation evolves gradually. There is no external force like God or Supreme Power that helps creation for its evolution. Thus, this theory denies the existence of God. However, there are some scholars of *Sankhya Darshana* who do not deny the existence of Supreme Power. They advance the logic that nature is lifeless and unconscious. To cause motion and consciousness in nature and its creation, a conscious as well as an all pervasive and powerful energy is needed. This energy is God.

Yoga Darshana

The system of Kapila (the *Sankhya*) is called the atheistic *Sankhya*, and that of Patanjali the theistic *Sankhya*. Yoga means union of the mind with God. In the Yoga system, meditation is the uppermost whereby the individual establishes closeness to God. In other words, Yoga means concentration of the mind to a fixed point without any variation of mind, and the fix point is nothing but God, where there is no variation. In this system, the practitioner of Yoga has to delink all his thoughtful relations with the world, remain firm towards meditation of God and realize oneness with Him. It has eight stages – *Yama* which means restraint; *Niyama* which means religious observances; *Asana* (posture); *Pranayama* (suppression or control of breath); *Pratyahara* (restraint of the senses); *Dharana* (steadying the mind); *Dhyana* (deep contemplation); *Samadhi* (profound meditation towards giving up all the links with the mundane world). The system of *Nyaya* is analytical and original while *Sankhya* is synthetic and a form of imitation or replication. *Vaisheshika* is supplement to *Nyaya*. It establishes a particular *visheha* which is a predicable of atoms. Kanada enumerates six such categories only to which the seventh was subsequently added.

Yoga Darshana like *Sankhya* recognises all the twenty-four natural elements mentioned below:

1. Five *panchamahabhuta* – sky, fire, air, water and earth;
2. Five objects of *Panchamahabhuta* – *shabda*, *rupa*, *rasa*, touch and smell;
3. Five *jnanendriya* – eyes, nose, ears, tongue and skin;
4. Five *karmendriya* – legs, hands, mouth, genital organ and *guda* (anus); and
5. Four elements of inner-heart (*antaḥkarana*) – mind, wisdom, ego and *cit*.

All these aforesaid natural elements are lifeless because they emanate from nature which itself is lifeless. Hence, *Yoga Darshana* adds one more element that is God who is conscious and all powerful. *Ishvara*, the *Paramatma*, is eternal, all comprehensive, all powerful, omnipotent and omnipresent. He loves devotees and helps them. The primary aim of life is to personify God and achieve salvation. Yoga is the subscribed method following which one may realize or personify God.

Vimansa Darshana

This *Darshana* is based on logical concepts. Logical discussions and logical conclusions are nearer to the truth. It is quite near to the philosophy of *Vaisheshika Darshana*. Here, things or elements are examined, analysed and discussed. It accepts the method of *karmakandas* mentioned in Vedas. The basic object of its thinking is Veda or Sruti. It is not only realistic but pluralistic as well. According to *Vimansa*, God has no role to play in creation since creation is the result of action. The energy or power of creation is present in the subtle cause. Soul is different in different living beings. However, a soul is immortal. It does not perish after death of the body. It survives to take another birth, to enjoy the remaining fruits of actions. Each matter possesses quality (energy). For instance, a seed has the quality to germinate and grow. Fire has the energy to burn things.

Regarding creative action, it recognizes the theory of atom. Here, it is very much similar to the atom theory of *Vaisheshika Darshana*. It further recognizes that the *para-prakriti* is endless and limitless. All materials of the world are the products of atoms which reside in *para-prakriti* in subtle forms. Neither *para-prakriti* nor the subtle atom is destructible. Hence, they exist even after dissolution of the creation. As soon as new creation takes place, subtle atoms, having collaboration with *panchamahabhutas*, takes their forms.

Vedanta Darshana

Vedanta Darshana is, in fact, the most valuable and knowledgeable Vedic literature. The literature was produced at the end of the Vedas. So, it is called Vedanta. A major portion of the Vedantic literature are Upanishads that are full of deep and divine philosophy. The ultimate goal of the Vedas have been discussed and described in Vedanta. It is said that as oil is hidden in oil-seeds, Vedanta is enshrined in the Vedas. *Mahanarayana Upanishad* says that the knowledge of Vedanta, which is the most mysterious knowledge, has been described in the last part of the Vedas. (*Mahanarayana Upanishad*, 10.8) Besides the Upanishads, *Brahma Sutra* is also the most important creation of Vedanta. The Upanishads are in the form of dialogues between a teacher and disciples, and the facts are scattered. So, to consolidate these Vedantic facts *Brahma Sutra* was produced. *Bhagavad Gita* that is full of spiritual philosophy is another part of Vedanta.

Smritis and Puranas

Smritis are law books or code of human life. These are *Dharma Shastras* and religious texts that lay down civil/criminal laws – the inventory of rights and duties of people. These Smritis are known after the name of the authors such as – Manu, Atri, Vishnu, Gama, Harita, Yajnavalkya, Ushnas, Angiras, Apastamba, Samvarta, Vasishtha, Vyasa, Shankara, Likhita, etc. After the Srutis, the Smritis are the founding base of Hinduism. There are also the *Grihya Shastras* (thirteen in number) which deal with the social life of the Hindus. Their authors are Sankhyayana, Ashvalayana, Gobhila, Khadira, Praskara, Apastamba, Hiranyakeshin, Nandhyana, Manva, Kathaka, Bharadwaja, Vikahanasa, and Kaushika respectively. They speak about the rights and duties of the people in their day-to-day affairs.

Puranas are those religious books of ancient India which teach religion, cosmology, and laws through an elaborate network of tales and legends. Every Purana deals with five subjects – *Sarga* (creation), *Pratisarga* (cycles of dissolution and renewal of the worlds), *Vansha* (genealogy of gods and sheers, the great periods, each of which is headed by the primal ancestor (Manu) of the human race and the history of the great dynasties whose origins are ultimately traced back to the Sun and the Moon. All Puranas do not deal with such five things exactly. There are 18 Puranas written by Vyasa Muni. Name of the Puranas are given below:

1. *Brahma Purana*
2. *Padma Purana*
3. *Vishnu Purana*
4. *Shiva Purana*
5. *Bhagavata Purana*
6. *Narada Purana*
7. *Markandeya Purana*
8. *Agni Purana*
9. *Bhavishya Purana*
10. *Skanda Purana*
11. *Vamana Purana*
12. *Kurma Purana*
13. *Matsya Purana*
14. *Garuda Purana*
15. *Varah Purana*
16. *Vaivarta Purana*
17. *Linga Purana*
18. *Brahmanda Purana*

Closely associated to the Puranas are the two *Itihasas* (History) known as the *Mahabharata* and the *Ramayana*. They are literary classics, but full of religious thoughts. Kautilya's *Arthashastra* and Vatsyayana's *Kamasutra* which are also religious texts of India.

Conclusion

It is evident that the Vedas are Srutis. It has not been produced by a single rishi or a sage of any particular time period. There are various rishis of ancient India who being curious, about the wonderful nature of the world and the universe; and establishing mental contact with the supernatural powers, received their holy language relating to the creation of the universe, its cosmic order, its divine nature and purpose of divine creation, dictated the received divine knowledge to their disciples who were also devoted to the holy knowledge. It took centuries to complete the Vedas. Thereafter, various great rishis and munis, devoted to supernatural knowledge, took the troubles to memorize the sermons of their Gurus, presented various religious philosophical scriptures like Smritis, Brahmanas, Aranyakas, Upanishads, Puranas, Sutras etc, enriching Vedic knowledge. The Vedas in original form were too vague to understand easily. Hence, different Bhashyas and commentaries were written with a purpose to highlight the Vedic knowledge and expand its scope. It is notable that the Vedic literature mentioned above does not present a new philosophical theme going out of the range of the Vedas. Rather their views and thoughts are closely related to the Vedas. The Vedas remained the basic source of their knowledge. What they said is an elaboration of the Vedas. However, the philosophies and knowledge what they presented in different Vedic literature are very much logical, scientific, convincing and useful. A deep and thorough study of these ancient religious as well as philosophical presentations, leads one to say that the ancient great Indian rishis and sages were devoted not only to religion, but to the happenings of the great transcendental world which is inconvincible to the common mind.

Thus, they founded, with their true devotion to godly atmosphere and natural order in the universe, the strong and beautiful base of Indian culture and civilization. The inhabitants of ancient India, who were called Hindus, adopted the new way of civilization and culture whole-heartedly. The philosophy and religion they presented was not non-secular, but secular in spirit and universal in nature. The Dharma which they spoke of, is universal and *Sanatana*. If it is understood in the right perspective, it is the only light that may save the world of today from disappearing religion, falling morality, and controversial philosophical thoughts.

Notes and References

1. Majumdar, RC and others, 1978 (4th edition) *An Advanced History of India*, Macmillan Publishers, Delhi, p 24.
2. Ibid.
3. Ghosh, Ramachandra, 1988, *History of Hindu Civilization*, Kaushal Prakashan, New Delhi, p 2.
4. Ibid, pp 1-2.
5. *Shatapatha Brahmana*, IV 6, 7, 1, also see, *Aitareya Brahmana*, V, 32.
6. *Atharvaveda*, VII, 64.2; *Rigveda*, X, 90, 9; *Taittiriya Samhita*, 1, 2, 3,
7. Muller, Max, *The History of Ancient Sanskrit Literature*, pp 70, 526 ff.
8. Weber, Max, *History of Indian Literature*, p 148.
9. Lassen, *Indian Antiquities*, III, 379ff

4

Impact of Vedantic Philosophy on Indian Religion and Civilization

Veda means knowledge. The Vedas which have been handed down by the early Indo-Aryans carry a vast treasury of knowledge related to the wonder of universe, its origin, its expansion, its infinity, its forces, its powers comprising of various gods, goddesses and supernatural beings, their nature and the mechanism of the universe as a whole. The Vedas talk of laws, order and thought of Divine Beings. The Vedas contain the thread which links the present with the past. It mentions about the most convincing religion of antiquity which throws sufficient light on the rise and growth of various religions across the human world. In the words of Ramachandra Ghosh, "To the Vedas must be attached an undying interest and an ever increasing value not only for their greatest antiquity, but also for the immense flood of light which they throw on the primitive state of Indo-Aryan society, Indo-Aryan speech, and general mythology."[1] The Vedas are the primeval sources for studying and understanding Indo-Aryan theology, philosophy, morality, ethics, society, religion and politics. They abound in the knowledge of theology, philosophy, astronomy, geometry, etc. Ramachandra agrees that, "In process of time, the Vedic religion, whatever it was, has become through the corruptions and prejudices, of a most revolving type, of successive ages a heterogeneous medley of theology, philosophy and science."[2] The age in which the Vedas and their appendages were produced, has exercised the blandest influence upon all succeeding periods of Indian history. Every later branch of literature is closely connected with the Vedic traditions. The religious and moral ideas have been derived from them, and the Indo-Aryan life, in all its aspects, has been moulded by traditional precepts.

Vedas

The word Veda is significantly employed to designate those ancient Sanskrit works, in which is laid the foundation of Brahminic belief, and these works were originally three in numbers – the *Rigveda*, the *Samaveda* and the *Yajurveda*. The prayers in metre (verse rhythm) are called Rik, and those in prose are denominated *yajus*, while those intended to be chanted are named Saman. Again, the complete collection of hymns (*Mantra*), prayers and thanksgivings, belonging to the Vedas is called its Samhita. The fourth Veda, namely *Atharvaveda* is a later addition. The *Rigveda* is the Veda of hymns, the *Samaveda* is the Veda of chants, the *Yajurveda* is the Veda of sacrificial formulas and the *Atharvaveda* is the Veda of incantations.[3] The *Rik Samhita* was composed on the banks of the river Indus. Their final redaction certainly took place when the Aryan tribes had moved from Punjab to the eastern plains, and the Brahminical elements had become predominant. Before migration to various parts of India and their final settlement in this country, the Aryans carried with them the hymns which were given their final shape after they had permanently settled here.

The *Rigveda* consists, with a few exceptions, of detached prayers dedicated to divinities (now no longer worshipped). In point of time, and even in a point of literary development, it is the oldest of the books and the earliest depository of Aryan faith. The hymns, indeed, do not show what the primitive creed of the Indo-Aryans was, but on the other hand, they reflect a strong light on the original articles of belief of humanity itself. Though the hymns lack literary development, they contain moral ideas and spiritual hopes and aspirations. It were these values that helped India to develop a society or a country, giving top priority to moral, human as well as philosophical, values not only inside but also outside the nation. Today, India abounds in international morality, brotherhood, humanity and spirituality due to its historical background that is abundantly available in Vedic as well as in its appendage literature. Thus, it was the ancient ancestors who laid the foundation of India's moral and philosophical base upon which the strong and attractive Indian cultural, as well as religious, mansion was built.

Origin of the Vedas

Regarding the origin of the Vedas nothing definite can be said because the hymns were developed during different phases by different families. That is why there is heterogeneity in the Vedas. The hymns are arranged in order of the deities addressed, and in accordance with the families of various rishsis. Through various hymns, homage or depreciation has been paid to various objects like mountains, rivers, springs, trees, plants, the horse, the cow, the dogs, which keep watch over dwellings, the birds which reveal the future, the sacrificial implements, the war-chariot, offensive and defensive weapons, the plough and the furrow, etc. The hymns are addressed to Agni, Indra, the Vishvedevah and other divinities.[4] Prayers and admirations have been made to various natural as well as supernatural powers with the expectation to obtain blessings and goodness. In that way the vastness and supremacy of the deities are described. It shows that they were fully convinced of natural as well as supernatural forces and they expected blessings from them by offering sacrifices and doing prayers. Vedic hymns are appraisal of natural as well as supernatural energies of the universe.

It is said that there is a faculty of faith in man, a power independent of senses and reason, the primordial source of any religion, which enables man to apprehend the Infinite. It is true that Nature 'does not speak of itself, but of One Who speaks by it.' Nature is definitely infinite, but greater than it is the human soul. Religion, in fact, "is a spontaneous sentiment", an intuitive perception, in which the mind unconsciously draws its breath and has its being. It is not the product of reasoning. It is the hidden fount of faith, which gushes up within man. Man in all the entirety of his complex nature "cries out for the living God. Human reason cries out for God, because it cannot rest on its onward march till it arrives at an Intelligent First Cause."[5] It is all because in this vast universe man needs a Supreme authority that can guide him towards better ways, protects him from troubles and calamities and helps him to fulfil his desires. Some philosophers have rightly said that if there is no God, we have to create one for our guidance, support, protection and dependence.

Soul is an integral part of divine force that is Infinite and the primeval cause of everything. God that represents that infinite, eternal and everlasting power attracts each and every soul towards Him. It is that attraction which attracts each soul and the latter in search of the centre of attraction speculate more and more, imagine more and more, wander onwards with the ambition to merge with the Godly centrifugal force. Philosophy and religion, what have been discovered hitherto, are human unceasing efforts to personify the Supreme Power and obtain permanent peace and pleasure. Since that Divine Power is infinite and beyond reasonable comprehension of mankind, man uses the faculties of his imagination and emotions which ultimately results in religion. Primitive Aryans were more emotional than rational in efforts of their research to deities. The Indo-Aryans imagined the highest and contributed the best. The hymns of the Vedas are unceasing efforts of the Aryans to know God and find out ways and means to please Him for blessings, nearness and ultimately merging in Him. Prayers and devotions are the most convincing ways to please such unseen and unknown power and obtain his blessings. The vital question is not whether human prayers reaches the supreme power, but it is the essence of the prayers that gives one confidence that he has been heard, and makes one convinced that he is under the protection of the most powerful of the universe. With this faith and confidence he can do what he likes. Nothing definitely can be known about the infinite universe, but something definitely can be imagined about infinity. Indo-Aryans tried their best to imagine and know about the world of ambiguity and vagueness.

The Indo-Aryans recognized the presence of the divine in the brightest aspect of nature, and therefore, they called the blue sky, the fertile earth, the genial fire, the bright day, the golden dawn as their deities. In the words of Ramachandra, "The flaming orb of the mighty brilliant sun, the rattling thunderstorm, the flaming lightening, the rolling thunder, fitful whisperings of the forest trees, the furious blasts, rain, mist and hail awaken bright fancies in the mind of the thoughtful and poetic man. These, indeed, are the powers that thrilled and awed our ancestors; and made a tremendous impression upon their desponding mind."[6] The early Aryans either Indo or others were too much curious about natural happenings, and they tried to penetrate into the ultimate cause of such happenings. Such curiosity did not made them scientists, but made them philosophers because they penetrated into abstract not into concrete. This led them towards search and research of reality which took several centuries.

The hymns of the *Rigveda* are apparently of different periods, spread over several centuries; some among them being older and some more recent.[7] Max Muller designates the most ancient portion of the hymns by the term *chhandas*, and those that are comparatively modern as Mantras.[8] The authors of the new hymns borrowed many thoughts and words from the old ones. The originality of ancient Vedas remained intact. The *Rik Samhita* is the product of joint efforts of various rishis who took not less than one or two generations to complete it. During the period when it was given shape, the Aryans moved from place to place, carrying their social, religious and political values. The Vedas do not appear to be the creation of one and the same author or even of the same age. According to Max Muller, "In the most ancient Sanskrit literature, the idea even of authorship is excluded. Works are spoken of as revealed to and communicated by certain sages, but not as composed by them."[9] It was impossible to grasp such vast knowledge by one or two authors at a time and produce it in any language. In fact, knowledge of the absolute is permanent, immortal and eternal. It never dies or disappears. It remains present even after annihilation of an entire creation. It is all because knowledge of the absolute is the Supreme Idea from which all things, either material or spiritual, emanates and survives. Supreme Idea is the permanent abode of knowledge. The creation is woven in the knowledge possessed by the creator. The ancient sages of India, perhaps, went into deep meditation and visualized the absolute knowledge revealed to them. They were *drashta* (seer) of knowledge. It was the personification of absolute knowledge, revealed to Indo-Aryans from time to time, which came to be known as Vedas. The Vedas have been handed down to us by our ancient sages. The earlier rishis who contributed to the growth of Vedas did not claim that they were not inspired by divine forces. They knew and believed themselves simply to be the authors of the hymns of the Vedas. It does not mean that they were unconscious of divine influence. They seem to have attached high value to their productions, which, as they believed, were acceptable to the gods whom they addressed and prayed.[10]

There are also a great multitude of passages in the *Rigveda* which ascribes a supernatural character to the earlier rishis.[11] It was believed that hymns uttered by them were of Divine influence. The rishis are said to have held intercourse about sacred truths with the gods.[12] On the other hand, some among them professed their ignorance of all matters either human or divine.[13] There are many hymns in which it also appears that the consciousness of some affinity with the divine nature was upper most in their mind. They likewise believed to have been 'endowed with super wisdom', and to have possessed the knowledge of the deities.[14]

Thus, it is evident that the rishis who were involved in production of the Vedas were of high mental as well as spiritual character. They were people of penance and meditation. They were sacred and their vision was transcendental. Absolute truths or ideas are eternal that always prevail. The people of transcendental vision have approach to such truths even today. The earlier Aryan rishis were of the kind who could establish link with the absolute truth through meditation and *samadhi*. It seems that they had personified the truths and the gods. What they received was not their experience or learning, but the revelation of the truths. The rishis sought from their gods every kind of temporal blessings, such as long life, food, riches, strength, offspring, cattle, and rain.[15] They believed that those gods were merciful and able to grace the blessing to devotees. It is believed that these rishis were themselves people of superhuman character and what they contributed was meant for human beings to understand creation and follow the path prescribed by them. The words said by the rishis in the Vedas are infallible. The truth contained in the verses is beyond criticism and doubt. These are to be believed inclusively. The claims as to divine and infallible character of the Vedas must have been set up gradually. However, such claim and height of the Vedas were denied when Buddhism appeared in India. The Buddha, who believed in the philosophy of atheism and denied the existence of gods, opposed the infallible character of the Vedas and challenged the practice of Brahminism which ultimately resulted in direct clash between Buddhism and Brahmanism.[16]

Views and Opinions of Indian Scholars about Vedas

Indian authors held the opinion on the origin of the Vedas as springing from the mystical sacrifice of *Purusha*.[17] It is believed that the *Rigveda* sprang from *Skambha*; *Atharvaveda* from the mouth of Brahma, Indra, Agni, Vayu and Surya; Manu and *Shatapatha Brahmana* from Prajapati. In short, belief prevails that various parts of the Vedas, Puranas, Brahmanas, Smritis and Upanishads have sprang from various gods. Since the hymns and narrations mentioned in them are godly, their sanctity and sagacity cannot be doubted. The Vedas are self-existent. The creator brooded over three worlds, and thence produced three lights, fire, the air and the sun, from which respectively were excreted the Rik, Yajus and Saman. In like manner, many other authorities might be cited to the same effect, but they are puerile and contradictory to themselves. The rishis designated the older hymns, and of the later period by various names such as Arka, Uktha, Rik, Gir, Dhi, Nitha,

Nivid, Mantra, Mati, Sukta, Stoma, Nick, Vachas Suman, Yajus, Manaman, Manishi, Sumati, Dhiti, Dhisana, Stuti, etc.[18]

The authenticity of the Vedas or connected religious scriptures of India is a subject of controversy. In the scientific age there are many who are to deny the Vedas' authenticity relating to its origin and sanctity, but it is a fact that the Vedas are still fresh in the Hindu mind and they have played a great role to constitute India's Hindu society. The remarks of Whitney related to the significance of the Vedas are notable. He says:

> "At whatever time the work may have been performed, it constituted a decided era in the literary history of India. Thence forth, the text became a chief object of the science and industry of the nation, as their contents had always attached its highest reverence and admiration; and so thorough and religious was the care bestowed upon their preservation, that, notwithstanding their mass and the thousands of years which have elapsed since their collection, hardly a single various reading, so far as is yet known, has been suffered to make its way into them after their definite and final establishment. The influence which they have exerted upon the whole literary development of after ages is not easily to be rated too high."[19]

Among the four Vedas the *Rigveda* has the greatest significance. The *Rigveda* is the most earliest. Numerous hymns of the *Rigveda* have been repeated in other Vedas. Its rishis are referred to even in the other Vedas. However, all its original verses are not traceable. Whatever has been preserved, is of great interest. It attracted the attention of the renowned scholars of the world. It serves as "an oasis in the vast desert of ancient Asiatic history, and it is the only real Veda, the *Rigveda*, the earliest existing record of the whole Aryan race."[20] The Vedas are written in an ancient form of Sanskrit. They abound in obsolete and peculiar expressions made up of the more recent grammatical forms with such irregularity as leads to the inference that the language was too unsettled and variable to be brought under subjection to a system of rigid grammatical rules. The language is too vague and too difficult to understand easily. It is said that the Vedic dialect is to be understood as the least altered representative of that original tongue from which are descended the languages of the leading races of Asia and Europe.

> "The language of the Vedas is an older dialect, varying very considerably, both in its grammatical and lexical character, from the classical Sanskrit. Its grammatical peculiarities run through all departments: euphonic, rule, word formation and composition, declension, conjugation, syntax."[21]

It has already been mentioned that the Vedas were produced in different periods. Max Muller divides Vedic Age into four distinct periods. The first is the *Chhanda* period, second is the Mantra period, third is Brahmana period and fourth is the Sutra period. During the *Chhanda* period the oldest hymns were prepared, and this period, in fact, furnishes us with a fair picture of the primitive society of the Indo-Aryans at a time when no particular system of religion was prevalent. There existed neither *varna* nor caste system. But in the Mantra period religion came to be regarded in great estimation. During this period the more hymns were composed, and everything was placed together and arranged into one Samhita. Three other Samhitas were also collected and arranged systematically for distinct theological or sacrificial purposes. During this time the system of priesthood came into practice. The priests elaborated a most highly complex system of sacrifices. From here the Brahmana period began, and the principal theological and liturgical books appeared. Thereafter, theological speculations obtained greater pace. In the Sutra period the ceremonial precepts of the earlier time were reduced to a systematic form. The works of the period are not all written in the enigmatical form of Sutras, but some are in verse and others in prose. The Vedas have their own Sutras and Brahmanas, and the Brahmanas do not refer to them. It is proved that the Brahmanas period must have proceeded the Sutra period. In the Brahmana and Sutra periods the Sanskrit language must have undergone considerable modifications. The Sutra period extends far into the Buddhistic time. During this period occurred certainly one of the most remarkable changes in the Indo-Aryan religion and society.

According to Max Muller's estimation the *Chhanda* period might have existed from 1200 to 1000 BC; the Mantra period from 1000 to 800 BC; the Brahmana period from 800 to 600 BC and the Sutra period from 600 to 200 BC. But this estimation does not seem appropriate because it is too narrow. In the absence of dates, it is not possible to exactly divide these periods of ancient Sanskrit literature. So, uncertainty hangs over the exact chronological order of these periods. The dates of preparation of ancient Sanskrit literature are based on approximation. There is no unanimity among the scholars to decide about the exactness of the period or dates of such literature. Sir William Jones and Colebrook assigned to the composition of the *Rigveda*, a period fourteen or fifteen hundred years before Christ. Ramachandra has rightly remarked that "There are no milestones in Vedic literature. The classification of ancient Sanskrit literature has now become a theme for discussion by every Sanskrit scholar. But where it is to end is not easy to surmise. It has been questioned whether the basis of the classification is scientific or ritual or theological. But whatever may be advanced against such an arrangement, we have every reason to place our faith in the distribution of Vedic literature into distinct periods."[22]

Chhanda and Mantras in Vedas

Each Veda has two folds – the Mantra and Brahmana. The part of the Veda that contains the Mantras, the material hymns or prose forms of prayers, is called its Samhita. The Brahmanas stand to the Mantras in the same relation as the *Talmud* (compendium of Jewish laws and teachings) does to the Mosaic (the first five books of the Old Testament) code. The former presupposes the earlier existence of the latter. And the proof that the Mantras are far older than any other portion of Indian literature is to be found particularly in the character of their language. The Brahmana portion of each Veda is posterior at least to some part of its Samhitas, for the former evidently refer to, and contains extracts from the latter. The Mantras are generally in verse while the Brahmanas are entirely in prose. The Mantras, in fact, for ages remained unwritten and carried out in memories. Although the Veda is formed both of Mantra and Brahmana yet as the Brahmana consists of an explanation of the Mantras. It is the latter which were at first recorded. Sayana in his commentary on the *Brihadaranyaka Upanishad* also says that "the Mantras are the sources of the Brahmanas."[23]

Brahmanas

Most of the Brahmanas are collective works and there are old and new Brahmanas. Several of the Brahmanas have no trace today. The Brahmanas, in fact, were the productions of the schools of Brahminic priesthood. They are characterized by dogmatic assertion, and by flimsy symbolism. However, they contain too many theological and ceremonial values. The oldest rituals, the oldest linguistic expositions, the oldest philosophical and mystical speculations are found in them. Regarding their origin and age they occupy a mind of intermediate position between the transitions from a simple Vedic mode of thought to the Brahminical vagaries.[24] It is believed that these transitions were brought by Brahmanas only. They drew them up with a view to enforcing various ceremonies and sacrifices, to illustrate the use of the hymns and to enjoin the duties of the different classes of priests.

The Brahmana was originally a theological tract. It was so designated because it owed its origin to Brahmana or prayer. The entire collection of Brahmanas gives the impression of having undergone a secondary alteration. It came into being in the later course of the religious or theological history of Indo-Aryans. The belief of the statements of these compositions is related to religious practices. In the words of Ramachandra, "They are very useful for an explanation of the principle of belief because they were composed with the distinct object in the intellectual history of the Indo-Aryans; but in literary point of view they are altogether without any interest. They are in the main marked by serious reasoning, full of genuine thoughts, lofty expressions, and valuable traditions; but their general characteristics mainly consist in their archaisms, grammatical irregularities, antiquated and tautological style, and antiquarian pedantry."[25] One finds pantheistic system in the Brahmanas. The system was adopted simply for the explanation of Vedic deities. They put emphasis on ritualism comprising of *vidhis* (ceremonial procedures) and *artha-vidhis* (ceremonial procedures with meaning). They also talk of various battles fought between Devas and Asuras. There is mention of four *varnas* (Brahmin, Kshatriya, Vaishya and Shudra) and their social status. In fact, the Brahmanas are the history of one of the most important periods in the social and mental development of India. They establish the importance and also the efficacy of the Vedas. In other words, they came into being to support and explain the Vedas.

The Brahmanas supported the Vedas, no doubt, but it provided a new direction to Hindu society where Brahminism got fertile land to flourish. From here ritualism and *karmakanda* began. The class of priests who assumed the responsibility to perform sacrifices came to be known as the most respectable class. Among the four *varnas*, they came to be known as the Brahmins and others as the Kshatriyas, Vaishyas and Shudras. The social division took place. However, the base of the different *varnas*, in the beginning, was not the birth or heredity, but the jobs or professions that they followed. It was the Vedic religious beliefs, propounded and explained by the Brahmanas, which served as the strong base of social division.

Aranyakas and Upanishads

From the Brahmanas sprang those mystical and theosophical writings, the Aranyakas and the Upanishads. By the word Aranyaka, Panini understands a mere forester. If the theological works called the Aranyakas were extant during his time, he would have recognized them as a portion of the sacred literature. The Aranyakas is so called, according to Sayana, because they were read in the forests. Of the Aranyakas there are four extant, the *Brihad*, the *Taittiriya*, the *Aitareya* and the *Kaushitaki*. They contain the quintessence of the Vedas, and they treat only the science of Brahma. They are anterior to the Sutras, and likewise, they are posterior to the Brahmanas, to which they form a kind of appendix. The Aranyakas discuss about the obscure points of religion and philosophy, the nature of God, and subjects of a like nature. There is no mentioning of authorship. It is notable that they exhibit the very dawn of philosophical thought. They also abound in passages which are unequalled in any language, for grander, simplicity and boldness.

Upanishads are the soul of the Indian metaphysical philosophy. They talk of universal transcendental God, His nature, attributes, and His relevance with our world. The original Upanishads, or the mysteries of Theosophy, had their place in the Aranyakas and the Brahmanas. The most important of them are full of theosophy and philosophy. The Upanishads belong to *Parishads* or settlements. The ideas and even the expressions contained in them are apparently common to most of them. Those ideas again did not grow up in one and the same locality; but they must have had an independent growth which was of course determined by local influences and individual opinions. The Indo-Aryans began to cultivate philosophical thoughts from an early age. In the course of research to find out the origin of the creation, they developed such philosophical investigation. They developed the philosophy of Vedanta (Absolutism and Advaitism) and discovered the theory of *Maya*, establishing the fact that nothing is true and permanent except God alone. What we see and observe in this world is not reality, but a mirage, which has no real existence. Socrates, Plato and many other Idealist thinkers of the world followed the same line regarding metaphysical philosophy. The Vedanta talks of the God who is alone, without anyone, and whatsoever one sees or observes in nature is nothing, but a mirage because their existence is temporary and they are subject of decay. On the other hand, God about whom they speak is eternal, permanent, all pervasive, all powerful, unseen, and shapeless, beyond the reach of the sense organs and the human mind. In the *Bhagavad Gita*, Arjuna says to Lord Krishna:

> The Supreme Brahman, the Supreme Light, the Supreme Purifier art thou. All the rishis declare Thee as Eternal, Divine *Purusha*, the Primal God, Unborn, Omnipresent....[7] (*Bhagavad Gita*, X/13).

When Arjuna witnessed the *Virat Rupa* of the Lord, being surprised he said:

> Thou art the Imperishable. The Supreme Being worthy to be known. Thou art the Great Abode of this Universe. Thou art the undying Guardian of the Eternal Dharma, thou art the Ancient *Purusha*, I deem. (*Bhagavad Gita*, XI/18)

Max Muller has surmised that the word Upanishad "meant originally the act of sitting down near a teacher, of submissively listening to him," whence it came to mean "implicit faith, and at last truth or divine revelation." With regard to the Upanishads, Schopenhauer, the founder of a new school of philosophy, in a high stream of appreciation of Upanishads has said: "In the whole world of literature there is nothing to be compared with the Upanishads. They have been solace of my life; they will be the solace of my death."[26] Upanishads are communally in the forms of dialogues. The oldest among them may date as far as six century BC. Some noted Upanishads which are available today are – *Brihadaranyaka, Aitareya, Chhandogya, Taittiriya, Isha, Shvetashvatara, Kena, Prashna, Katha, Mundaka* and *Mandukya*. All these Upanishads are old and genuine. They are also called classical. The verses or prose of the Upanishads are very primitive. The greater portion of them expresses the deepest thoughts on religion and philosophy. The ordinary enumeration of the Upanishads exceeds a hundred, but most of them are apocryphal. Of all the Upanishads fifty-one were translated into Latin and published by Anquetil Duperron in 1801 under the title of *Oupnekhat* or *Theosophia Indica*.

Significance of the Upanishads

The Upanishads are the words of Gaudapada Shankaracharya and other renowned philosophers. The theological and philosophical views of the Upanishads are the deepest thoughts of the human mind. In the words of Ramachandra, "They are the most ancient monuments of philosophical conceptions, and as such they are far more advanced, both in the depth and loftiness of their ideas and opinions than any of the Greek schools prior to Socrates, except that of Elea. They contributed much towards the formation of civil and domestic policies, and directed the whole tone of moral ordinances. They are considered some show of reason as the highest authorities on whom the various systems of philosophy are said to rest."[27] The basic objectives of the Upanishads had been to unfold the darkest point of philosophy and religion, to discuss the creation of the world to descant on the nature of God, and to elucidate the relation of man with God and the like. The emphasis has been laid down on the fact that human soul is a reflection of the universal soul, and they are one in nature as well as qualities. Soul of every creature, being an integral part of the universal soul, is immortal and eternal. Nothing can destroy it. Each soul residing in any living being reflects God's qualities. Since each soul is a reflection of God, all creatures or living beings are similar in spirit. On the basis of this philosophy the Upanishads teaches the doctrine of non-violence, universal brotherhood, and humanity. God is the creator of the universe and soul is God's representative. It is as pure and sacred as God himself. Since the soul has been captivated by the *Maya* or nature, its release is possible provided it can come out of the captivity of ignorance. Upanishads prescribe several means and ways to liberate the human soul from the captivity of *Maya*. The most viable way to liberate the soul is to establish close links with God through worshipping God with absolute faith and devotion. Man being the victim of lust and *trishna* has indulged in the material world for temporal pleasure. Due to ignorance, man, instead of getting pleasure, has fallen the prey of pains and troubles. The status in which living beings have fallen down would continue till salvation is obtained. To get salvation one needs the blessings of perfect spiritual gurus and the compassion of God.

There is no systematic uniformity in the Upanishads, and the philosophy contained in them is sublime. It is, in some places, puerile. They talk of spiritual existence. They have successfully made the distinction between concrete existence and abstract beings. The philosophy that reflects in the Upanishads is the subject of criticism, no doubt, but its significance lies in the greatness of religion. The Upanishads contain mythological as well as theosophical elements. They exhibit a freedom of thought which was, in fact, the beginning of Hindu philosophy. Emphasis of the Upanishads is on the term 'know thyself', and understands the universality of the self and its relationship with the Universal Self. The Upanishads, from the beginning to the end, consists of texts which teach the unity and the transcendent nature of the Self, and that all this world is the One Eternal Self – the one spiritual reality. From it all things proceed, in which everything subsists and into which all things ultimately merge. Except the Universal Self, nothing is permanent. It is the originator, sustainer and destroyer of things. The entire universe emanates from it, remains and prospers in it and lastly merges into it. The Highest Soul is the starting point of all phenomenal manifestations.[28] The doctrine of metempsychosis takes its root from the Upanishads.

According to Upanishads the world is an illusion because of its transitory stability. Here is ignorance which is the root cause of transmigration of living beings from one birth to another. The circle of transmigration of the individual soul is ceaseless till it obtains salvation. The illusion separates the personal self from the impersonal. The only way to destroy such illusion is to obtain real knowledge that has been prescribed in the Upanishads. Upon the rise of true knowledge the individual self attains freedom from further new births and reaches the spiritual height from there is no fall again. In the words of Ramachandra, "The means of liberation from metempsychosis is not the performance of sacrificial rites, but the knowledge of the identity of the self with the Eternal Self. They inculcate pantheism of one kind or another; but, beyond doubt, their pantheism is of a very spiritual kind. And unity, indeed, is not opposed, but is indispensably necessary to the idea."[29]

Pantheism that emerges later is a belief whereby it is understood that God is all pervasive and He envelops everything. God has manifested in numerous ways and many other gods and goddesses are God's representatives because they have originated from Him and they draw all qualities as well as powers from Him. They have been assigned to different performances in the universe to uphold it and support it in its development. However, there is only one God who is Supreme and All Powerful. However, the Upanishads speak of the Unspeakable and define the Indefinable. "The Unspeakable or Indefinable of the Upanishads is not God, but the Self; and, on the whole, their system is a system of spiritual absolutism."[30]

Concept of Brahma, the Creator

Various modes and fashions of the Self and Supreme Self has been discussed in different Upanishads.[31] It is said that Brahma, the creator, comprehends all things, both objects of perceptions and those that are beyond the reach of perception. Nothing could be imagined or understood of the latter because it is either non-manifested or beyond the reach of human senses. Brahma has four modes of existence, the waking state, the state of dreaming, the state of profound sleep, and the fourth state being quite different from any of the former. This state is the state of *turium* in Sanskrit language which means a state about which nothing can be said because it stands above the manifested world in the absolute subtle form. This state is indiscernible and indescribable. It is the state where all manifestations cease. It is blissful and without duality. The *Mandukya Upanishad* finds the Infinite Spirit in its primitive notion where there is no activity. It is the state of complete tranquility. There is neither motion nor time. It has no relevance at all with the manifested universe. It is not only invisible but traceless as well. But there is something. It is this something that is unspeakable and indefinable. The rishis, maharishis, yogis, mediators, poets, and philosophers have been imagining this state in various ways, but what they conclude is neither universal nor final. Regarding realization of God by meditation, the *Bhagavad Gita* amply says:

> With the mind intend on Me, O Partha, practising Yoga, and finding refuge in me, how in full without doubt thou shalt know Me, that do thou hear. (*Bhagavad Gita*, VII/1)

It is further said:

> Meditating with the mind engaged in the Yoga of constant practice, not passing over to anything else, one goes to the Supreme *Purusha*, the Resplendent, O, son of Pritha. (*Bhagavad Gita*, VIII/8)

However, what the ancient Indian as well as modern philosophers have spoken about such Unspeakable is the wisest of all the knowledge discovered and presented by scholars of the world.

The Upanishads and the *Bhagavad Gita* are expansions of the Vedas.[32] However, among all of the Vedic works that were the last composition. The *Taittiryankas* speak of Brahma as true, they give proofs of their having been impressed with the idea of power. It was discovered that Brahma, a conceptual force of ultimate power, is neither masculine nor feminine, but neuter. The Chhandogyas speak of a *Sat* (a divine infinite force or energy) which has the capability to be many. It was the desire of that *Sat* to be many and, thus, the creation came into being. So, creation is expansion or materialization of the desire of the *Sat* (*Paramatma*). It is also said that the creator is *Akshara* (beyond destruction), and it remains even after end of creation. *Akshara* is the basic source of creation. Regarding *Akshara*, the *Bhagavad Gita* says, "*aksharam brahma paramam*" (The Indestructible, transcendental living entity is called *Brahman*). (*Bhagavad Gita*, VIII/3). Manifestation or creation that takes place emerges from that *Akshara*. It is said that Rudras, Adityas, Vasus, and Sadhyas, Vishvas and Ahsvins, Maruts and Ushmapas, host of Gandharvas Yakshas, Asuras and Siddhas, etc, emanate from the *Akshara* and they all look at the Supreme Lord Godhead being astonished. They all pray to the Imperishable God. (*Bhagavad Gita*, XI/22)

The Mantras, the Brahmanas, the Aranyakas and the Upanishads are designated under the term of Sruti. The term Smritis includes the Vedangas, the Sutras. Sruti means revelation of divine truth or hearing of divine truth while the meaning of Smritis is a collection. What has been mentioned or discussed in the Sruti is not the thought of the thinkers, but of the truth that were revealed to the rishis and yogis who had gone into deep *samadhi*. Hence, the statements of the Sruti is true and beyond doubt. The Smritis are the later part of the Vedanta and the facts mentioned in them have been collected from various authentic sources. Smritis are the memories of the rishis, and as such the memories vary and lack authenticity. Like the Sruti. The Smritis have no claim to an independent authority, but derives its sanctions from its relations to Srutis.

The Mantras are either metrical hymns or prose forms of prayer, in which the praises of gods are celebrated for the attainment of their blessing. The hymns of the *Rigveda* and the *Samaveda* are in the forms of Mantras that praise deities of gods of like Agni, Vayu, Savitri, Surya, etc. The Brahmanas arose out of the hymns, and so they stand next to the Mantras. The former embrace liturgical (fixed form of published worship) prescriptions regarding the ceremonial employment of various rites and sacrifices. It is these Vedic Mantras which gave rise to rites and sacrifices. Thus, the origin and practice of Hindu rituals and *karmakandas* are the Mantras mentioned in the Vedas. The rites and sacrifices, falling in the hands of priests which appeared later on, became too rigid and orthodox, inviting critics.

Conclusion

While concluding the chapter it may be said that the Vedas and their appendages which developed during the ancient period of Indian civilization is the base of India's Hindu civilization and culture. They contain the philosophy that is related to both transcendental as well as mundane worlds. They present a vast picture of the transcendental world that is non-manifested; and that is the primal source of all kinds of manifestations including living and non-living things. What we talk of God that is the divine concept, both manifested and non-manifested; in the Vedas that concept is *Brahman* which is the ultimate sources of creation from Brahma down to the single blade of grass. The non-manifested (*Avyakta*) is the sleeping state of Brahma. Out of that, all manifestations (*Vyakta*) are manifested when Brahma awakes. (*Bhagavad Gita*, VII/18) The *Avyakta* is also called *Akshara*, the Imperishable that is the highest place of God and one reaching there never returns to the mundane world. (*Bhagavad Gita*, 8/21). The living creature, right from Brahma to the smallest living being, is nothing but a reflection or manifestation of the *Brahman*. The mundane world is a material world which is completely wrapped in *Maya* (illusion) which is a product of *Prakriti*; and the living beings of this world, though they are an integral part of Absolute God, are ignorant of their real nature with the result that they have been wandering after material prosperities that are the subject to transitory existence. Falling into the lap of *Maya*, which contains fastening elements like desire, greed, lust, wrath, etc, all the living beings of the mundane world are subjects of bondage, facing various troubles and pains like birth, death, oldness, diseases, scarcity, etc.

The Vedas teach people how to be liberated from such bondage of *Maya* and return back to the immortal place, reaching where no one comes down to the mundane world. That is called salvation. In other words, Vedas describe not only the nature of *Brahman*, but also presents the ways to mankind for revival and liberation. *Karmakandas* prescribed in the Vedas are the means to please various gods and goddesses to satisfy the longings of man. While practising *karmakandas* a man comes to realize the divine significance and ultimately he is inclined towards the power of ultimate resource. His desires are gradually satisfied by performing sacrifices and his knowledge as well as wisdom develop, to such an extent that he gradually lands into the land of God where there is neither ignorance nor bondage. He learns from the Vedas and its appendages like Sruti, Smriti, Puranas and Upanishads, etc, the glories of God. That makes him pure and fit for grasping divine knowledge that result in devotion to God. He realizes his true nature (soul) and establishes close links with God and His blessings. At such a stage of his spiritual development, his illusions disappear; and he develops the qualities that takes him to the divine plane which is immortal, perfect, pure, free from all types of pains like birth, death, etc. This is the place that stands above the land of destruction. Here there is neither *Maya* nor ignorance. If there is anything, that is the never-ending divine rays of non-manifested *Brahman*. It is Sanatana (without beginning and end), full of divine bliss, illuminated without suns and moons, and beyond the approach of *Maya*. Thus, the Vedas and their appendages help one to realize his soul and its nature and its relationship with God and adopt the devices to emancipate himself from the bondage of *Maya* and ignorance. The Vedas present the nature of God and explains the advent of the creation of the world, its qualities and nature and also the relationship between spiritual as well as material worlds.

Religion, religious faith and traditions play vital roles in giving shape to a society. In case of India, Hindu society and civilization have Vedic religion. There is no aspect of Hindu life which directly or indirectly has not been influenced by Vedic religious philosophy. The Vedas and other literature related to the Vedas created the religious faith and provided the ways of life that are still fresh in the mind of the Hindus. Besides Hinduism, other religions like Buddhism, Jainism, Sikhism, etc, which developed on Indian soil, wear the print of Vedanta. If it is not exaggerated, Indian society has been, from the beginning, the product of ancient Vedic literature, Vedic philosophy, Vedic beliefs and Vedic thinking. Vedic literature has not only influenced Indian people and society but has also formed the base of the development of Hindu religion, and almost all social, political and moral aspects of life. The faith of Hindus in God's blessing is indispensable. Their efforts to obtain salvation giving up worldly lust may still be discerned among many of the Hindus. The religious places or the places of pilgrimages are witness to the fact that Hindus of India are theists having absolute faith in power of the Almighty. It is the Vedic belief that made India the land of gods and goddesses (*devabhumi*). People of India visualize gods and goddesses in every single particle. They worship mountains, rivers, plants, birds, etc, knowing that God resides in all of His creation. If Vedic philosophies are removed and taken away from the life of a Hindu, he is dead.

Notes and References

1. Ramachandra Ghosh, 1988, *History of Hindu Civilization*, Kaushal Prakashan, Delhi, p 2).
2. Ibid.
3. *Atharvaveda* X. 7, 20; *Chhandogya Upanishad*, VII. 1, 2; *Brihadaranyaka Upanishad*, II. 4, 10).
4. *Rigveda*, I. 162, 163; IV. 57, 4; VI. 55, VIII. 101, 15; X. 12, 169, 165.
5. Ramachandra, 1988, op cit, p 170.
6. Ibid, pp 171-72.
7. *Rigveda*, I, 12, 11; I, 27, 4; I, 60, 3.
8. Max Muller, *History of Ancient Sanskrit Literature*, pp 70, 525ff.
9. Ibid, p 623.
10. *Rigveda*, V, 45, 4; V, 85, 1; VII, 26, 1, 2; X, 23, 6.
11. Ibid, VII, 76, 4; III, 53, 9; VII, 33, 11f; VII, 87, 4; VII, 88, 3 ff; X, 14, 15; X, 62, 4, 5.
12. Ibid, I, 179, 2; VII, 76, 4.
13. Ibid, I, 164, 5.
14. Ibid, I, 31, 1; III, 21, 3; V, 29, 1; VI, 14, 2; VIII, 6, 11; IX, 107, 7.
15. Ramachandra, 1988, op cit, p 31ff).
16. The conflict and clashes between Buddhism and Brahmanism in India has been discussed separately in the succeeding chapter of this book.
17. *Rigveda*, X, 90, 9.
18. Ramachandra, 1988, op cit, p 32ff)
19. Whitney, *Oriental and Linguistic Studies*, p 22.
20. Max Muller, *Chips from German Workshop*, I, p 5).
21. *Journal of the American Oriental Society*, III, p 296 ff.
22. Ramachandra, 1988, op cit, p 44.

23. *Bibliotheca Indica*, II, pp 855ff.
24. Max Weber, *History of Indian Literature*, p 12.
25. Ramachandran, op cit, p 49.
26. Max Muller, *History of Ancient Sanskrit Literature*, p 319.
27. Ramachandra, 1988, op cit, p 65.
28. Banerjee, *Dialogue on Hindu Philosophy*, pp 14, 42 ff
29. Ramachandra, op cit, p 67.
30. Ibid.
31. For detail study of types of the Upanishads and their spiritual concerned, see Ramachandra's *History of Hindu Civilization*, op cit, pp 67-74.
32. Ibid, p 77.

5

Discovery of Divinity and Deities by Indo-Aryans

The human mind is a wonderful treasury comprising of many abstract elements like reason, faith, emotion, sentiment, curiosity, etc. Man has always been inquisitive by nature since he arrived on this planet. It is this inquisition of human beings that enabled him to penetrate into the depth of a surrounding atmosphere, wonders of nature, vast territory of the earth, moving planets, shining moon, bright sun and infinite galaxies of stars. Man, being curious about his surroundings, has been searching causes of their origin, system of their working, powers and energies contained by them and their utility. The human faculty of reason works through its different senses or sensual organs like eyes, nose, ears, tongue, etc. Besides that, man has the faculty of faith, intuition and emotional sentiment which are independent of reason. The intuition of mankind has no limit and it may go up to the point where reason can never reach. It may transcend to any part of the universe and form perceptions about the world that is transcendental. The soul of mankind is greater than nature itself. It is the soul from which intuitive perception rises and establishes links with supernatural forces or powers. Religion, which is the product of spontaneous human sentiment and intuitive perception, is not the product of reason. The pace of reason has limits while intuition can go to any length. Reason is scientific, which seeks causes of every effect, but intuition is based on faith. It is the power of intuitional perception that enabled man to discover various gods as well as goddesses in the universe and establish links with them.

Man, in all the entirety of his complex nature, cries out for the living God. Human reason cries out for God, because it cannot rest on its onward march till it reaches an Intelligent First Cause where his intuition helps the reason to grasp the reality. The human concept about deities and idols may not be rational, but it may not be false also. It has been experienced even today that while going into the deepest intuitional *samadhi* one discovers the transcendental truth that stands beyond the boundary of reason. The ancient ancestors of the Indo-Aryans (rishis, maharishis, munis, mahamunis) while producing the Vedas established close links with supernatural powers who were found holding and controlling various creational activities. Their journey towards divinity began with polytheistic concept of gods, no doubt, but slowly and gradually they realized that various gods and goddesses are nothing, but manifestation of the Ultimate Supreme *Brahman* that is one and only one. His opulence, attributes, energies, qualities, etc, are incomparable. They discovered that such Supreme Power which is called God is infinite and eternal.

Discovery of Objects of Worship by Early Indo-Aryans

The Aryan predecessors carried with them their religion along with certain procedures of how to worship unseen forces, when they began their primitive home. However, their concept about gods developed slowly over time. The Vedas contain no real system and they never classify or define the objects of worship. The objects of worship came into being when the commentators of the Vedas expressed their views. While producing the objects of worship they differed from the original Vedic concept of gods. Every object in the universe awed our earliest forefathers, and roused them from stolid wonderment to think and ponder on the greatest problems of life. It is said that in the childhood of their faith they looked for the infinite in the moon, in the sun, in the sky, in the storm, and in the flash of lightening. So, they first called it the builder of the thunderbolt, the giver of rain, the bringer of light, the giver of food and life. At last they framed their creator, the king, the father and the god of gods. Concept of gods developed along with the development of religious thought. Hence the relationship between gods and religion is indispensable. In the words of Ramachandra, "All that we see is that they (early Aryans) felt the presence of God in every object in the universe; and that they tried to rise from nature up to nature's God. Indeed, we see a real transition from the known to the unknown, from the visible to the invisible, from the finite to the infinite. In fact, the infinite underlies the finite."[1]

The real history of India may be traced out in permanent settlements of the Aryans in Indian territories. From here the history of their traditions and civilization began. Real history of India began with the arrival of the Aryans or who first settled in the valley of the river Sindhu (Indus). Excavations at several places in the northwestern part of the Indian Territory bears witness that the people who had settled at Harappa and Mohenjo-daro were well civilized. Ruins of well-built cities and seals, surprisingly similar to those discovered at different places of the ancient world have been found in the Indus valley. The people who evolved this culture were Aryans. Their religion was normally devoid of icons or one in which images played no part. In their pantheon the female element was subordinated to the male and a place of honour was given to deities like Indra, Varuna, Mitras Surya, Agni and other supernatural beings, who seem to have been quite unknown to the originators of the Indus culture. According to Majumdar, "unfortunately the early literature of the Aryans, called Vedas, cannot be dated even approximately, and it is impossible to say with absolute precision in what chronological relation the civilization portrayed in Veda stood to the Indus culture of the third millennium BC."[2] Max Muller hesitatingly placed the beginning of the Vedic literature to the latter half of the second millennium BC. In the words of Ramachandra Ghosh, "Our Aryan fathers handed to us the scriptural Vedas, which have been canonized as time wore on; and which, notwithstanding many puerilities and repulsive legends, arrest our thoughts and inspire us with keen interest. They looked upon their venerated scriptures as the foundation of their power and prestige. Our heart grows warm when we find the Vedas to be strewn with original and at the same time sober and profound ideas, pure and sublime conceptions, and lofty sentiments which were by no means unworthy of our most distant ancestors."[3]

It has already been stated that the Vedas are the highly developed ancient literature of the world presented by Aryans. It is the literature that attracted the attention of some of the best scholars of Europe and America. The word Veda is significantly employed to designate those ancient Sanskrit works in which is laid the foundation of Brahminic belief, and these works were originally three in number, ie *Rigveda*, *Samaveda*, and *Yajurveda*, which have already been discussed in detail in the preceding chapters of this book. Frequent mention is made in ancient Sanskrit literature of the Indian scriptures under the name of *traividya* or the triple science.[4] The prayers in metre arch called Rik, and those in prose are denominated *yajur* while those intended to be chanted are Saman.[5]

The hymns of the *Rigveda* themselves are apparently of different periods, spread over several centuries BC. Some among them being older and some are of much later period. Max Muller designates the most ancient portion of hymns by the term *Chhandas* and that are comparatively modern Mantra.[6] The *Samaveda* is an anthology and purely a derivation. This Veda was at one time the most comprehensive of the four Vedas. However, it is nothing more than a recast of the Rik, being composed with some exceptions of the very same hymns which are in their Rik-form. The *Yajurveda* is in double form – the *Krishna Yajur* or the *Taittiriya Samhita* and the *Shukla Yajur* or the *Vajasaneyi Samhita*. These in the main have the same matter, but they seem to differ from each other only as regards their details and arrangement. In the *Krishna Yajur* the formulas for the entire sacrificial ceremonies are generally accompanied by dogmatic explanations and ritual supplements, while in the *Shukla Yajur* the case is quite different. There they form subjects that are entirely distinct from one another. The White embraces the texts that are not found in the Black. The *Atharvaveda*, though next to the Rik is the most comprehensive and valuable of the four collections. It is almost entirely a *Rigveda*, but it has many points of contact with the *Yajur*, and there is also no room for doubt that its songs rank chronologically with the Brahmana of the Rik, the *Saman* and the *Yajur*.[7] The *Atharva Samhita* is rather a supplement to the *Rigveda* than one of the four Vedas, and has very little coincidence with any of them in its general character.

Thus, it is obvious that there lies a long journey for mankind to arrive to the concept of modern God. That is why the mankind's concepts related to God has been changing from time to time. The religion, if it means the concepts related to

God, existed from the early Vedic period, but without a proper name. The name of a religion came into being when the religious concepts were codified and institutionalized by a certain class of people. The Vedic religion came to be known as the religion of the Hindus named as Hinduism as it were developed by the people who came to be called as Aryan-Hindus.

The Indo-Aryans recognized the presence of the divine in the bright aspects of nature. The blue sky, the bright sun, the blowing wind, the thundering of cloud and the flash of the lightening, rain, mist, night and day, etc, made them enchanted, and they began to observe them as powerful heavenly agencies. The natural powers in various forms made a tremendous impression upon their desponding mind. The human mind at the primitive stage could hardly be convinced that these forces were natural events. So, the simple Aryan people, being afraid of such natural happenings, began to pray to them and offer sacrifices for protection and blessings both. At this primitive stage the birth of certain gods was conceived. And such birth can have no other than a physical meaning.[8] So, the primitive gods carried physical meaning. Such gods were very much near to the worshippers and gave them power of understanding and to face natural happenings boldly. These gods served as symbols of inspiration, understanding, wisdom, courage, and foresight, enabling people to proceed ahead and create history.

The Vedas know of no images. The idols or images are the development of later part of the Vedas. According to Raja Rammohun Roy, "The Vedas hold out precautions against framing a deity after human imagination, and recommend mankind to direct all research towards the surrounding objects, viewed, either collectively or individually, bearing in mind their regular, wise and wonderful combinations and arrangements.[9] Max Muller also says, "The religion of the Vedas knows of no idols. The worship of idols in India is a secondary formation, a later degradation of the more primitive worship, worship of ideal gods."[10] On the other hand, Bollensen does not agree to the views mentioned above.

In the absence of a religion the faith of the primitive people (not Aryans) resided in animism. The animist people worshipped stone, trees, cloud, etc, believing that they possessed power. It is true that the primitive people, being either in wonder or afraid of natural happenings, established their faith in different objects giving them the shape of idols for worshipping, but in case of the early Indo-Aryans, it cannot be said with emphasis that they were idolatry. They were people of deep poetic temperament and of a delicate imaginative nature. The gods which they discovered 'received a variety of ideal or human forms and epithets'. The *Rigveda* mentions of several epithets like '*rupa*', '*vapus*', *nripesas*', etc, in metaphorical sense. Their imaginations penetrated even beyond nature. They discovered the force and power amalgamated with nature and also the root of such natural powers.

Mythology and Worship

Mythology is closely connected with worship, and the ceremonies appear to be imitations of celestial phenomena. The mythologies of the Vedas connected with worship, which were originated by different divine rishis at different times, are of two categories – the Solar and the Meteorological (Psychologico-Lingual Theory). In both the groups, both male and female may be discerned. The male elements are the Sun and the Agni, and the female elements are the Dawn and the Cloud. Mythology was at first 'anthropopathy' and then gradually became 'cosmic.' A myth in its early stage is a legendary story. It developed as human civilization grew, carrying some meaning related to the primitive stage. It helps people to understand the past. It is said that "Myths are, in fact, formed independently of one another; they regard the same object in different aspects, and among different objects they seize the same relations. As they radiate from diverse centres, they mutually interpenetrate each other and issue of course in a certain syncretism." It is believed that nature has been the place for origin of all mythological legends. In case of India, various rishis viewed nature from different angles and originated different mythological legends about the same object. Max Muller has attempted to explain Vedic mythology by producing the solar theory. According to him the development of that mythology was owing to the solar influence in its various manifestations. Max Muller is of the view that the Aryans were highly imaginative, and they gave various names to the same object, but they soon forgot the importance or rather the import of the original names, and from this, the mythology consequently arose. Vedic mythology was in its first stage, but language was never at rest to spin it. He held the view that mythology was "the bane of the ancient world, a disease of language."[11]

History changed into fable, which is not without peculiar charms, and which is also full of interesting problems that supply ample material for the history of Aryan thoughts. And it is at the same time most valuable to the students of history, not only in philological, but also in philosophical, and more especially in a psychological point of view.

The *Rigveda* does not mention tangible things like stones, shells, bones, etc, as objects of worship. However, the semi-tangible objects of worship like trees, mountain, rivers, the earth, and the sea, and the intangible objects like the sky, the stars, the fire, the sun, the dawn, the moon, etc, have been mentioned in the *Rigveda*. They all took the forms of deities of the Vedas. The mighty agencies were at first idealized; and thus most of the gods are merely poetical names, which gradually assumed a divine personality. In the words of Ramachandra, "The Indo-Aryans were never taught to subordinate their imagination to their understanding; nor did they ever learn to conquer nature; they rather easily succumbed to her ... and abstractions ever became persons. The names not being those of attributes, but of things, appearances, and forces, led the hymnists to personify them; and to create a mythology."[12]

Thus, it is evident that the interests of the Indo-Aryans were neither in physiology nor in physical construction of the world, but in ideology, and spiritualism. They viewed and observed the vast universe from the spiritual point of view. Their purpose was not to know or study the physical phenomena, but to discover the root cause of these phenomena; and to achieve the purpose Indo-Aryan rishis identifying gods, personified them. What was gross in the merely physical idea of a god was subsequently refined into a more spiritual conception. To quote Ramachandra again:

> "Those names (of gods) were sometimes used merely as appellatives; and sometimes as names of gods. It thus is seen that various names were taken from the most impressive phenomena of nature, owing to the utter helplessness of the worshippers, to express their ideas as representing the true nature and character of Deities. Indeed, names after names were invented to express the infinity and the majesty of the divine, and this only was suggested by the consciousness of the insufficiency of those names that had already been formed and used to convey such ideas in the infantile development of religious conceptions which arose, as it were, from a Divine nebula."[13]

Search of Indo-Aryans for Supreme God

The Indo-Aryans were inquisitive by nature and their search was not confined to the natural world, but they were curious to know something beyond the physical phenomena and to know the basic cause of their happenings. In that course of the curious mental journey they discovered the ultimate cause of various causes. The idea of Supreme Power existed in their minds but in a 'vague and hazy form'. In course of their search and research about something an unknown Power, they discovered some celestial agencies, one after another, actively engaged in celestial happenings, but their spiritual cravings were yet unsatisfied. They wanted to reach to the point from where celestial agencies appear. They named these deities as per their understanding. Every name was fixed with a distinct purpose. The names given to various gods by different rishis at different times gradually came to signify distinct divinities. The rishis invented names after names to grasp and comprehend God. Though their aim and objective were to identify with the Ultimate Power, yet they discovered the origin and growth of deities, who came to be known by various names like Agni, Surya, Rudra, Vayu, Indra, Vasu, Sabita, etc. Since their goal was to discover the first cause of creation of the universe, the deities which they visualized were taken sometimes, as the first cause or ultimate power. So, they prayed to them with hymns. To them, sometimes, Agni present in nature was the first cause, and sometimes they felt that Indra, in the form of rain and water, was the primal God. In that course, the researchers went on and on towards the search of their final goal and discovered various powers whom they named differently. This is evident from the names of gods mentioned in the Vedas. The gods of the *Rigveda*, though remain the same in the other Vedas, but their ranking and power changes. For instance, Rudra of the *Rigveda* becomes Shankara of the *Yajurveda*. This is all due to the broadening concepts of the Aryan rishis. The names after names which were given were not as important as the concept hidden behind these names. And in such names there must have been, as it were, some presentiments of monotheism. In the words of Ramachandra, "they were evidently meant to express the Beyond, the Invisible behind the visible, and the Infinite within the finite, the Supernatural above the Natural, the Divine, the Omnipresent and the Omnipotent."[14]

During pre-historic times, the Indo-Aryans presented polytheism by recognizing God too vividly in His manifestations. Thereafter, they proceeded towards monotheism. It took centuries to establish the Eternal Deity. Various deities discovered by different rishis possessed different nature. Born of the conscience and the heart, their very names have moral and religious import. They were treated like friends, protectors, beholders, sympathizers, benefactors, givers without prayer. To them all are truthful, beneficial, gracious, omniscient, omnipotent. All bestow life and inspire knowledge. All are invoked for the same blessing; and all are supreme. The hymn of the *Rigveda* says, "None of you, O gods, is small or young. You are all great."[15] Thus, it is evident that the early Indo-Aryans while propounding the concept of the Ultimate Supreme Power, consciously or unconsciously, talked of different attributes of the same Power. In due course of time these different powers assumed particular names which are still in practice. They are all gods and goddesses because they, being aloof from the physical world, behold and control all physical activities of the world of ours. However, today it has become universal fact that the different celestial forces called gods or goddesses are expanded energetic divine forces who all belong to one Supreme Power. They are the reflections of the Mighty Force who is actively serving various causes of creation. Appearing differently, they are not different. Rather they represent only one God. It appears that the gods mentioned in the Vedas bear different names and it also appears that they exist differently, but it is not so. Reality is that in the root of their existence there is only one Supreme

Power. The *Rigveda* says that there is one God but rishis and scholars call Him by different names. The Western scholars, too, agree to the view that in the root of polytheism monotheism exists. The great ancient Indian rishi Shaunaka, in his creation, the *Brihaddevata* says that gods are opulence of one God who is called by different names. (*Brihaddevata*: 1/71.) Thus, it is crystal clear that concepts of various gods and goddesses are nothing, but manifestation of the Ultimate Force who is the base of creation.

Doctrine of India's Polytheism in Search of Monotheism

Critics of the Hindu religion are of the view that it supports polytheism which is an attack upon the divine concept of monotheism. Reality is that the critics fail to grasp the reality of Hindu religious philosophy. It is all because the critics lack full knowledge of Hindu religious philosophy enshrined in the religious scriptures and *Dharma Shastras*. Truth is, Hindu religious philosophy propounds the concept of Absolute God. The Hindu religious scripts, while talking about metaphysics, talk of an absolute non-manifested God (*Brahman*), who is absolutely alone, having no shape, but pervading everywhere. The doctrine of polytheism was developed in search of that universally pervading God while explaining and interpreting different aspects of the manifested God which is known as polytheism. Other religious scriptures talk of the concept of monotheistic God where there is no place at all for the existence of any subordinate or inferior God. Their angle as well as approach is limited to the God, who is called *Nirguna-Nirakara* (devoid of any attributes and shape). The Vedas and its appendages talk of *Nirguna-Nirakara* God along with *Saguna-Sakara* God as well. Other religions like Islam and Christianity describe about a non-manifested single God, no doubt, but they do not talk about attributes of God that pervade after His manifestation while the latter explains in detail various divine attributes and powers of God after His manifestation. Such God is popularly known as *Saguna-Sakara* (divine manifestation with qualities and shape).

It is the Hindu religious scriptures that present, evidently, the nature and features of God, His absoluteness, pervasiveness, supremacy, independence, eternity, etc. The Vedas begin with monotheism, and in support and explanation of Vedic monotheism, the Indian rishis began to visualize polytheism.[16] Various gods are nothing, but a reflection of the Ultimate Supreme God in the creation having different assignments to support, and uphold the creation. They are manifested aspects of God. That is why they appear like God, possessing various qualities and powers. The Indian rishis, sages, munis and philosophers discovered and recognized the energy of God present in each atom of the universe. The questions that puzzled them were, what is the universe? How does it exist? How did it come into existence? Who is the creator of the universe? Replying to these questions, they invented not only the Vedas and their appendages, but also discovered the community of gods and their performances, that are nothing, but expanded forms of God. Thus, it is evident that the theory of polytheism is not different from the theory of monism.

The rishis of the Indo-Aryans penetrated into the mysteries and the complex innumerable systems of the universe, and discovered the Sole and Ultimate Power (God) from whom the entire creation emanates, in whom it resides and prospers and lastly, it dissolves into the unfathomable ocean of eternity, and above all that God resides. Their concept crossed above the *mahashunya* (absolute nothingness) where no religion of the world could reach. This is the unique feature of Indian philosophy. They also discovered that from that Ultimate Source of Power intelligence, wisdom, non-illusion, patience, self-restraint, calmness, pleasure, pain, birth, death, fear, and security appear. He is the beholder of equanimity, contentment, austerity, beneficence, fame, shame, etc. Everything evolves from Him. They recognized Him as the Supreme *Brahman*, the Supreme Light, Purifier, Eternal, Divine *Purusha*, the Primal God, Unborn, and Omnipresent. They found Him as the ultimate source of all glories, both heavenly and non-heavenly. Different gods are an extension of his powers and expansion of his divine glories.

The entire cosmic manifestations, moving and unmoving, are manifested by different activities of the Supreme Godhead. The energy we witness in the universe including the sun and the moon is manifested attributes of God. Except God no one is independent. All depend upon Him. He is the source of everyone. In this regard in the *Bhagavad Gita* Lord Krishna declares:

> I am the father of this universe, the mother, the dispenser, and grand sire; I am the knowable, the purifier, the syllable 'Om', and also the Rik, the Saman, and the Yajus also. I am the Goal, the Sustainer, the Lord, the Witness, the abode, the Shelter, and the Friend, the Origin, Dissolution and Stay, the Treasurer-house, the Seed Imperishable. (*Bhagavad Gita*: IX/17-18.)

Speaking about mystery of such God, Lord Krishna further says:

> Neither the hosts of the gods nor the great rishis know my origin; for I am the source of all the gods and the great rishis. (*Bhagavad Gita*: X/2.)

The non-manifested *Brahman* is the source of:

> Intelligence, wisdom, non-illusion, patience, truth, self-restraint, calmness, pleasure, pain, birth, death, fear, and security; innocence, equanimity, contentment, austerity, beneficence, fame, shame (these) different kinds of dispositions of beings arise from Me alone. (*Bhagavad Gita*: X/4-5).

Thus, it is quite evident that what the Indian ancient religious scriptures talk about gods and God are not different. Rather, they are manifested energies of the single God who is alone in spirit and energy. What have manifested in the universe are his energies that never perish. He alone is the Supreme *Brahman*, the Supreme purifier, eternal, divine, the primal god, unborn, omnipresent, and what not. He is the source of demi-gods and even inferior energies like Gandharvas, Apsaras, Asuras, Rakshasas, Pitras. According to divine genealogy, Brahma is the original creature born out of the energy of the Supreme Lord called Narayana, who is known as Hiranyagarbha. From Brahma all the seven great divine rishis, and before them four other great divine Sages named, Sanaka, Sananda, Sanatna and Sanat Kumara, and the fourteen Manus, are manifested. All these twenty-five great sages are known as the patriarchs of living entities all over the universe. There are innumerable universes, and innumerable planets within each universe, and each planet is full of population of different varieties. The traditions and civilizations, what the Hindus of today follow, emerged from the wisdom expressed by the aforesaid great personalities of India. It is another fact that, scientifically or chronologically, it cannot be proved when and where these towering personalities expressed their highly advanced views and opinions. However, the wisdom expressed by them is useful not only to the Hindus, but to each inhabitant of this planet. If it is taken in the right secular spirit, devoid of any biases, it is universally beneficial and applicable to all the seekers of truth.

Vedanta□s Doctrines of Monism and Monotheism

In Indian Vedic philosophy two distinct trends developed – Monism and Monotheism. The former is a doctrine of one reality and not only of one God or absolute. *Brahman* and

Brahman alone or Absolute and Absolute only is the sole reality. *Jiva-jagata* or this universe of souls and matter is *mithya* or false. So, there is only one *Brahman* and one Reality. Monotheism is a doctrine of one God only and not of one Reality. There is only *Brahman*, no doubt, but there are three realities – God or Absolute *Brahman*, *Jiva* and *Jagata* (God, Soul and Matter). According to Shankaracharya, *Brahman* or Absolute is *Ekemevadvityam* (*Chhandogya Upanishad*, 3.14.1). It means there exists, permanently, only one *Brahman* and everything that comes out, follows from Him. The *Brahman* is *nirvishesha* or without quality or *vishesha* or *bheda* or difference of any kind, whatsoever. So, *Brahman* is *Nirvikara* (Absolutely pure), eternal and all pervasive. He is absolutely changeless. He is totally free from any kind of qualities that are the major cause of change. He is *Nirguna* (without quality). The attributes of *Brahman* are *nirvikara, nirguna, nirakara* (shapeless) *nistriya*, *shuddham* (absolutely pure) free, without sin.

Shankara's doctrine of *Ekemevadvityam* was modified by Ramanuja, the great Indian philosopher who appeared after Shankaracharya. Though he accepts oneness of Absolute *Brahman;* he denies that He is *Nirguna*. Rather He is *Saguna*. He is not *nishkriya* (without action) but *sakriya* (having activities). He possesses heavenly qualities and powers. He is the Creator. He being unchangeable, He changes in the form of universe of souls and matter. He is *niranjana* (non-visible), absolutely pure, sinless and perfect. *Jiva* is the part of *Ishwara* or *Brahman*. The difference between *Brahman* and *Jiva* is like the sky and the sky surrounded in a jar. Once the jar is broken, the surrounded sky in the jar merges into the greater sky. It is *Maya*, *avidya* (ignorance) that has been covering the soul. Once it is removed, the soul is free and pure. According to Ramanuja, *Brahman, Jiva* and *Jagata* are different in attributes otherwise they are identical in nature (*swarupa*), and so they are inseparably connected and form a beautiful synthetic harmonious organic whole or unity like a tree with its different branches, leaves, etc.

Ramanuja founded the Bhakti Marga, the way of devotion. Since soul is encircled by *Maya* that is all pervasive and powerful, the only easiest way to be emancipated from the clutch of *Maya* is devotion (*Bhakti*). Since God is kind and merciful, He listens to devotee's prayers and grants him blessings. God is the soul of souls, rescuer, protector and supporter and controller of all beings. He is kind and listens to prayers. He is our father, mother, friend and sympathizer. He is harmless. The need is to call him or his pious name with devotion and surrender to his will. Thus, here the concept of *Saguna Brahman* begins.

Varieties of Gods in Hindu Religion

There are different kinds of gods, and their number precedes even thirty-three crores.[17] They are divided into great and small, young and old.[18] It is notable that this distinction is denied in another passage.[19] They are described as immortal, but nothing is mentioned about their self-existence. It means they are not eternal as it has been substantiated later on that they exist so long as the creation exists.

There are gods called *Dyasu* and *Prithivi*. *Dyasu* is connected with a root *div*, which means to shine. The name has no hint of cloud or rain. But in the later form *Dyasu* became a god of rain and thunder. Before the dispersion of the old Aryan stock, *Dyasu* was the chief divinity. Since he is a very powerful deity, he is capable of gracing blessings to mankind for their prosperity and happiness. They are described as possessing physical, moral and spiritual characteristics. Both *Dyasu* and

Prithivi are jointly called universal parents. In another place *Dyasu* is called heaven father and *Prithivi* heaven mother. They are parents not only of men but also of gods. They are also known as creator and sustainer of everything in the universe. Somewhere it is mentioned that Indra created them and elsewhere it is stated that they are the creation of Somas, Pushan, Dhatri and Hiranyagarbha. It is also believed that they came about of Tvashtri and to be supported by Mitra, Savitri, Varuna, Indra, Soma and Hiranyagarbha.

There is another concept of a goddess named Aditi. Aditi is a Sanskrit word which means infinite. The concept of Aditi developed out of the idea of extensive plains. It was such an idea which culminated in infinity, and at last she became an important goddess, the mother of all gods and demons. She is a great power. In the *Samaveda*, Aditi is represented with her sons and brothers. Her sons are called Adityas like Mitras, Aryaman, Bhaga, Varuna, Daksha, and Amsa. Their number is not fixed. Somewhere they are said to be seven, somewhere, eight and somewhere nine also. They are described as sleepless, many-eyed, vast, strong, bright, holy, pure, golden, sinless, blameless, etc. They witness every activity of all creatures and award them with blessings and punishments in accordance with their *karmas* (duties). The entire universe is in her hold. She is capable of blessing her worshippers anything. In modern sense, Aditi is infinite space from which is born everything, from Brahma to grass.

It appears that the concept of Aditi represents *Prakriti* (infinite space). There are two *Prakritis* – *Para-Prakriti* and *Apara-Prakriti*. Both are infinite, but the former is higher, pure, invisible, all pervasive, great or imperishable source of all energies and capable of giving various forms of living and non-living beings. It is quite subtle. The first element that appeared from it is called *Mahadtattva* (the subtle, bright, invisible divine element full of divine energy). *Apara-Prakriti* that is next to the *Para-Prakriti* is the abode of *Maya* (illusion) that has covered divine wisdom, centred in the inner-heart of every living being. It is called Nature which represents attributes of *Purusha*, who is none other but Supreme God. So, *Prakriti* is next to Supreme God. It may be said that *Prakriti* is manifested energy of the non-manifested *Brahman*. It is the *Brahman* that manifested in the form of infinite *Prakriti*. The relationship between *Prakriti* and *Purusha* is like the sun and its rays, the ocean and its waves and flowers and their smell. Apparently they are different, but inherently they are one. It is also known as *Kshetra* (*Prakriti*) and *Kshetrajna* (*Purusha*). The latter is the knower of the former. The energy which one finds in *Prakriti* is not its own, but it is the attribute of God. *Prakriti* is the beholder of that energy. Various elements of the world of nature including three great energies – *Sattva*, *Rajas* and *Tamas* – are inherently God's attributes but apparently they are natural forces which cause changes in the universe. All twenty-four natural elements like *Panchamahabhuta* (earth, water, air, fire, and sky); five *Tanmatras – Shabda, Rupa, Rasa, Sparsha* (touch) and *Gandha* (Smell); five *jnanendriyas* – eyes, ears, nose, tongue, and skin; five *karmendriyas* – hands, legs, mouth, *guda* (anus), genetic organ; and four elements of inner-heart – mind, wisdom, ego, and *chit* reside in *Prakriti*. They are lifeless, but coming in contact with the *Purusha* (soul) they all became active and seem as if they are all alive.

Other Vedic Gods

Other Vedic gods are Mitra and Varuna. The Vedas put much emphasis on Varuna while Mitra is occasionally celebrated. Mitra etymologically signifying measure was originally the name of the day, and Varuna etymologically signifying the coverer (night). Varuna takes its root from the word *var* which means to cover, enclose. Since day and night follows each other after a certain period, they are closely related. The constellations are the holy act of Varuna. The moon moves by his command. He is called the source of light. He grants wealth and avert evils. He is the sovereign of his own abode and a king both of gods and men. He is mighty, fixed, foresighted and visible to his worshippers. He is the master of the cosmic world. It is said that he created heaven and earth. He possesses a high moral character in comparison with other gods. Varuna was an older god than Indra. In due course of time, with changing religious concepts of the Indo-Aryans, Varuna worshipping declined and Indra assumed a superior place.

Indra was human and his original name was Vindra which meant the obtainer. In Vedas, he is known as 'Destroyer of Virtra'. Virtra was an Asura, the common enemy of the Indo-Aryans and Persa-Aryans. Indra is all powerful and the destroyer of enemies. He conquered heaven by austerity. In the words of Ramachandra, "During the first period of civilization the conception of Indra was that of the leader of a gang of hunters, described as savage, intoxicated and impetuous. During the pastoral period he was conceived as a shepherd for a hook is mentioned as being his weapon. When the Aryans gave up their wild habits, and betook themselves to agricultural pursuits the nature of Indra was transformed; and so he is spoken of as having a patriarchal family ... and at last during the period of chivalry he was elevated to the rank of a king, and now he was invoked as a god of war and victory."[20] Today, Indra stands as the king of all gods. His most powerful weapon is Vajra, and he used an elephant as a means of transport.

Another Vedic god is Vayu, the blower, who is always found to be associated with Indra. In the *Rigveda* his place is not as important as Indra. He is also known as the son-in-law of the god Tvashtri. He is very much powerful. He is the transformer of power from one place to another. Rudra is also a very important Vedic god. He cries high and he is the god of anger. He is also known as the god of thunder and storms. The character of Rudra is identical to that of Pushana, who is the harvest god and nourishes crops. Rudra is very much powerful and he has the capacity to destroy the creation. Due to his destructive ability he is said to be represented as the lord of evil spirits. He was originally an object of worship by the aborigines. There are gods like Maruts and Mars who are closely connected. According to Prof $$$Kuhn, the Maruts were primarily understood as the souls of the departed, and as such souls were taken as winds, or ghosts or spirits. They gradually assumed the character of Storm-gods. But this opinion is not assented by the Vedas. Maruts are regarded as sons of Rudra and Prishni. Their origin is from the ocean. They worship Indra.

Agni is also a very important Vedic god. He is invoked at all sacrifices. So, he is the sacrificial fire. He serves both man as well gods. The offerings or oblation given to gods in sacrifices are carried to the projected god by Agni. He invites the gods to the ceremonies. He is always fresh and young. He is the source of effulgent light, and emblem of purity. He is known under various appellations, and many deities inferior to him are purely his manifestations. He is identical with Varuna, Mitra, Indra, Aryaman, Yama, Amsa, Tvashtri, Rudra, Pushana, Savitri, Bhaga, Aditi, Hotra, Bhrati, Ila, Saraswati and with the Eternal Vedas. The Vedas speak a lot about his austerity, quality, power, activity, immortality, etc. He is the divine king and is as strong as Indra. He is the protector of the universe, and he may bless his worshipper with whatever he desires. He was the divine king worshipped by Varuna, Mitra, Maruts and other gods. However, during the period of chivalry, Indra and Soma superseded Agni.

Surya and Savitri are related to the Sun. Under these two epithets, the Sun is chiefly represented in the Vedic hymns. Surya is also known as Aditya. It is said that Surya is born by gods like Indra, Agni, Soma, Mitra and Varuna. Like Agni and Indra he, too, is the source of light. He is all seeing, and he beholds the good and bad deeds of the mortals. Only three Suktas in the first book of the *Rigveda* are devoted to Surya. These Suktas do not talk about 'expressive acknowledgment of his supremacy.' The expression contained in the hymns relating to this deity exhibit a careful and loving observation of Nature. He is spoken of as coming "from a distance" and "removing all sins." As the divine Sun, he is supplicated to take away the "sickness of the heart" and the "yellowness of the body."

There are gods called Ashvins who are connected with Surya. They are the twin sons of Vivasvat and Saranyu. They are described as young, beautiful, ancient, strong, bright, terrible and skilful. They grace the worshippers with the force to defeat their enemies. Their business is more earthly than heavenly. Later, Ashvin came to be known as Ashwini Kumars, whose mother was the second wife of Sun called *Chhaya* (shadow). They are said to be masters of medication and doctors of gods. They have two elements – cosmic human or historical. The cosmic element refers to their luminous nature while the latter element to the wonderful cures of diseases.

Tvashtri is the Vedic god who is known as Vishvakarma today. He possesses wonderful skills to construct wonderful mansions for gods within no time. Thus, he is the divine artisan, the skilful worker and the creator of all forms. He is expert in all magical devices. Soma is the god who plays an important part in the sacrificial act of the Vedic Age. The worship of Soma refers to the feudal and chivalrous period. He also comes under the category of divine god. He is talked as the lord of gods and men and the generator of the sky and the earth, of Agni, Surya, Indra and Vishnu. He is wise, strong agile and thousand-eyes. During the post-Vedic period he came to be known as the Moon and its regents. Usha was described as a goddess. She was also known as Dawn. Her connection is with Surya. She too, is divine, and is presented as the affluent, as the giver of food and bringer of opulence. She is always young and fresh. She goes to every house and does not despise the small. She carries brightness. When she appears, the birds begin to chirp in their nests. She is said to be the daughter of night. She is also known as the faithful wife of Surya.

God Brihaspati is described as the offspring of two worlds. He is styled as the father of gods. It is said that he possesses all divine attributes. His notable characteristics are, nobility, purity, opulence, clear-voiced, and remover of all diseases. He is also known as the priest of gods and he leads gods towards prosperity and goodness.

There are a number of minor gods like Aptya, Ahirbudhnya, Aja, Ekapad, etc. They are all connected to different gods mentioned above. Tritya is connected with Maruts, Vayu and Indra. The abode of Aptya is hidden. Ahirbudhnya is a dragon of the deep and resides in the atmospheric ocean. Aja Ekapad is said to be a storm-god. Saraswati is the goddess of the *Rigveda*, who is celebrated sometimes as a river and sometimes as a deity. She attends sacrifices with other goddesses like Bharati, Hotra, Varutri, Mahi, Ila, Dhisana, etc. Aranyani is mentioned as the goddess of forest solitude. Various shapes of the Moon have been given different names. For instance, Rakha signifies full moon, Anumati, the moon one digit less than full, Sinvali stands for the last day before the new moon.

A close analysis of the names of gods and semi-gods found in the Vedas reveal the truth that the Indo-Aryans were very much sensitive and intuitive by nature. So, they comprehended about Nature and found out different forces enshrined in it and active everywhere. As they were poetical, they provided different names to the power present in Nature and called them gods because they were celestial bodies associated with the universe. Nature is full of energies of various kinds. Though the ultimate resource of these energies is solar world, yet they (energies) reflect through various natural happenings. Indra, Vayu, Agni, Asvani (*vanaspati* or vegetation), Usha (Dawn), Surya, Savitri, Mitra, Rudra, etc, are natural forces which have been designated by our Aryan ancestors. Not only that, their vision penetrated into space, and they recognized heavenly gods governing heaven and hell both. They designated them and treated them like deities. It shows their deep understanding and that their philosophic vision was great. Variations in the Vedas regarding their names, relationships and powers are due to the presentation of these facts by different rishis and thinkers in different periods. Hymns produced, relating to these gods and goddesses, were not prepared at a particular period or time. Their search continued for long. In the primary stage their vision was vague. As the years rolled down, their understanding got mature and vision was sharpened. The facts, what they produced helped a lot to their successors to grasp the meaning of Ultimate God and expression of His celestial reflections through Nature. The spiritual path constructed by the ancient Indian rishis may be rough, but it was the later Indian sages, thinkers and philosophers who could succeed to present a clear vision of Monotheistic God.

Uniformity between God and Gods

Apparently God and gods appear different, but inwardly they are the same. Gods are manifested energy and divine attributes of the *Brahman*. Shankaracharya in *Sivanand Lahri* writes that creation of universe is God's play. What exists in the universe is a reflection of God's energy and power. God Himself has assumed different forms in His creations. Hence, gods in different forms represent God only. Their all divinities, powers, beauties, and opulence are derived from God only because He is the ultimate source of energy for everyone. Different ornaments made from gold appear different so long as they are in ornamental forms. In reality these ornaments are modified shape of gold. Like that there is only one God from whom different gods have appeared in the creation, and so long as they are in the creation, they seem to be different, but after the dissolution of the creation their existence is no more because they all merge into the infinite eternity where nothing exists except God.

Entire Hindu religious scriptures unanimously agree that there is only one God who has neither a beginning nor an end. He is, but without birth and death. Entire creation is His *Lila* (play). So long as He is non-manifested; nothing can be said or imagined about Him. His manifestation is his creation where he resides in each atom of creation. Right from Brahma down to grass, it is God who reflects. The qualities, energies, shape, forms, colour, etc, what are visible in the universe, are due to God only. He manifests in different forms to support and uphold creation. It is He who desired to manifest into many, and He manifested into many. (*Ekoham Bahu Syam*). He Himself appeared in the form of Brahma, the Creator; Vishnu, the Sustainer; and Shankara, the Destroyer. These three (*trimurti* or trio) were called Mahadevas. Thereafter, a number of gods having different assignments came into being to uphold and expand creation.

The concept relating to various gods may be different, but in essence it is the same. *Brihadaranyaka* calls gods as life, vitality, soul and *Parabrahma*.[21] *Rigveda* is of the view that Indra, Mitra, Varuna, Agni, etc, are manifested forms of God. It is God only, who is being prayed and worshipped to, in different names and shapes. Sruti speaks that all living beings including gods originated from the divine source and survive in the same source, and it is that source (God) which is knowable, and it is that source that is only Brahma. In the *Bhagavad Gita*, Lord Krishna says to Arjuna:

> I am the Self, O Gudakesh, seated in the heart of all beings; I am the beginning and the middle, as also the end, of all beings. Of the Adityas, I am the Aditya; of the radiances, the resplendent Sun; I am Marichi of the Maruts; ... I am Vasva of the gods, and of the senses I am the mind, I am the intelligence in living beings, ... of the Rudras, I am Shankara, of the Yaksha and Rakshasas the lord of wealth, and of the Vasus, I am Agni, of the mountains I am the Meru.[22]

God is indefinable, but to have some understanding about God there are a number of adjectives that indicate His divine glories and power. God is Infinite Being, Imperishable (*Akshra*), Splendid, Immutable, Divine Glory, Abode of the Universe, Primal God, Supreme Abode of all beings, Immeasurable, Unchangeable, etc. Speaking about divine glories of God, Lord Krishna speaks to Arjuna:

> I am the father of this world, the mother, the dispenser, and grandsire; I am the knowable, the purifier, the syllable 'Om', and also the Rik, the Saman, and the Yajus also. I am the Goal, the Sustainer, the Lord, the Witness, the Abode, the Shelter and the Friend, the Origin, Dissolution and Stay, the Treasure-House, the Seed Imperishable."[23]

The Lord further speaks:

> Neither the hosts of the God nor the Great Rishis know my origin; for I am the source of all the gods and the Great Rishis.[24]

Arjuna in his vision sees in Lord Krishna as:

> The Rudras, Adityas, Vasus, and Shadhyas, Visvas, and Asvins, Maruts and Ushmapas, hosts of Gandharvas, Yakshas, Asuras, and Shidhas...."[25]

Thus, it is very much obvious that God is reflecting through various gods. Various gods are worshipped in various forms, no doubt, but according to the *Bhagavad Gita*, it is Supreme God who is really worshipped, and it is He who is the right source of blessings. The divine powers of various gods are the powers of the Supreme God. Gods are expansions of the *Parmatma*. He is seated at the apex of creation. All the energies, qualities, activities, and affluences available in the universe are coming out of infinite divine bright light (*tej*) of God which is too subtle to speak of. Scriptures say that God is a heap of accumulation of unending and unfinished consciousness and divine light. He is the ultimate source of accretion of all living beings. Nothing is without God. From the view to understand God in different categories, gods are the divine category nearest to Him. If God is viewed from different kinds of species (*yonis*), gods are the first species. If species are viewed from the angle of superiority, gods are the superior most species among other kinds of living beings. Despite all that, truth is that God stands above all; He is the best, all powerful and all pervading. Creation is his divine *Lila*. Wise is he who personifies God in all particles of creation whether animate or inanimate. Differences between God and gods exist so long as one does not know the real nature of God and his divine play. Once real nature of god is realized, illusion automatically disappears.

Affluences of Gods

As gods are extended energies and powers of God, they seem to be affluent and powerful like God. They are sovereign, powerful and all pervasive like God. They are capable of gracing worshippers with blessing. In *Nirukta* it is said '*danad devh*' which means a god is he who gives or attributes. The community of gods donates their divine energy and power to create things in the universe. According to the Vedas gods are basic cause of origin of the animate and inanimate things in the universe and within the universe. In other words, the different elements pervading in the universe like fire, air, sky, water, earth, etc, and changes that take place in the universe causing birth and death of animate and inanimate things of the universe happening due to combinations of these different elements, is called divine activities where gods play different assigned roles.

Advent of Rituals

According to the *Brahma Sutra* and *Deva Sutra*, gods are capable of accepting oblations offered to them in *yajnas* and sacrifices anywhere in the universe at any time. When invited with devotion, honour and love, gods appear in subtle forms at the place where a *yajna* is performed. According to scriptures, they possess all *siddhis* (extraordinary powers), and after being pleased they may grant these powers to their devotees. If a god is pleased, he may bless the worshipper with the desire what he likes. They may be present at several places at the same time to accept the oblations. They also reside in temples where the statue of a god is to be installed with prescribed rituals, and accept worshipping. They possess *siddhis*, and are capable of moving in the sky; making their bodies subtle and gross; appearing in different forms; overpowering anyone; having vision to see anything anywhere; capacity to enter into the body of anyone; meeting death as per their desire; having vision to see present, past and future; and to do things what they like. Thus, the power and capacity of gods are great because they are next to the Supreme God and their purpose is to assist Him. They administer the universe and control its various activities.

There are different categories of gods. According to Hindu *Dharma Shastra*, there are thirty-three crore gods, but thirty-three gods are the most important. They are twelve Adityas, eleven Rudras, eight Vasus and two Ashwini Kumars. Their appearance is related to the very origin of creation. Some gods appeared later on. These categories of gods are those who avail the opportunity to join the rank of gods due to their good performances in human life. They obtained divine power by their hard penance and they remain in heaven and enjoy heavenly pleasure so long as their *punyas* are with them. Gods are present everywhere in the universe. Lord Vishnu is said to be the god of space, Vayu of the sky, goddess Durga of Agni, Ganesha of water, Shankara of earth. These five gods – Vishnu, Surya, Durga, Ganesha and Mahesh (Shankara) are upholder of sky, fire, water, wind and earth. They are called *Pancha Brahma* (five Brahmas). According to Hindu *Dharma Shastra*, no *yajna* is complete until these five Brahmas are worshipped first. Among them the worship of Ganesha is first. Since he knew Brahma first during his childhood, he was allowed to be worshipped first during the occasion of any religious performance.

In due course of time a number of rites, having relation to religious scriptures, came into being where priests availed the opportunity to handle the affairs. Rites are processes to worship gods and please them. Religious rites are prescriptions prescribed by *Brahmanas* that teach how to worship and what to be offered to gods. They also prescribe norms about how to worship them and at what times. They also developed rites to worship *pitras* (departed souls), Yakshas, Gandharvas, ghosts, etc. In course of time various Mantras were developed to worship them and establish near relations with them. All these rituals became traditional and left a big impression on the mind of the common people. That is why even today they are found engaged in various religious performances where priests play a vital role. The rituals and *karmakandas* became so vague and traditional in Hindu society that they took entire section of the people in their strong grips. The rites and rituals remained confined not only to processes of *yajnas* and sacrifices, but to every aspect of individual life as well as social behaviours. It was religion and religious rites that prevailed everywhere, and to get rid of such faith and belief became impossible. They brought forth a number of evils in the society and the whole society came under the influence of ritualism. The essence of ritualism disappeared, but its blind faith remained in practice. The class of Brahmins was more benefited because no ritual or religious performances could be completed without their presence and participation, and for that they had their economic share. That is why during the sixth century BC Buddhism appeared as a protest against the orthodox practice of ritualism and *karmakandas* in the Hindu society. Since Buddhism has been discussed somewhere else in this book, here it is enough to state that Buddhism was the product of blind Hinduism which could hardly allow reason to view things in the right perspective. Rather it propagated ritualism and *karmakanda* making people become blind followers of Hinduism.

A Journey from Natural Gods to Spiritual God

In the beginning, these gods were products of the poetical minds of the ancient rishis, and the names which were given to most of the gods were poetical. The mighty natural agencies were thus, poetically idealized. These names remained confined to sensuous objects. These names obtained divine personality gradually. Originally, they had material meanings, but gradually they came to be used in the spiritual sense. In the words of Ramachandra, "What was gross in the merely physical idea of a god, was subsequently refined into more spiritual conception."[26] The ancient Indian rishis had grasped the infinity and majesty of the Divine, and in the process of providing divine powers, certain names they discovered, and called them by different names. However, they knew well that these gods are not different from the Supreme Power. Rather they are expansion of the same Supreme Power. Every name of god had some distinct purpose and meaning. In search of the Ultimate Power they went on searching the gods. The idea of god existed in the mind of the early Indo-Aryans "in the vague and hazy forms", who was not yet "defined and properly named." The Indo-Aryans conceived one god after another, but each "was found powerless to satisfy their spiritual carvings." They invented names after names of gods to comprehend the *Brahman*. To quote Ramachandra once more, "They were evidently meant to express the Beyond, the Invisible behind the Visible, the Infinite within the Finite, the Supernatural above the Natural, the Divine the Omnipresent and the Omnipotent."[27] Their search for Ultimate God continued till they approached or realized the existence of the Supreme Power, upholding the entire universe in His fold and reflecting Himself in different ways. Getting convinced of the single Supreme Power whom they called God, the ancient Indian rishis realized that Indra, Mitra, Varuna, Surya, Aditi, Savitri, etc, are not different from God. Rather they are an extension of the same God with the purpose to uphold various jobs in the universe.[28]

The early Indian rishis, in their curiosity and simplicity, had established close relations with natural forces, and treated them as their friends, protectors and sympathizers. They expected, from them, divine help during times of calamities and troubles. They worshipped them to obtain wisdom and avail their favour and blessings. The deities of ancient Vedic period represented not only the conspicuous processes of external nature, but also the higher relations of moral and social life. The songs with which the Indo-Aryan "invoked" the gods clearly show that they sought them for their spiri ual as well as for their material welfare. Ethical considerations are not, therefore, wholly alien to these natural outbursts of the pious mind. The distinction between "good and bad was clearly made in a moral sense; and law and virtue were also recognized."[29] They believed that gods are destroyers of evil doers.[30] They also prayed to the gods to forgive their sins and also the sins of their forefathers. They believed that gods forgive and punish sins.

The primitive Indo-Aryans, while travelling from one place to another, were in need of blessing of unseen powers so that they could successfully continue their journey to find out a favourable settlement. They needed courage, bravery and wisdom to come across natural inconveniences and win over their enemies so that they could settle peacefully at the place which attracted them most. Gods being the symbol of inspiration and source of encouragement, provided them enough wisdom and courage to move ahead and settle well. In other words, they carried with them their religion and worship, when they started from their primitive homes and spread over various territories of the earth. The religion and way of worshipping kept them united even though they were spread over different parts. The Indo-Aryans were the first who in the early stages speculated largely on supernatural matters; and their religion was an important feature of their civilization. The Vedic religion in all its aspects is the true expression of the view, which the simple minded, but highly gifted ancient Indian thinkers imbued with deep religious feelings. The religious feelings and thoughts which originated first in the single mind gradually expanded when it was taken over by others, and in that process the early religion or religious thinking got refined with the advancement of time.

Indian Religion whether Monotheistic or Polytheistic

Barth is of the view that "India is radically pantheistic, and that forms its cradle onwards."[31] He is correct in some respect, but it is not the total truth. What religion was to the early Indo-Aryans were, indeed, faith, worship, hope and reverence for the gods. They had 'fervent religious sentiments', but the religion of early India basically differed from pantheism which differ from polytheistic because they represent each deity as independent of all the rest. In the *Rigveda* there are various passages that somewhere speak about monotheism, somewhere polytheism and somewhere pantheism. Somewhere hymns appear to be speaking of atheism also. Some of the hymns are monotheistic as they recognize the existence of one personal God; some are polytheistic as they do not deny multiple divinity; some are pantheistic as they reject the personality of a Creator and hold everything to be God; and others are atheistic as they deny an absolute eternal Supreme Being. The pre-historic stardust of all the systems may properly be called pantheism not in its exclusive sense. It is not philosophical abstraction, but intense realization.

Whether the Indian Vedic system is monotheistic or polytheistic is a matter of debate, but it is a fact that monotheism could hardly precede polytheism. The approach of the ancient Indian rishis was polytheistic, no doubt, but their goal was monotheistic. Monotheism is the later development when their thought developed and became matured. However, it was not possible for them to ignore original cognition and take itself to the vagaries of naturalism, and to the worship of multifarious deities of the 'Vedic Olympus'. Concept like monotheism or polytheism has little significance at the time when the idea about divinity was non-existing. However, the idea about entity and non-entity was very well familiar to the ancient Indian rishis.[32] There are some scholars who are of the view that the idea of single God originated from the mist of polytheistic and idolatry phraseology. But this view is not universally applicable. In case of India, the ancient rishis had conceived of a single supernatural power, but they were not able to name that power properly. Hence, they moved towards polytheistic idea which resulted in discovery of various gods having the same nature and power. To them there was no word available to express the abstract idea of an immaterial and Supernatural Being. It is true that they adopted polytheism in search of monotheism. Idea of monotheism achieved perfection during the era of the Upanishads. During this period the Indian thinking about monotheism became more precise and clear. It was found that a single God pervaded everywhere in the form of gods and goddesses. The Upanishadic thoughts made it crystal clear that there is only one God who is the ultimate source of all powers, energies and opulence in the universe.

The early Aryans presented mythical, sacramental, polytheistic and even pantheistic ideas. However, in the words of Ramachandra, "In the childhood of the world the Indo-Aryans possessing simple and reflective minds solved the mysteries and difficult problem of the production of the existing universe in various ways. They interpreted a great number of different conjectures with regard to cosmology.... They ascribed sometimes to physical and sometimes to spiritual powers. And as speculation gradually acquired vigour, different opinions asserted themselves, and they naturally became perplexed."[33] Under the circumstance of perplexities, various questions regarding origin of the universe, gods, heaven and hell, etc, appeared that needed proper answers. It was asked: Who created universe? Who controls the universe? Who is the originator of heaven and hell? Who supports the universe?

It appears that the early Indo-Aryans had not fully and clearly comprehended the objects of their worship. The conception of Godhead indicated in the hymns of the Vedas is of a fluctuating and undecided character. But the search continued. And a time came when they deduced that the universe has sprung out from complete darkness where there existed nothing. There was no sky, no space, no life, no water, no sun, no day and night, etc. If there was anything, it was 'pre-existing chaos.' According to the *Rigveda* the Indian rishis themselves were ignorant of the beginning of all things.[34] That is why they deduced different doctrines relating to the origin of creation and they prescribed various deities like Indra, Agni, Aditi, Dhatri, Pushna, Soma, Varuna, Rudra, Savitri, etc, who play roles in creation as well as destruction of things in the universe. In course of time it was confirmed that different gods are manifestations of a single God with the energy and power to sustain and support the creation of God-like human beings and other species that are performing various jobs in the universe to carry on the incessant processes of the universe.

Concept of Next World, Immortality of Individual Soul, and Rebirth

The ideas of ancient Indian rishis which were originally related to Nature gradually took the moral, religious and lastly, philosophical shape and discovered several doctrines related to present, past and future life of mankind. In that course of thinking, concepts related to soul, death, birth, sacrifices and salvation, etc, came into being. In the ninth and tenth *mandalas* of the *Rigveda* there are some distinct references related to future life. The Aryan ancestors who had conceived about immortality and eternity of God treated human soul as the integral part of God and believed that souls, too, are eternal and immortal. It exists even after decaying of bodies.[35] They conceived the idea of soul from the sun who is regarded as the soul of all things changeable or unchangeable.[36] Since souls are indestructible, they exist even after death. Hence, the souls of deceased ancestors exist in another world. In the *Brahman*, immortality is promised to those who rightly understand and regularly practice the rites of sacrifice. Those who fail to do so, and depart to the next world before the expiration of the natural term of life, are weighed there in a balance.[37] The doctrine of the *Brahman* is that after death all are born again in the next world, where they are recompensed and the wicked punished.[38] The producers of the Upanishadic thought substantiated the fact that how the departed soul proceed to heaven or hell according to their *samskara*, and how long they have to live there.

The Aryan ancestors established their faith in eternal laws of God, and in that course, they realized that in the kingdom of God both good and bad prevail together. The course of human fate is decided after death according to man's performances in the present life. Good behaviour brings about good results while bad activities result in suffering and pain. In this way they gave forth morality and religion together. Those who perform righteously in the present life are sent to heaven after death for better enjoyment and pleasure. On the other hand, the sinners, after death, have to suffer badly in hell for long. It is evident that the ancient Indo-Aryans had grasped the idea of the next world where one has to pay an account after ones death.

As they developed faith in rebirth, and also in a Pitriloka, where the departed souls are carried by Yama Deva (the god of death for, award and punishment), and the departed souls are allowed to stay there till their future course of life is decided according to their performances in the mundane life. The *Rigveda* talks of funeral hymn offered to Agni which also confirms the future life. Hymns also talk of the Pitriloka where departed souls live.[39] Once they discovered the idea of immortality of souls and their rebirths, it was natural for them to discover the idea about salvation which means cessation from the incessant circle of birth and death. Since this fact has separately been discussed in the following chapter in detail, it is enough to say here that the idea of salvation (*moksha*) is a unique discovery of the early Indian rishis upon which the entire texts of Hindu religion has been constructed.

Thus, it is quite obvious that the ancient Indian rishis who possessed poetic sense and who were philosophical minded, presented the edifice of religious as well as common philosophical thoughts that put India at the apex of the philosophical world. The Vedas and their appendages attracted various famous scholars of the world, to investigate into the philosophies presented in these creations. They all, except those who were jealous and envious of India's ancient philosophical stock or those who could not understand it, appreciated the religious scriptures of ancient India on the ground that when the philosophical horizon was unapproachable to other parts of the world, India was talking about the philosophical as well religious concepts which helped Indians to established a civilization based on morality, humanity and sanctity.

Notes and References

1. Ramachandra Ghosh, 1988, *The Hindu Civilization*, Kaushal Prakashan, Delhi, p 195.
2. Majumdar, RC and others, 1978, *An Advanced History of India* (4th edition), Macmillan, Delhi, p 24.
3. Ramachandra Ghosh, op cit, pp 195-96.
4. *Journal of the German Oriental Society*, XXII, p 587ff.
5. Barth, *Religions of India*, p 25.
6. Max Muller, *Lectures on the Science of Language*, II, p 519.
7. Max Muller, op cit.
8. Ibid.
9. Raja Rammohun Roy, *Introduction to the Abridgement of the Vedas*, p vii.
10. Max Muller, op cit.
11. Max Muller, *Hibbert Lectures*, p 198 ff.
12. Ramachandra Ghosh, 1988, op cit, p 187.
13. Ibid, pp 187-88.
14. Ibid, p 189.
15. *Rigveda*, VIII, 30, 1.
16. Chandrika Singh, 2008, *Parmatma ka Sachha Swarup aur Mukti ke Marga* (Hindi), Janki Prakashan, Patna, p 25
17. *Rigveda*, III, 9, 9.
18. Ibid, I, 27, 13.
19. Ibid, III, 30, 1.
20. Ramachandra Ghosh, 1988, p 179.
21. *Brihadaranyaka*, 3/9/9
22. The *Bhagavad Gita*, X, 20, 21, 22, 23.
23. Ibid, IX, 17/18.
24. Ibid, 2.
25. Ibid, XI, 22.
26. Ramachandra, 1988, op cit, p 188.
27. Ibid, p 189.
28. *Rigveda*, IV, 53, 2; Ibid, I, 25, 20; Ibid, VII, 32.
29. *Rigveda*, II, 28, 5, 29, 1.

30. Ibid, I, 35, 3, 11; I, 36, 14' I, 115, 6. Also see Johnson's *Oriental Religions*, p 119.
31. Barth, M, *Religions of India*, p 8.
32. *Rigveda*, X, 72.
33. Ramachandra Ghosh, 1988, p 200.
34. *Rigveda*, X. 129.
35. Ibid, I. 12, 5, 56.
36. Ibid, X. 58, 1.
37. *Shatpatha Brahmana*, XI. 22,7,33.
38. Ibid, VI. 2, 2, 27; X. 6, 3, 1; XI. 7,2,23.
39. *Rigveda*. X. 16.10.

6

God and Universe: Creator and Creation

Our planet, a small particle in the wonderful mysterious universe, is full of astonishments. The elements and energies it possesses speak of the greatness of the earth and its creator on the one hand, and make one curious about its origin, natural happenings and mysteries on the other. When one glances at the luminous galaxies of stars in the sky, it creates more wonder and astonishment in the mind of the viewer. The question that immediately strikes the mind is what is all these and how did it came into existence. Is it eternal or has it been made by someone? Perhaps this is the curious question that brought forth philosophy to discuss about both the worlds – physical and metaphysical. Idea emerged that in the universe nothing is without its cause, and creation of universe is the biggest effect of the greatest cause. The power that has created such a vast and limitless universe is greater than the greatest, bigger than the biggest, wonderer than most wonderment and superior to the superior most. From here, probably, divinity emerged, and the idea of God prevailed. Once it is accepted that the vast, unfathomable, mysterious, wonderful universe is God's creation, God, must be all powerful, luminous, pervasive, and capable of doing anything. The entire cosmic world is interwoven in wisdom having perpetual cosmic laws. The question is what is wisdom, and from where such wisdom comes. The human mind that is sensitive and imaginative both, has been engaged in knowing about the mysteries of the universe and greatness of its creator. In course of their research, a number of great thinkers, philosophers, religious poets and seers produced different theories related to God and His creation. Their contributions to understand God and His creation and also in penetrating into the divine mysteries, produced various branches of philosophy on the one hand, and set up different branches of religions on the other. What they have produced is not universally applicable and scientifically acceptable; however, it helps one to understand the power of divinity and mysteries of the universe.

The role played by ancient Indian rishis, maharishis, munis and metaphysicians in this regard not only is greater but more conceivable as well as logical. Their angle and approach have been better than others so far the philosophy of divinity and religion is concerned. That is why India is still the richest in the field of philosophy and especially of metaphysical philosophy. In the field of philosophy India was entitled as *Jagat Guru*. The concept of God and His role in creation, maintenance and destruction of the universe discussed and described in the Indian religious scriptures is not a futile attempt. Rather their presentation, scattered in the Vedas, Upanishads and other religious scriptures, are systematic, scientific, and convincing.

God is a Mystery

It has already been thoroughly discussed in the preceding chapter how the concept of God or Supreme Power was discovered. It is not only Hindu religious philosophy that presents the concept of God, but almost all the religions of the world begin with the idea of God who is supposed to be the creator of everything on this planet, and in the universe. What is God, is a question that has not yet been answered satisfactorily. There have been and there are still some who disagree with the view that there is God or a Supreme Power sitting somewhere in the higher sky, with the purpose to control and command the universe. Since neither the existence of God may scientifically be proved nor can His greatness be easily understood, it is futile to talk about such a great power. So, there are many who neither deny the existence of God nor accept His presence. They are called agnostics, atheists, sceptic, etc. But those who believe in the existence of God and His greatness possess, especially eyes (divine eyes), through which they penetrate into the divine mysteries and what they present about God's attributes and opulence attract many to be inclined towards God and obtain His blessings. Religious are those who, having absolute faith in and great respect for God, abide by the laws and opinions produced by religious scriptures. Such believers have no doubt at all about greatness, mercifulness and kindness of God. To them God is not a subject to analyse, examine and prove. Rather, it is a subject of belief and feeling which demands full obedience and complete surrendering. To understand God one must be sentimental and emotional. There is neither script nor a language to write or speak about God since He is beyond languages. Neither man's intelligence nor his wisdom may catch God because He stands above all where their intelligence, wisdom, language etc, have no approach. In other words, God is unspeakable and beyond human understanding where except intuition nothing goes. However, enough indication is available in the world that indicates about the presence of Supreme Power. The need is to study the indications and understand them. Emergence of a religion is the effort in this regards which help to know and understand God and His creation.

In reality, God is a wonderful subject, a deep mystery, an unspeakable story and an unthinkable heap of divine energy and divine consciousness. It is the light that illumines even the sun and the moon including stars, planets and sub-planets. It is beyond mind, wisdom and language. To present a real picture of God, there is neither a language, nor a poem nor any other means. Expression of God is in silence. It is said that God is *Nirakara* and *Sakara*, *Nirguna* and *Saguna*. In the eyes of wisdom (mind) He appears like *Nirakara* but in the eyes of heart He becomes *Sakara*. Religious scriptures say that God is eternal, has no beginning and is endless. It has neither beginning, nor middle nor end. The Vedas say that God has no face and no colour. He is neither true nor untrue. No one is there to create God. He appears automatically, so He is called *Swambhu* (self-born), completely independent, self-willed, unrestrained, without any cause and spontaneous. There is no authority to control Him. Rather, He controls, right from Brahma to the level of grass. Entire universe is his creation and it (universe) evolves, expands, survives and lastly meets to the fate of annihilation at His will. No one could search out his final abode. Nothing definitely could be said about His nature, will, existence and merits. Whatsoever has been said or is said, even today, is not final. There are still much to be said about God. So, He is an unfinished story, untellable tale and unthinkable thought. However, what has been talked and said about God, till today, by various rishis, munis, scholars, thinkers, philosophers, poets, etc, help one to grasp and conceive the meaning of God and get an introduction to God's greatness. That is why seekers of truth and lovers of God study all the philosophies related to God, all that have been produced from time to time by a number of seekers of truth. It is universally acceptable that God is great, wonderful, mysterious, endless, beginning less, incomparable and beyond any measurement. What has been said so far about God is the inner-feeling of ancient rishis, munis, saints, sages, etc. In the religious scriptures what have been said about God and His great *Lila* is the inner-feeling of his great devotees and seekers of final truth.

Two Aspects of God

For understanding, God is divided into two aspects – *Nirguna-Nirakara* and *Saguna-Sakara*. The former, being spread everywhere, is shapeless, formless and without quality, while the latter is the primary source of all qualities and He may appear in form at any time anywhere. Lord Krishna, talking about some attribute of *Nirguna Brahma* in the *Bhagavad Gita* presents the following attributes of *Nirguna-Nirakara* Brahma:[1]

1. *Aksharam* (imperishable);
2. *Anirdeshyam* (without direction);
3. *Achintyam* (Unthinkable)
4. *Avayaktam* (unmanifested);
5. *Achalam* (immovable, constant);
6. *Srvatryagam* (all pervasive);
7. *Kuthastam*; and
8. *Dhruvam*.

Aksharam is that which never perishes. In any circumstance, place and time, its presence is not destroyed. Because *Akshara* is non-manifested, it is not accessible to words and therefore it may not be defined. As God is beyond destruction, it is called *Aksharam*. He is permanent, eternal and ceaseless. He was present in the past, He is present now and He will be present in the future also. The second attribute is *Anirdeshyam* which means that which can neither be directed anywhere nor can be pointed out. Questions like who is he, where is he and what is he may not be answered properly. So, He is called *Anirdeshyam*.

Since God can neither be directed nor be recognized, He is entitled as *Anirdeshyam*. In other words, one which may be felt in the inner-heart, but cannot be expressed in words or languages is *Anirdeshyam*. The element that has a class, qualities, and activities in time and place may be described, but that which is devoid of all these attributes, may not be directed and indicated. Except feeling nothing definitely can be said about God because he is beyond time and space. God is spiritual.

Achintyam is that which can neither be thought of, by the human mind and in words, for both are incapable of approaching God. God being spiritual stands above creation. Mind and languages are created things. Creation can never know the reality of the creator. Therefore, both mind and language are unable to say exactly what is God. Mind has its own sphere, much below the sphere of the Almighty. Mind cannot cross its limit. While reaching the apex of its own sphere, mind becomes inactive. It can feel about God, but cannot produce His exact picture. So, God is *Achintyam*. God being *Nirakara* is pervasive. There is no place where God is not present. God is Brahma, spreading everywhere. Influence of God is invisible, but it can be felt. What one sees and observes in the universe are the products of the Brahma. Brahma is a divine subtle element that exists everywhere. The element of the Brahma is capable of doing anything. So, there is no difference between God and Brahma. Rather Brahma is the manifested part of the *Brahman*. There is no atom where God is not present. The entity of an atom is due to the presence of God in it. So, God is called *Srvatryagam*. Everything is situated in God. In other words, place, time, sky, living and non-living beings and other materials are from the omnipresent as well as omnipotent *Brahman*. They all emanate from *Brahman*, remain in it, spread and evolve in it and lastly, merge into it.

God is the ultimate source of their living, working and disappearing.

God is also called *Kutstham* which means changeless. It always remains as it is. It has no defect, no alteration and no change. Changes occur in a thing which is within the sphere of time and speed as well as influenced by the three *gunas* of nature. Since God stands above the limit of time and speed, where there is no effect of *gunas*. He is constantly and absolutely pure and without any defect. Defects or impurities are only in *prakriti*, not in God. Since God is never involved in any activity of creation, He is always and absolutely pure. No impurity can touch God. If impurity touches God, it may also be pure without any delay. So, God is *Kutstham*. The entire activity of creation, which is full of *vikaras*, is within the sphere of God, no doubt, but God always remains pure because of His non-involvement in the natural spheres. Though God is the creator of the universe and supplier of the natural energies in the universe, He remains totally unaffected, absolutely aloof from natural activities and completely far away from any kind of impurities. It is all because He is *Kutashtha*. Being involved, he is non-involved. Being creator He is non-actor, and being the ultimate source of qualities He stands above all natural qualities.

Another attribute of God is *Achalam* which means no movement at all. Because of His permanently stable position He is immovable. All natural objects are within the motion but God is above motion. He is stable like sky. The motion is in the nature. Due to motion things are in constant change. Changes in the universe are natural phenomena, but God is immune from effects of any change. Happenings take place in the sky without influencing it. So, all activities are there within the sphere of God, but God is never influenced by such activities. Another feature of God is *Dhruvam* which means always, eternal and permanent. God remains forever. He exists even after complete annihilation of creation. *Dhruvam* adjective of God clearly indicates that God is beyond destruction. The continuity of His existence is without any break or pause. He was; He is; and He will be because he is eternal. The adjective *Dhruvam* identifies that existence of God is beyond doubt. God is called *Avyaktam*. It means God is, no doubt, but non-manifested. He is non-manifested because He is *Nishkala* (without any shape or form). He is shapeless, formless, and colourless. *Nirakara* God is beyond concepts like deities and idols. Manifestation, in fact, is presence of God, but in concealment. What has come into manifestation is not God, but due to God. That is why He is called *Nirakara* that which has neither shape nor kind.

Thus, it is obvious that the concept of *Parmatma* is peculiar, wonderful, supernatural, transcendental and imperceptible. He is beyond the catch of human mind and wisdom. *Nirguna-Nirakara* Brahma may be felt, but cannot be described. What so ever is said about Him is incomplete. His story is endless; His glory is wondrous; His abode is hidden; His qualities are mysterious; His feeling is full of pleasures and bliss; and His Abode is source of all energy and power. *Nirakara Brahma* is the subject of *Sankhya Darshana* where He is discussed as absolutely as spirit and known as the Supernatural Transcendental unseen power that is the primal cause of the creation of all elements of the universe. He is also known as the great endless ocean of power, energy, light, consciousness that illumine celestial bodies and give senses to the living beings to understand the universe and its creator. By knowing creation of God that represents God's greatness one may hardly feel something about God.

However, it is notable that *Nirguna-Nirakara* Brahma being shapeless without mouth, eyes, nose, ears, hands, legs, etc, accepts and eats offerings, sees everything, hears voices, smells objects and speaks about things. In the *Bhagavad Gita* Lord Krishna says to Arjuna:

> With hands and feet everywhere, with eyes and heads and mouths everywhere, with hearing everywhere, That (God) exists enveloping all. Shining by the functions of all, the senses (yet) without the senses; unattached, yet supporting all; devoid of qualities. (*Bhagavad Gita*, 13/13-14)

The aforesaid statement clearly indicates that God has countless mouths, eyes, ears, legs, hands and senses. Being non-manifested, He is capable of seeing all, eating whatsoever is presented to Him, smelling things and walking everywhere. It is also said that God, without hands and legs, accepts offerings and moves fast in all directions. He sees without eyes and hears without ears.[2] Thus, God being the base of qualities (*gunas*), is not evolved in *gunas*; being illuminator of sense-organs, He stands above their effects. He is not in bondage like other living beings. Nothing can influence God. He is not visible but everything is visible to Him.

Saguna-Sakara Parmatma

Aspects of *Saguna-Sakara* God are different to that of *Nirguna-Nirakara*. The former is mere Supreme Abstract Idea while the latter being abstract is capable of taking concrete form and appears before His trustworthy devotees. True devotees of God having firm as well as unbreakable faith in God's supremacy, kindness, benevolence, compassion and sympathy want to see Him face to face. Unlike the followers of *Nirguna-Nirakara* God, the devotees of *Sakara* Brahma believe strongly and feel inwardly that God is merciful, kind enough and lover of devotees. So, for the sake of devotees who have totally surrendered to Him, and who are desirous to see Him, may not take much time to appear in beautiful attractive form before them. Here *Nirakara* Brahma being merciful and kind enough turns immediately into *Sakara* Brahma for the sake of his trustworthy devotees. He appears before them in the charming and attractive divine form. The devotees of *Saguna Brahma* firmly believe that God who is *antaryamin* (knower of inner-heart), all pervasive, all powerful, having all qualities, and listener to prayer, would definitely appear in the divine shape hearing the devotees' inner-voice and sublimed prayer. They also believe that God, being devoid of *gunas* remains the constant resource of *gunas*; being invisible to living beings is the base of visibility; capable of converting a mountain into an atom and an atom into a mountain; able of giving life to lifeless and making living beings dead, can appear before His devotees hearing their distressed cry. With such ambition and hope devotees desire not only to see God face-to-face but also like to be God's friends, parents, brothers, slaves, etc. It is believed that *Saguna-Sakara* God along with the liberated souls live in His Dhama (Abode) which has been given various names like Divine Loka, Goloka, Baikuntha, Swarga, Kailash, etc.

Nirakara and *Sakara Brahma*: Two Aspects of Single Coin

In reality God is indivisible, and he cannot be divided into parts. Both the concepts – *Saguna* and *Nirguna* or *Sakara* and *Nirakara* – are the angles of followers who view God from their respective angles. In broadened sense God is everything. Appearance of God depends upon the angle of the viewers. According to *Shvetashvatara Upanishad*, God is "the one, the luminous, hidden in all beings, all-pervading, the Inner Self of all, the superintendent of all acts, of all beings, the witness, perceiver, alone and free from qualities."[3] God takes the shape according to consciousness of viewers. It is very much difficult to assign a single form to God. He is applicable to his devotees or followers according to their emotion and sentiment. The *Bhagavad Gita*, in this regard, says:

> Howsoever men approach Me, even so do I reward them; My path do men follow in all things O son of Pritha.[4]

God reward men with things they desire, in accordance with the way in which they seek God and the motive with which they seek Him. In the consciousness of the followers of *Nirguna Brahma* He is beyond the reach of their sense organs, mind and emotion. On the contrary, in the consciousness of the followers of *Saguna Brahma* He appears as fire appears from wood after trial. According to *Bhagavad Gita*, God is *'Samoham sarvabhuteshu'* (present in all beings in equal manner). It is said that:

> The same I am to all beings; to Me there is none hateful or dear, but who worship Me with devotion, they are in Me, and I am also in them.[5]

Love and Devotion for God

Love and devotion are complementary to each other. Where there is love, devotion appears automatically. Love is the fountain of devotion. Love demands nothing. Rather, it renounces everything for love. Love is attraction while devotion is complete surrender. It is love that brings forth devotion. Love without devotion is meaningless. Love is first to appear broadening the path for advent of devotion. A lover becomes devotee of his/her beloved. Love has no barrier, no boundary. There is no secrecy between lover and the beloved because hearts of the both become similar. Both remember to each other. They do not like separation. If there is separation both equally suffer. During the phase of separation, they remember each other in memory. A true devotee of God loves Him not for any gain, but for His goodness. Nothing in this world is dearer to the devotee than God. Even memory of God gives pleasure to the true devotee. Greatness of God is so dear to him that he always talks and thinks about God's glories. In memory of devotee there is neither logic nor reason. If there is anything, it is sentiment and emotion. Firm faith, unbreakable hope and unforgettable memory of God always occupy the heart of a devotee. Here is the relationship of kinsmanship. To a devotee God is no one else but He is completely his own. The relationship between a devotee and God is like devoted couple who owns nothing separately, but shares everything jointly. They are one in spirit. When the heart of a devotee in absence of God drowns into the ocean of Godly love, tears roll down from his eyes automatically; his hairs stand on ends; and quintessence of love automatically erupts from his heart that ultimately drenched God. At this moment God has to appear before his devotee to embrace him/her. This is the climax of love and devotion. *Srimad Bhagavatam* says:

> I am under my true devotee. I am not independent of my devotee. My simple and saintly devotees have established possession over my heart. They love me and I love them. (*Srimad Bhagavatam*, 9/8/63)

In this regard the *Bhagavad Gita* says:

> By devotion he knows Me in truth, what and who I am; then, knowing me in truth, he forthwith enters into me. (*Bhagavad Gita*, XVIII/55)

God's devotee may be of lower nature, having impurities, but love and devotion (*Bhakti*) for God makes him pure removing his all impurities. Thereafter, he is entitled to avail salvation. It is said:

> Soon he becomes righteous and attains eternal peace; do thou, O son of Kunti, proclaim that my devotee never perishes. For finding refuse in Me, they also who, O son of Pritha, may be of a sinful birth – women, Vaishyas as well as Shudras – even they attain the Supreme Goal. (*Bhagavad Gita*, IX/31-32)

Thus, it is very much obvious that God is both *Saguna-Sakara* and *Nirguna-Nirakara*. Being non-involved in the creation, He seems to be involved in it, living far from the creation, He seems to be quite near to it, keeping aside from natural qualities, He seems upholding all qualities and being devoid of merits, He seems to have the merits like beauty, pleasantness, gracefulness, benevolence, etc. When God is viewed from an intellectual angle, He looks quite subtle, invisible, unknowable, unthinkable, unspeakable and unapproachable because at the heat of knowledge the *Saguna-Sakara* form of God begins to melt and becomes thinner and thinner, subtle and subtle like water vapour which ultimately disappears. But when one approaches Him with love and devotion, *Nirakara* Brahma at the coldness of love and softness of devotion begins to fridge taking the shape of *Saguna-Sakara Brahma*. Falling in gravity of love God appears before the lover to make him happy, to know his well-being and to protect him from any kind of trouble. Love binds God and makes Him to live, eat and dance with devotees. His entire mysteries disappear when his true devotee comes to Him. There are various examples in human history when God appeared before His devotees. God is present everywhere. He may appear in any form before His devotee. It is evident from the statement of the *Bhagavad Gita*. It is said:

> According to the Vedas, Narayana, the Supreme Person is residing both outside and inside of every living-entity. He is present in both the spiritual and material worlds. Although He is far, far away, still He is near to us.[6]

He is hidden in those who is either atheists or whose devotion to God is still suspicious. To approach God the ladder of devotion made of belief and trust is needed. Due to His engagement in transcendental bliss, the common man with material eyes cannot see what He does. So, He is known as unknowable. But one who has his purified eyes, mind and senses may witness His opulence and obtain His direct blessings. According to the *Brahma Samhita* the devotee who has developed love for the Supreme God can see Him always, without cessation. At the desire of Arjuna, Lord Krishna appeared before him in divine form as *Chaturbhuja* (four arms) Narayana and said:

> Not by Vedas, nor by austerity, nor by gifts, nor by sacrifice, can I be seen in this Form as thou hast seen Me. But by undistracted devotion can I, of this Form, be known and seen in reality, and entered into, O harasser of the foes.[7]

Thus, it is clear that God is one, but there are different paths to approach and reach Him. The path whether it is *Nirguna* or *Saguna* both lead to one God. Both the paths are able to take one to the Abode of God. *Moksha* can be availed following both the paths. Hence wise is he who without falling in the disputes of *Nirguna* and *Saguna*, love and worship one God who is omnipotent and omnipresent. Rather the path of *Nirguna* is more difficult because it needs more wisdom and understanding which is impossible for common people. *Saguna* path is easier because it needs love, devotion and faith. Removing the doubt of Arjuna regarding Supremacy of the Paths between *Nirakara* and *Sakara* or *Nirguna* and *Saguna* the Lord Krishna declares:

> Those who, fixing thought on Me, contemplate Me, always devout, endued with supreme faith, those in my opinion are the best *Yogins*.[8]

The *Shvetashvatara Upanishad*, talking about the nature of God, says that only one God is secretly sitting in the heart of every being. He is knower of the inner-heart of all. He is embodiment of consciousness and giver of consciousness to all living beings. He alone is the witness of all universal activities, and He awards the fruits of actions of all living beings. He is absolutely pure and above the three natural *gunas* – *Sattva*, *Rajas* and *Tamas*. Being pure embodiment of consciousness He seems inactive, but He alone is the controller of countless living beings. It is He who creates universe.[9] All this world is pervaded invisibly by the Highest Being. In the non-manifested form of the Highest Being all beings live from Brahma down to the plant. No being devoid of the Self can ever become the subject of experience. God does not dwell in other beings because of absence of contact with others, unlike corporeal things. However, He is certainly the innermost essence even of the *akasha* (sky) that is unconnected with any object, and it cannot be contained anywhere as though in a receptacle. The Sruti speaks of an attached condition of the Self, seeing that He is unconnected with any object. It is said "Devoid of attachment. He is never attached."[10] Speaking about pervasiveness of God in creation, Lord Krishna says:

> See, O son of Pritha, My heavenly forms, by hundreds and thousands, of different sorts, and of various colours and shapes. Behold the Adityas the Vasus, the Rudras, the Asvins and also the Maruts; Behold many marvels never seen before.[11]

Parmatma is *Sachidanand*

It is not that only Sanatana Dharma of Hindus speaks about divine glory of God, but all other religions like Islam, Christianity, Sikhism, Jainism, Judaism, etc, speak about greatness of God and His divine opulence. They, too, believe in one Absolute non-manifested God being the source of entire creation. This is another fact that, if spoken neutrally, the conceptual aspect of Almighty God spoken by Sanatana Dharma is more tangible, more explicit, more enlarged and more conceivable. God spoken by the Sanatana Dharma is *Sachidanand*. He is embodiment of *Sat*, *Chit*, *Anand* (truth, consciousness and bliss). *Sat* means imperishable truth that remains as it is forever and that is beyond any change. *Chit* means consciousness, the base of feeling, understanding, knowing and thinking. All sense organs of living beings and their mind and wisdom are active due to their constant contact with *Chit*. *Anand* means bliss that presents immense pleasure. All the earthly objects have their utilities which attract living beings. Utilities contain pleasure. So, people like to be in close contact with the objects that give them pleasure. The ultimate source of pleasure is God because He is everywhere. He is in everything. The Godly bliss known as *Brahmanand* is *paramanand* (the highest imperishable pleasure) which cannot be described in words. It is the subject of feeling and enjoying. Since essence of God (bliss) is present in everything, either living or non-living, they are useful. It is the usefulness of things that attracts living beings and they run after them. Utility is not permanent. It changes with change of the nature of things. Notable fact is that the process of continuity of utility inaccessibly continues. Things disappear, no doubt, but the essence of a thing passes into its inheritor. So, bliss of God is permanent. It is this bliss which gives perpetual rejoice.

God and His Incarnation

It has almost universally been recognized that universe is a creation of the power that is the superior most and there is a great power that upholds the entire universe. Disputes and controversies are there regarding His shape and aspects. It is undisputable fact that the universe depends upon certain cosmic orders. Even the slightest disorder may cause a big catastrophe. There is decided a cause behind every happening. Everything, either living or non-living, is bound to act according to its nature. It is the Dharma of things to behave or act in direction of their decided fate. To act differently means to create disorder, inviting devastation. The sun, the moon and the stars, all have bounded duty to act properly. If they act differently, ruin of the universe along with their existence is a must. Air is bound to blow, water is bound to remain cool and liquid and fire is bound to be hot and produce heat. Likewise, human beings are bound to follow the decided course of actions. Various gods and goddesses have to abide by divine rules and cosmic laws. Even God, the maker of such rules, cannot deviate from such divine rules without any specific purpose. If anyone acts against the decided course of action it is sure that a number of inconveniences as well as confusions may occur in the society and it would ultimately result in anarchy and ruin. *Dharma Shastras* of each religion prescribe certain social, religious, economic and moral behaviours for mankind. It is the moral duty of the people to act in the right direction, to protect themselves protecting creation. Experience shows that man falling victim to material lust and greed forgets his moral duty and to satisfy his *trishna* adopts a ruinous path with the result that whole of the social as well as religious orders come in stake. In such situations man is surrounded by a number of troubles and pains. It appears that the entire edifice of creation would fall down. The number of greedy, immoral, people of demonic nature, selfish, etc, increased, who hardly allow others to live in peace and security. To them there is neither God nor any godly rule. They believe in might as well as fight. Their misbehaviour and selfish attitude cause total anarchy, especially for those who have faith in God and godly life. They become enemy of religion. To them there is no God except themselves.

At such critical and painful satiation God being merciful take incarnation on the earth with the marked objective to destroy such irreligious and anti-social elements and re-establish religion or right order. It is evident from the statement in the *Bhagavad Gita* where Lord Krishna speaks:

> Whenever there is a decay of religion, O Bharata, and an ascendency of irreligion, then I manifest Myself. For the protection of the good, for the destruction of evil-doers, for the firm establishment of religion, I am born in every age.[12]

There is a deep integral relationship between the creator and his creation. No one wants to see ruin of his creation. Since entire creation is product of God's will, He does not like to see that, His creation, is ruined by harmful forces. When peace-loving people find themselves unable to meet ruinous forces on the earth, they pray to the Almighty to appear on the earth and protect them. So, God being kind enough incarnate on earth to serve the purpose. Nothing is dearer to God except His devotees. There are certain devotees who like to live with Him being His relatives on the earth. With a purpose to satisfy the devotees' desire God takes human form on earth and enjoys with them. It was the pure love of Gopis of Gokul that compelled Lord Krishna to incarnate in Gokul and do *Raslila* (divine dance) with the Gopas and Gopis, who were true devotees of God. Lord Rama incarnated to liberate Bharata (India) by killing demons like Ravana and others. The traditions established by incarnated God or His messengers on earth refresh people and serve as a precedence to be followed by coming generations. Thus, incarnations of God protect the earth and its species including human beings by finishing demon-like people on the one hand, and re-establish forgotten religious, moral as well as social traditions in the interest of all on the other.

Creation of Universe

Creation is a continuous process of becoming something. It also means to come into existence and remain active. For each action there is one actor. The universe comprising of subtle and solid materials which can be seen, imagined and felt, is the creation in which the actor is God. Universe, comprising of all subtle and solid materials that are seen, understood, imagined and felt, came into being due to the close contact of *Purusha* and *Prakriti*. The former is God while the latter is God's creation. God's creation is mysterious, that which cannot be understood easily. However, it is knowable. Universe, that is full of mysteries and wonders, indicates the greatness of God. It is the subject of experience that things come into being, evolves and lastly fades away. Appearing and disappearing is the continuous process of creation. It is difficult or rather impossible to say how and when did it come into existence. Various theories have been presented relating to the origin and evolution of the Universe. Religious theory has its own stories and statements.

According to *Matsya Purana*, during the period of *mahapralaya* (complete annihilation of universe) there was nothing except acute and impenetrable darkness covering the sky. There was nothing which could be imagined, nor there anyone to think about. There was no race or sign of existence of anything. Everything had disappeared. If there was something, it was God alone, about whom nothing could be said because there was no one to say and no one to listen.[13] It is further said that at that very time, imperishable God, who is beyond the reach of the sense organs and subtler than subtle, greater than great and, self-born, appeared alone, penetrating darkness with the purpose to create universe.[14] The *Shiva Purana* says that the entire universe had met the fate of complete destruction and nothing was there except deep darkness, which had devoured up all elements along with their subjects. There was neither the sun nor the moon. No planet or planetary directions were available. There was neither day nor night; neither fire nor earth; neither water nor air. If there was anything it was the great empty sky only which was full of darkness that could not be penetrated into. In that situation the *tatsad brahma* (imperishable truth), which stands non-manifested and above the reach of knowledge and understanding, was present alone. He thought of *ekoham bahushyam* (becoming many from one), and then the creation of the universe came into being.[15]

Theory of the Divine Bang

According to the statements said above, it appears that creation of the universe is a desire or *Lila* of God. To remove darkness light is needed. It is believed that in the upper sky (*para-prakriti*) a big bang occurred, resulting in a huge ball of bright light that soon spread all over the sky removing all the darkness. It is a matter of common experience that during the night everything comes under the shadow of darkness, but in the morning, with the appearance of the sun, entire darkness automatically disappears within no time. Similarly, with the big bang, the light which appeared was not like the sun's light, but it was the spiritual light that further caused to the birth several crore suns and moons and uncountable stars and planets in the sky. Vedas and Upanishads say that the spiritual light which first emerged was wonderful transcendental light emitting sharp, quick-running and astonished divine energy that served as the first cause of creation of the universe. In other words, that divine light which suddenly occurred in the sky was the embodiment of Almighty God and the beginning of creation. It is this spiritual light, being the embodiment of Mahavishnu according to the Hindu religious scriptures. The concept of

Mahavishnu is the symbol of divine light which pervades every nook and corner of the universe, and that is the main cause of emergence of things in the universe.

The first energy in the form of divine light is called *para-prakriti*, or *Adi Shakti* (the first manifestation of divine energy). The *Adi Shakti* manifested everywhere, giving birth to Brahma, Vishnu and Mahesh – the great *Trimurti* of the universe – who appeared with the purpose to create living and non-living beings, sustaining their existence and lastly finishing them up, respectively. Thereafter, various gods and goddesses came into being to uphold the universe. *Adi Shakti* is called the mother of not only *Trimurti* but also of the entire universe because they all appeared from the great womb of *Adi Shakti*. It appeared from the great womb of *para-prakriti*. Thus, it is obvious that creation is the result of the union of *Purusha* (God) and *Prakriti* (manifested aspect of God). These two aspects appear differently, but in reality they are originally one. *Prakriti* is the integral reflection of godly power. In the *Bhagavad Gita*, Lord Krishna says to Arjuna:[16]

> All beings, O son of Kunti, go into my *Prakriti* at the end of a *kalpa*. I send them forth again at the beginning of (the next) *kalpa*.

It is further said:[17]

> By Me presiding, *Prakriti* produces the moving and the unmoving; because of this, O son of Kunti, the world revolves.

The *Prakriti* is not God, but manifestation of his energy that is "one, the luminous, hidden in all beings and is all-pervading, the Inner-Self of all, the superintendent of all acts, the abode of all beings, the witness, the perceiver, alone and free from all qualities."[18] The statement indicates that the base of creation of every being is the hidden spiritual light in the centre of the heart of a being. This is the soul that supplies energy, making things continuously active. The soul, hiding inside in a being, acts independently, but not involving itself in the act.

According to the *Shiva Purana*, Lord Shiva is *Purusha*, *Parampurusha, Ishvara* of all, Self-born, the Creator of the universe and Abode of imperishable energies from which creation takes place. *Shakti* is embodiment of manifested Shiva that is called *prakriti*. Whatsoever one sees, hears, imagined and felt, is all in *prakriti*. In entire creation there is nothing except Shiva and *Shakti*. Activities among the living and non-living beings and movable and immovable things are due to *Para-Shakti*. As no issue can be born without the union of man and woman, creation cannot take place without meeting of Shiva and Shakti. It is said, as there is no difference between moon and its light, sun and its rays, Shiva-Shakti are inseparable. The countless waves of an ocean rise from it and merge into it. They have no independent existence. Similarly, entire energy of creation, existing in different forms, emerge from Mahashiva, the great *Brahman*, and lastly merges into that *Brahman*. As without light the moon has no charm, Shiva without *Shakti* has no attraction. Neither Shiva can live without *Shakti* nor can *Shakti* exist in the absence of Shiva. Both are one and complementary to each other.[19]

Appearance of Mysterious Syllable *Om*

Om is the mysterious syllable or Holy monosyllable that symbolizes Lord Shiva. It is said that entire creation is within *Om*. So, it is called *Pranava* (God). Vedas, Smritis, Puranas and other religious scriptures talk a lot about the greatness of *Om* with honour and regard. Knowledge of *Om* brings one near to *Shiva-Shakti* because both Shiva and *Shakti* appeared in the form of *Om*. God is expressible truth and *Om* expresses God. *Om* is monosyllable (*Ekakshar*) which is called *Pranava*. The word *'pra'* means the world that has emerged from the *Para-Prakriti*. The word *'nava'* means boat, which takes one from one part of the river to another part. It means *Pranava* helps living beings to cross the ocean of the mysterious and illusive world (*Bhavasagar*). No one can get across the mundane world without the mercifulness of *Pranava*. In other, yet simple words, no one can obtain salvation without the blessings of Lord Shiva, nor may one get pleasure in this world without His blessings. Hence, those who are ambitious of obtaining salvation or to live with pleasure in this world must worship Shiva.

The syllable *Om* has five parts – *Akar* (a), *Ukar* (u), *Makar* (m), *Bindu* (.) and *Nada* (voice). All these five aspects are symbols of God. *Akar* and *Ukar* symbolize non-manifested Shiva, while *Makar* symbolizes *Shakti* that is manifested. In other words, God Mahashiva is the non-manifested *Brahman* which is called *Nishkala* (without any form). It is *Nishkala* that is *Nirakara*. *Shakti* is *Shakla* (*Sakara*), manifestation of *Nishkala Brahman*. According to *Shiva Purana*, *Nishkala* is *Alinga* (without any shape), while *Shakla* is *Linga* (having shape). It is believed that with the desire of the *Brahman* to be many, a big transcendental eruption, having a puzzling roar, hollow sound, and emitting immense bright light, automatically took place that covered the entire sky within no time. It was that divine noise which took the shape of *bindu* (.), the half syllable. It was this *bindu* that became *Om* or *Omkara*, emitting echo, reverberation, resonating prolonged sound that is still available in the universe. Yogis with the concentration of their mind hear the divine sound that is wonderful, charming, pleasant, attractive and beautiful. The divine sound became the base of creation because of its divine energy. The vowels and consonants as well as grammar in which all languages are interwoven, emerged from the divine sound *Omkara*.

Thus, *Nada* (the divine sound) is Brahma which is present everywhere in the subtle sky. It is the mother of creation of the abstract and concrete world, human languages, etc. Scientists call it ether. The *Nada Brahma* is, thus, first manifestation of *Nirakara* Brahma.

Entire creation is first in the *Shabda Brahma* (*Omkara*), then it is in the world of creation. It is *Shabda Brahma* that is the first art of *Paramatma* which has enwrapped the whole of the sky. All the elements present in the creation are the products of the *Nada Brahma*. *Bindu*, *Nada* and *Shabda* are so subtle, so great, so subtly manifested and so wondrous that nothing definitely can be expressed about them in human language. They are the subjects of feeling only. However, it can be said that *Om*, the *Ekakshar* is the primal divine seed from which entire creation has appeared like millions and billions figures take shape within the original figures from one to ten. As a great tree of banana is concealed in its very small seed, entire knowledge from Brahma to the mundane world is located in the divine monosyllable *Om*. That is why great Rishis, Munis, sages, poets, messengers etc have spoken a lot about *Om* with great humbleness. All the religious scriptures especially of the Hindus adore the greatness of *Om*.

According to *Katha Upanishad*, all the Vedas which substantiate the truth, all the penances that like to obtain the truth, by mercy of which follow the celestial life, that (truth) is *Om*, only *Om*.[20] It further states, Brahma is that *Akshara Om* that is the best of all. By knowing that *Akshara* one gets what he likes.[21] *Taittiriya Upanishad*, in praise of *Brahman* (*Om*) expresses that '*Omit Brahma Omitam Sarvam*' (*Om* is the only Brahma, and it is everything.)[22] Again, The *Chhandogya Upanishad* says that as all leaves are covered by numerous thin stems, similarly, that entire world is covered with *Om*.[23] Talking about the great significance of *Pranava*, the *Mandukya*

Upanishad states that *Pranava* is *Upper Brahma*, and *Pranava* is called Brahma. It is (*Pranava*) that is extraordinary, without pause and obstruction. There is nothing before, after and beyond *Pranava*. It is imperishable. It neither decreases nor increases. It remains as it is.[24] It is further said that *Pranava* is the beginning, middle and end of everything. *Pranava* is sitting and witnessing God in every heart.[25]

Thus, it is evident that significance of *Om* is unspeakable. Whatsoever is said about *Om* or *Pranava* is insufficient. It is the primal source of creation. It is the reflection of *Brahman* in the entire universe. Everything is within *Pranava*. It is the great womb of creation. Nothing can exist beyond it. *Pranava* is the primary source of origin, existence and dissolution of things. It is perfection of knowledge. It is the embodiment of purity, power, energy, science, arts and what not.

Concept of *Trimurti* (Brahma, Vishnu and Mahesh) in Hindu Shastra

In the Hindu religious scriptures there is mention of three great gods – Brahma, Vishnu and Mahesh – who are known as the embodiment of *Ekakshara Brahma*, and they have great significance in the world of manifestation. Their roles in creation of the universe are indispensable. Being different in their appearance, they are virtually one. They are seen in three forms due to their different performances in creation. Like Absolute *Brahman*, they are all pervasive, powerful, omnipresent and omnipotent. It is Absolute *Brahman* who has appeared in these three different forms to handle the creational affairs. It is evident from the *Srimad Bhagavad Purana*, which states:[26]

> I (Absolute *Brahman*) am the first as well as the primal cause in the world, and I am Brahma and *Mahadeva*. I am soul of all, *Paramatma*, witness, self-illuminated, having no title. Accepting My

> three qualities of *gunas – Sattva, Rajas* and *Tamas*), I do creation, maintain and destroy the world. And I have adopted three titles like Brahma, Vishnu and Mahesh.... We Brahma, Vishnu and Mahesh are the same.

The first deity that appeared from the divine light of the Absolute *Brahman* was known as Vishnu because of his presence everywhere. Later on, Vishnu came to be known as *Sri Hari* and *Narayana*. Since the very purpose of advent of Vishnu was to do creation, he began the process of creation of the universe. It is believed that when Lord Vishnu was deeply engaged in hard penance, water began coming out from his body, and that spread all over the sky submerging Vishnu in it. In fact, the water, which is talked about, is nothing, but divine light (*Brahmajyoti*) which spread everywhere. Vishnu came to be called *Narayana* due to his sleeping into *Brahmajyoti*. So, *Narayana* means one who sleeps in *Brahmajyoti*. It is, perhaps, this *Brahmajyoti* that is known as *Kshira Sagara* (ocean of milk) in which Lord Narayana along with Goddess Lakshmi reside, sitting or sleeping on the bed of divine serpent Vasuki. What we talk of the *Gangages* is the powerful current of purity of thought that emerged from the ocean of *Brahmajyoti* and came down to earth. The *Gangage*, as a symbol of purity, is the current of pious knowledge emerging from Lord Vishnu. It has the quality to purify even the most corrupt person. Knowledge, especially about divinity, purifies people. Creation is interwoven in knowledge and knowledge itself is in *Paramatma*.

Lord Vishnu, sleeping inside water (*Brahmajyoti*) was thinking about creation. Meanwhile, a lotus, having countless petals, emerged from the centre of Vishnu's navel, and spread all over the great sky. It is said that the divine lotus was God's Hiranyagarbha within which sky, earth and *patal* (lower region of sky) were hidden. It has already been stated that a great divine bang occurred before creation. It was, in fact, an outburst, an eruption in Hiranyagarbha from where creation began. As soon as it burst, it was divided into two parts – upper and lower. The upper part appeared as celestial sky while from the lower part the earth and *patal* came into being. From that Hiranyagarbha appeared Brahma with four hands and five mouths. According to *Mandukya Upanishad*, Brahma appeared automatically.[27] *Matsya Purana* says:[28]

> From the womb of Hiranyagarbha, first of all, Aditya came into being. He was called Aditya because he was the first to come, and he was called Brahma because he was reading the Vedas. He, dividing Hiranyagarbha (in two parts), created heaven and earth. Between these two (heaven and earth) he created various directions including the imperishable sky. From the outer skin of the womb of Hiranyagarbha, mountains including Meru appeared, and from the outer membrane of the womb appeared lightening along with circle of clouds. From that Great divine egg rivers, Pitriloka (*Loka* of dead persons) and human beings came into existence.

In the creation, Lord Vishnu is the symbol of the inner-heart and the base of consciousness, while Brahma symbolizes consciousness. When consciousness meets the inner-heart (*antahkarana*) creation begins. So, Lord Vishnu and Brahma joined hands to begin the process of creation. Brahma holder of four Vedas (knowledge) created things while Vishnu provided them a base for evolution. It is said that there are five *sargas* (verity of worlds) created by Brahma. Brahma in the first *sarga* created the world of vegetation, in the second *sarga* the world of birds, in the third *sarga* the world of gods and goddesses. It has already been discussed in the preceding chapter that there are various types of gods and goddesses and their purpose is to uphold creation. In the fourth *sarga*, Brahma created human beings and in the fifth *sarga* the world of ghosts or dead. In all these *sargas* creation came out from Brahma's mind. It is said that despite the difficult efforts of Brahma his creation did hardly evolve with the result that he became sad and worried. No god or human being created by Brahma's mind liked to stay in his creation, and they all began to disappear. Thereafter, he personified Mahashiva, who handing over the responsibility of creation to Vishnu and Brahma disappeared.

Brahma being unable to continue the process of creation requested Shiva-Shakti to create beings within the sphere of birth and death. Since Shiva, who is the symbol of purity and kindness, denied creating the *sarga*, where miseries and death would prevail. Moreover, in such a creation human beings would always be engaged in various activities causing miseries and troubles. So, he asked Brahma to create such a world of creation where birth and death would be prominent. Such creation was not possible without copulation between two opposite sexes. So, need was felt to create sexual energy among male and female sexes. Sex, in fact, is the base of creation among living beings. It is a magnetic force that attracts opposite sexes, resulting in copulation. There is no creation without sexual intercourse between male and female forces. Such a process of creation still continues.

It was Lord Shiva who created power of sex in the universe with the purpose to expand and continue creation. To fulfil the need, Shiva, with the help of Shakti created the female sex. It is believed that the first female sex who appeared in God's creation was goddess Savitri, who later on came to be known as Gayatri. Savitri or Gayatri is the symbol of knowledge and Brahma, the creator, with the association of Savitri (knowledge) created different kinds of species in the universe. Gayatri is known as the mother of Vedas (knowledge) and Saraswati is the upholder of this divine knowledge. So, Saraswati is the expanded form of Gayatri. It is said that Brahma and Gayatri are the first divine couple who are still present everywhere in all creation, in a subtle form. *Matsya Purana* says that "Wherever God Brahma is present, Saraswati is also present there. Wherever Saraswati is present Brahma is also present.[29]

Thereafter, copulated creation began which is still in continuation. In creation there is no specie along with human beings which may develop their generation without copulation. Thus, female sex is an integral part of creation. Male sex is the carrier of seed which he puts the seed in the woman's womb. Thereafter, the female sex, carrying the seed, not only gives birth to new baby but also brings it up. Female sex is symbol of Shakti while male sex symbolizes Shiva. The union of both is the basic cause of creation. The first female sex who appeared in human form was known as Shatarupa while the first male sex was called Manu. According to Hindu *Dharma Shastra* Manu and Shatarupa are the first and foremost ancestors of mankind on the earth.

Mahakala and Death

So far the question of death of species or destruction of creation is concerned, it is a most painful incident, but to adjust the coming generation and release species from old age it is a must. It is said that Lord Shiva himself adopted that cruel and sad job. He appeared in creation in the form of Shankara, the symbol of Mahakala. *Kala* means time which is in constant motion. Mahakala is the emperor of time and ruler of all those who are in the great trap of time. All living beings are prisoners of time. Mahakala has *kalchakra* (circle of time) that is also called *mayajal* (net of illusions). It is a labyrinth, a zig-zag, a puzzle which has entangled those who either knowingly or unknowingly have fallen in its trap. To come across the *mayajal* is very difficult task. The current of time along with entire universe has been blowing ceaselessly from time immemorial. Gods, Gandharvas, Kinnars, Yakshas, Yatis, ghosts, human beings, birds, animals, insects, etc, have been caught in the great trap of *mayajal.* They appear and disappear in the ocean of time. In other words, they take birth and die, and the cyclic process of death and birth continues.

The *mayajal* (net of illusions) comprise of insatiable lust and desire for worldly pleasures like wealth, prosperity, fame, name, glory, reputation splendour, love and affection for family members and relatives, etc. It also comprises of hate, envy, temptation, emotions and sentiments. All these attract the living species towards worldly lusts keeping them engaged forever in worldly activities covering their eyes of real knowledge. The species falling into the traps of great *Mahamayajal* become and remain victim to sufferings and pain until they are liberated. So, creation of the universe is full of miseries and troubles.

Kala (time) has three aspects – past, present and future. Time has been in continuation without any pause from the beginning of creation. In the ceaseless movement of time everything is blowing automatically. No one is or nothing is static in creation. In the great womb of time the events that happened sometimes back are hidden. What is happening today is the present and many things are to happen that is hidden in the womb of future. Each present moment is in a continuous process of submerging into the dark coverage of the past living space for the coming moment. The space vacated by the present is covered by the future moment that is ready to come into the present. This process of time continues, moment after moment, that keeps the universe in a constant flux. There is no obstruction in the moving process of time.

Nothing can block its way. No one can catch time, rather time catches everyone. This is *Kalchakra*. All *mandalas* (spheres) of the universe, along with all living and non-living things are within the sphere of *Kalchakra*, the great bomb of time. They all are born in time and they will all die in time. Thus, time governed by *Mahakala* is all pervasive, all powerful and undefeatable.

All three aspects of time – past, present and future – are related to each other. Each aspect influences the other. Impact of present is influencing both past and present. Similarly, the past is affecting the future. Future is related to both past and present. Present converts into past. In real sense, present is the result of past and future. The status of future depends upon the present because it is the present that creates the future. That is why it is said that one harvests what one sows. Present *karmas* ripen and appear in the future as fruits. All living beings are in the captivity of time. Even great mountains, big rivers, the sun, the moon the galaxy of stars, etc, are prisoners of time. Everything is bound to act according to the will of the *Mahakala*. Destiny is the master of man. Man is to act only. Fruits are not in man's hand. Only action is in his hands. *Mahakal* is cruel, no doubt, but there is no chance of injustice in his empire. He gently offers the one his dues. In this regard the *Bhagavad Gita* says.[30]

> Thy concern is with action alone, never with results. Let not the fruit of action be thy motive; nor let thy attachment be for inaction.

So long as man has lust and desire to avail the fruits in the world of *Mahakala*, he is in illusion. Common people do hardly know that *trishna* and lust are the binding forces that keep man involved in *mayajal* where there is more suffering and pain. *Trishna* and lust have no end. They are insatiable. Their intensity goes on increasing more and more with the attachment of the world. Man will be a prisoner of *Mahakala* till he is totally detached from insatiable desires and lust. Salvation is the only way to come out of the cruel as well as merciless paws of *Mahakala*. It is *Mahakala* that devours up everything in the creation.

Thus, *trimurti* – Brahma, Vishnu and Mahesh are the three great powers in creation who perform duties of creating things, to sustain them and lastly to destroy those things. The process of creation, sustenance and destruction has been there from time immemorial or from the beginning of creation. In human creation it is *karma* (activity) that decides the fate of the human being. The base of creation is cosmic rules. Creation has purposes. It is not futile. The need is to understand what is creation and how does it function. Man will never be happy until he crosses the boundary of time and takes himself to the world of timelessness where God resides. *Dharma Shastra* teaches man how to get rid of the world of *Mahakala* and reach the sphere of *Akala* where there is neither death nor birth, neither the fear of disappearance nor the chance of reappearance, neither pain nor suffering, neither scarcity nor captivity.

Notes and References

1. *Bhagavad Gita*, XII/3-4.
2. *Shvetashvatara Upanishad*, 3/19.
3. Ibid, 6-11.
4. *Bhagavad Gita*, 4/11.
5. Ibid, IX/29.
6. *Katha Upanishad*, 1.2.21.
7. *Bhagavad Gita*, XI/ 53-54.
8. Ibid, 12 /2.
9. *Shvetashvatara Upanishad*, 6/11-13.
10. *Brih Upanishad*, 33.9.26.

11. *Bhagavad Gita*, XI/5-6.
12. Ibid, 4/ 7-8. Also see, *Ramcharita Manas* (*Balkanda*) 120/8.
13. *Matsya Purana*, 2-3/25-26.
14. Ibid.
15. *Shiva Purana, Rudra Samhita*. *Also see*, Chandrika Singh (2008), *Parmatma ka Sachha Swarup aur Mukti ke Marga* (Hindi), Janki Prakashan, New Delhi, pp 62-63.
16. *Bhagavad Gita*, IX/7.
17. Ibid, IX/10.
18. *Shvetashvatara Upanishad*, 6-11.
19. *Shiva Purana, Vayu Samhita*, 4/10-12.
20. *Katha Upanishad*, 1.2.16.
21. Ibid.
22. *Taittiriya Upanishad*, 1.8.
23. *Chhandogya Upanishad*, 2.23.3.
24. *Mandukya Upanishad*, 1/26-27.
25. Ibid, 1/28-29.
26. *Srimad Bhagavad Purana*, 4/7/50-54.
27. *Mandukya Upanishad*, 1/1.
28. *Matsya Purana*, 2-3/31-32.
29. Ibid, 3/8-9.
30. *Bhagavad Gita*, II/47.

7

Religion, Rites and Rituals

The concept of religion is as old as human civilization. Rather it may be said that it is religion that played vital role making man civilized. Man in the primitive age surrounded by forests, mountains, streams and rivers, knew no philosophy except being wondrous as well as astonished. The frequent cycles of seasons, happenings of storms, thunders, lightening, and of natural calamities like earthquake, flood etc, kept people under the reign of constant fear and terror. Being devoid of logical reason, they took such happenings as the causes of some unseen powers. So with a view to pleasing such power they began to make some sort of offerings to the natural powers of their imagination with the result that a tradition developed to believe in unseen power and please that power offering oblations. The fear of that mysterious power prohibited primitive people from doing wrong and harming other on the one hand, and led them towards the life of discipline and order on the other. Later on such thinking paved the way for the growth of the concept that came to be known as religion and the processes of worshipping of unseen power gradually expanded the path of religious rites and rituals. Concept of religion let people talk about mysteries, and procedures of worshipping brought them near to their imagined religious conception. The religious concepts gradually discovered the idea of the Supreme God. Religion, indeed, is basic subject related to existence, manifestation and supremacy of a power that has been named as God. Since the concept of God is completely pure, sacred, devoid of any demerits, splendid, having austerities, kindness, benevolence, love, etc, religion, too, is pious, sacrament and divine. Religion and God, in fact, are two aspects of the same coin. Religion helps one to understand God and apprehend godly qualities. Religion establishes postulates and precepts that help man to be pious and move towards the path of righteousness. It introduces man with God and provides him with ways to go near Him and avail His blessings. It also liberates man from the grip of worldly pains and troubles enabling him to obtain salvation.

Meaning of Religion

Religion is a vague concept because different philosophers and thinkers have conceptualized religion from different angles, and interpreted it in different ways. The point on which they communally agree to is its usefulness. Man, in the vast universe, has been applying his mental efforts to understand the universe, its beginning, and its purposes. His efforts have also been applied to know the advent of man in the universe and his purpose to live. In this course of human research religion came into existence. As stated above various natural phenomena like thunder, earthquake, volcanic eruption, birth, diseases, death, etc, made man wonder as well as curious on one hand, and terrified on the other. He tried to find answers to all that was happening, within his power of reasoning. In that course of research man found that there is some unseen power which causes events, and in pursuit of pleasing such power, he developed rituals which came to be known as religion in the early days of human history. Since the reasoning concept of mankind was limited, the first religion that developed came to be known as animism. As years rolled by, man's understanding developed. Various philosophical schools appeared, talking about both the transcendental world and the mundane world. The narrow concept of man about animistic gods broadened into Absolute God who governs the entire universe and creates human fate. Thus, religious philosophies, that appeared gradually, took the shape of a particular religion, inviting people to join and follow the established religious precepts and principles of a particular religion. People living on this planet migrated to different places in different groups in due course of time. Major groups of mankind carried along with them certain beliefs, customs and ways of life wherever they went and settled. Their faith and understanding related to the power of nature and sky were given high regard and honour. Each group developed the concept of God and interpreted God according to the understanding of their religious leaders. In the beginning, faith related to existence and nature of God which remained beyond any doubt and suspicion. But when the faculty of human reasoning developed, meaning of religion and concept of God began to change. Time came when religion, though unshakable so far, was questioned about the existence of ultimate supernatural power, yet various opinions appeared in the form of religions and their interpretations. In due course of time, religion was divided and lastly it fell into the grip of various religious sects that exist today. The concept of religion and God became so vague and controversial that a group of philosophers, namely, nihilists and atheists, began to discard religious as well as divine concepts, advancing the logic that there is no such power called divine, and the power that is enshrined in nature is something automatic. There is no such authority at all beyond the universe which controls and commands it and guides people. To them religion is nothing, but human weakness which forces one to live constantly under the perpetuation of an unseen and unknown power. Thus, religion and religious faith became the subject of controversy and conflicts. Even the Marxist thinkers called religion as opium, which keeps the followers of religion in perpetual slavery of selfish, wise and cunning people.

According to *Encyclopedic Dictionary of Society*, religion "is a system of belief, practice and philosophical values concerned with definition of the sacred, the comprehension of life, and salvation from the problem of human existence."[1] Religious tradition is the results of man's attempt to capture and enshrine his philosophical and spiritual insights so that they are available to individuals who face life and its stresses, confusion and complexities.[2] Again, "religion is a social phenomenon because it necessarily stresses fellowship in the development, teaching and perpetuation of religious insights and knowledge."[3] Religion deals with "the concept of the supernatural or path of salvation."[4] Hindu religion, that which is called Sanatana Dharma (having neither beginning nor end) is a "people's belief and practice towards their concepts of all that is beyond man's own power and mundane knowledge."[5] David Goodman Mandelbaum, an American anthropologist, talks of two aspects of religion – transcendental, which is ultimate, and universal gods and annual cyclical rites known by priests who are acknowledged to be the reservoirs of religious wisdom and learning.[6] In India, religion, which is also known as Dharma, is a concept developed out of the notion of *'Rita'* in the *Rigveda* which means right order and harmony in the cosmos and in the human world. In the human world it includes moral order. Dharma, which is duty, is a necessity in the life of an individual and also in the society, so that no one may deviate from the duty that has been endowed upon him according to his nature.

Religion, in general parlance, is a belief in an established system which talks about God, soul and the universe. It suggests ways and means to establish nearness to the Absolute Supreme Power. A religion is concerned with both the worlds – transcendental and mundane. According to the *Oxford English Dictionary* religion is "a particular system of faith and worship," and the "recognition on the part of man of some destiny, unseen power, as having control of his destiny."[7] It further states that religion is "a general mental and moral attitude resulting from the belief ... devotion to some principles, strict fidelity or faithfulness; conscientiousness; pious affection and attachment."[8] According to this, religion has been regarded as purely a faith in a power which is unseen, no doubt, but supreme, absolute, ultimate, omnipotent and omnipresent, which governs the destiny of any one, both animate and inanimate. Due to the possession of such eternal absolute the power of religion is entitled "to obedience, reverence and worship."[9] It deserves obedience because of its prevalent universal order and justice which it implies to uphold the creation. It commands reverence because it is loyal, benevolent and lovely to all. It is the subject of worship due to its divinity, compliances, purity and piety.

Religion is a system of expressing faith in and devotion to the power, popularly called God who has no comparison. There is no other power to counter it. Hence, faith in a religion must be unflinching and devotional. Religious faith in God generates mental and moral attitude in the individual or in a community devoted to religion. Religion affects human conducts and behaviours to make the people generous, noble, complacent, pure, kind and benevolent. The people, having complete faith in religion, follow the path of life which is linked to the goal of perfection and salvation. Religion needs a life of strict discipline, control of wild emotions and sentiments, unquenchable desires and suppression of egoist tendencies. It leads one towards the path of sacrifice, satisfaction with minimum, universal brotherhood and compassion for the poor, troubled, disabled and week creatures. Violence has no place at all in religion. It puts emphasis on self-restraint, self-sacrifice and life of simplicity. The teaching of religion is non-violence and reliance upon truthfulness. It calls upon its followers to be devoid of all sorts of deceits, violent acts and their evils. In short, religion does not permit dual personality, rather it wants to help the man to recognize his real personality which is hiding somewhere within the man of existence. Every religion of the world puts emphasis on honesty, sincerity, simplicity, kindness, non-violence, love for humanity, sympathy for poor and sufferers, and universal brotherhood. Religion, in fact, teaches man to follow the life of sanctity and sagacity. It is the subject of inner-consciousness and property of each individual.

Religion Institutionalized or Sectarian Religions

Today various sects of a religion have come into existence. There are various prophets or messengers of God who founded religions, and their disciples and followers, with a view to expanding religious scope and influencing others to join the bracketed religion providing it sectarian base, have provided various ways and means to adopt religion and personify God. As a result, religion has become sectarian in its character, and under such religious systems religion has become sectarian where creed and dogmas, whose primary aim is to dominate other religious sects, play a vital role to polarize the society. In the words of RP Sharma, a religion is "a feeling and a thought, spontaneity and a deliberation, a revelation and a strategy, a personal response to the ministries of life and a collective demand to an organization ... and a complex of rituals ... and inspired perception of ultimate truth and a system of thought."[10] Today, with the growth of sectarian concept of religion, such religious meaning is losing its ground and strength.

Sharma's view on religion is concerned with both the spiritual and the empirical aspects of a religion. So long as religion is a personal faith in Supreme Power, in established vision of the seers and revelation of mysteries, it is a spiritual force which is personal in character. But once a religion is given a sectarian form and institutionalized dogmatic character, it becomes the property of the institution which wants to establish religious hold and bring the entire world under its control and influence. Such a religion becomes rigid and its followers become fundamentalists which have no scope at all for religious tolerance as a result of which that religion becomes a subject of conflict, clash and tension. Sarath Jhingru has rightly observed that, "The religion institutionalized becomes interested in maintaining its hold on the populous and social institutions, and develops a rigid creed, set of rituals and laws which are declared as binding upon all its followers."[11] Here, religious postulates are given the character of infallibility and no scope is left for rational reconsideration and modification in its existing notion. Moreover, interpretation of religious principles is left in the hands of the fundamentalist priests whose words are treated as final judgment in this regard. The common people who know little about religious truth are bound to follow blindly the judgments of the fundamentalists that are launched from time to time.

A sectarian religion possesses all the good postulates and senses of a true religion, no doubt, but its preceptors, protectors and interpreters, whose intention is to dominate other religious groups, leave no stone unturned to provide a sectarian colour to the religion. Conversion as well as propagation either through force or temptation becomes the chief objective of the sectarian religion. Such activities ultimately results in religious confusion, feeling of religious intolerance and hatred towards its opponents on one hand, and intensifies communal riots on the other. If one goes a little back to the pages of religious history, there are numerous examples where religious faith of a powerful community was imposed upon the weaker sections of people either using force or giving temptation.

Universality of Religion

Religion in the spiritual sense is an intuitional or philosophical vision which stands above the personified religion. If a religion is a faith in God, it is only one, but its essence and rebuts reflect through various religious sects carrying the same message of love and benevolence. A religion does not recognize a community or a group. It is universal, uniformed, comprehensive and applicable to all in the similar degree of goodness. A religion, in the real sense, is the highest spiritual knowledge which "cannot be bought nor can it be acquired from books."[12] A religion is a way to God as well as man's relationship with his fellow beings. In the opinion of Swami Vivekananda,

> "religion cannot be found anywhere except in the core of the human heart. It is not a monopolistic dominance of a particular religious community or a group. Rather it is a system of belief, practice and philosophical values concerned with definition of the sacred, the comprehension of the life and salvation from the problems of human existence.... Religious traditions are the results of man's attempt to capture and enshrine his philosophical and spiritual insights so that they are available to the individual as he faces life and its stresses, confusion and complexities."[13]

No doubt, religion is a "social phenomenon because it necessarily traces fellowship in the development, teaching and participation of religious insight and knowledge."[14] However, it cannot be monopolized by a group. A religion is a science of vision related to the ultimate truth, its essence and values. Hence, its essence and values cannot differ in time and space. It must be the same among all religious groups. A true religion cannot invite religious conflicts and controversies. A religion which claims its superiority over other religions is, in fact, not a true religion but a sectarian creed under the guise of religious characters. It is the sectarian sartorial character of religion that has invited religious conflicts and the society resulting in communal riots where massacres committed keeping aside all religious morals and principles. Sectarian religion makes man a blind follower. The basic purpose of a sectarian religion is to bring the entire world under its powerful massive toes. It leaves no scope at all for free deliberation and tolerance.

Some Characteristics of Hindu Religion

Hindu religion is a "people's belief and practice towards their concepts of all that is beyond man's own power and mundane knowledge."[15] Mandelbaum formulated two complementary complexes. He calls the first one 'Transcendental' which is ultimate supreme derived from the Sanskrit texts and elates to system maintenance, long term welfare and ultimate goals; universal gods and annual cyclical rites; and is derived from the knowledge of higher priests who are acknowledged to be the reservoirs of religious wisdom and learning.[16] Another aspect of religion, according to Mandelbaum, is 'pragmatic' complex, compassed of lesser, regional or local deities of various types, including the spirits of the dead, the regulators of diseases, epidemic, natural disasters and community guardians.[17] In contrast to the transcendental, the latter includes personal and proximate gods of individual's welfare, the rites related to local deities and spirits and the ritual performances which are not necessarily equipped with the knowledge of Sanskrit Hinduism.[18]

Hinduism is generally believed to be an amorphous body of beliefs, philosophies, worship practices and codes of conducts. It is all because Hinduism has not been studied thoroughly and carefully. The depth of Hindu religion and religious philosophy is the deepest, which needs both patience and wisdom to grasp the actual meaning. Those who have fully investigated the Hindu doctrines of religion know better that Hinduism is not only a religion but it is also the most civilized way of life all over the world. The root of Hindu Dharma is not in speculation and imagination, but it is rooted in both manifested and non-manifested concept of *Brahman*, the Ultimate Goal, and the Primal Cause of creation, sustainer and destroyer. The scope of Hinduism is broader; the concept is larger; and the benevolence towards others is greater. Giriraj Gupta rightly remarks that the very nature of Hinduism leads to a greater tolerance of other religious thoughts among its adherents as they tend to believe that the highest divine power complement each other for the well-being of mankind.[19] He further says, "The quality of reliance, absorption and respect for other alternative ways of reaching the same goals, perhaps, are the characteristics which have general vitality in Hinduism from Millennium."[20]

Analysing and highlighting Hindu religion, Pandit Jawaharlal Nehru writes in his *Discovery of India* that Hinduism as a faith is vague, amorphous, many sided, and all things to all men. It is hardly possible to define it or to say precisely whether it is a religion or not, in the usual sense of the word. In its present forms, as well as in the past, it embraces many beliefs and practices, from the highest to the lowest, often opposed to and contradicting each other. Its essential spirit seems to live and let live. Talking about Hindu Dharma and

Indian spirituality, Swami Vivekananda once said, "India's strength is in her spirituality. India is the mother of seat of all true philosophy and metaphysics ... India must make religion the backbone of her national life if she is to live."[21] He believed that if there is any land on this earth that can lay claim to the blessed *Punya Bhumi* (land of divine goodness), to be the land ... where humanity has attained its highest towards gentleness, towards generosity, towards purity, towards calmness, above all, the land of introspection of spirituality" it is India.[22] He further said, "Spirituality has been always in India.... The eyes of the whole world are now turned towards the land of India for spiritual food.... We may be degraded and degenerated now; but however ... we can become great if only we begin to work in the right earnest on belief of our religion."[23] Hindu religion has penetrated deep into the mind and heart of every Hindu, either in India or abroad. It is all because of its greatness and benevolence. In other countries religion may the subject of religious preachers, but in India religion resides in every heart. Observing the spirit of Indian religion, Swami Vivekananda rightly says that, "We have yet something to teach the world.... This is the very reason, the *raison d'être*, that this nation has lived on, in spite of hundreds of years of persecution, in spite of nearly a thousand years of foreign rule and foreign oppression. This nation still lives.... It still holds to God, to the treasure house of religion and spirituality."[24]

However, Swami Vivekananda discards and condemns the practice of blind rituals in the name of religion. To him, religion means religious spirit related to wisdom and humanity. He disliked superstitions and blind customs in the name of religion or religious performances. To him, religion does not mean to follow customary rituals, but to live with religious spirituality where there is right understanding about right order of humanity. In the opinion of Vivekananda, true religion teaches one to look into his inner soul where there is no discrimination in the name of birth, caste and creed, etc. Speaking about the essence of Vedic religion he said:

> There are two sorts of truth we find in our *shastras*; one that is based upon the external nature of man ... the other with local circumstances, environments of the time, social institutions of the period, and so forth. The first class of truth is chiefly embodied in our Vedas; our scriptures; the second in the Smritis, the Puranas, etc. We must remember that for all period the Vedas are final goal and authority, and if the Puranas differ in any respect from the Vedas, that part of Puranas is to be rejected without mercy. The Vedas being external will be one and the same throughout all ages.[25]

Religion as Performance of Right Duty

Explaining the meaning of religion, the *Mahabharata* says that in this infinite universe and great world, the universal element which integrates different elements of the world is nothing, but religion. It is religion which combines both the external and internal worlds (physical and spiritual). Religion, in fact, is a quality which is inherent in every animate and inanimate. The explanation and meaning of religion are available in the Indian Vedas and other religious scriptures. Religion is a duty that has been prescribed in the Vedas and other *Dharma Shastras* like the Srutis, Smritis, Puranas, Upanishads, etc. Religion means to accept the commands prescribed in Vedic literature. The synonym of religion is pious duty and justice, and pious duty and justice have been mentioned in the Vedas and other Indian religious scriptures.

Religion (duty) is entrusted upon each and every component of the universe, living or non-living, visible or invisible. Everyone is bound to perform duty because duty is the base of the universe. To act against the prescribed duties in religious scriptures is irreligion. The sun, the moon, the earth, water, air, fire, and all gods/goddesses as well as semi-gods, etc, are bound to perform duty because duty upholds the universe. The duties prescribed in the *Dharma Shastras* are pious and meaningful. To go against such duties means to commit sin and follow those means to earn *punya*. Sin takes one to hell while *punya* preserves place for one in heaven.

Religion in Hindu philosophy is known as *'Rita'* which means duty. According to the *Rigveda*, *Rita* means a right order and harmony in the cosmos and in the human world. The *Mahabharata* presents a detailed and convincing elaboration of religion, which states that in this infinite universe and great world the universal element that integrates different elements of the world is nothing, but religion, the *Rita*, the Dharma or the right duty. The whole universe is fabricated in bounded duty of every object either animate or inanimate. Everyone assumes certain type of duty to perform actions according to its nature (*samskara*) which itself is the product of duty or dharma-karma. Dharma is, thus, the universal order which, if moving in the right direction, yields good fruit, and if in the wrong direction, produces bad fruit. According to the *Bhagavad Gita*, action is the base of creation, and everyone is forced to act accordingly, whether one likes it or dislikes. It is said, "None, verily, even for an instant, ever remains doing no action; for everyone is driven helpless to action by the energies born of Nature."[26] It is the fate of every creature to act and enjoy its fruits, either sweet or bitter, until one is liberated from the circle of birth and death. Even the sun, fire, moon, sky, wind, planets, earth, water, etc, are bound to uphold their duties with a view to keeping creation intact and propelling it upwards. To go against assignments or duties means to create disorder in the universe or to destroy creation. According to *Manu Smriti*, the base of Dharma is the conduct and behaviours prescribed in the *Dharma Shastras*.[27] In the Buddhist scriptures there is mention of Dhamma Chakra, the evolving wheel of Dhamma (duty). Action in the universe is universal and constant. It never ceases. The Dhamma Chakra moves both the ways – right and wrong. If it is propelled towards the right direction, it yields goodness, but once it turns towards the wrong direction, it brings damages even complete annihilation. So, the Dhamma Chakra, according to the Buddha, must be handled very carefully and consciously.

Religion gives wisdom to distinguish between good and bad actions and provides courage to perform Dharma (duties). According to Hindu philosophy, the term duty is related to religion which is an inherent quality of man. That is why the Vedas explain religion in the term of duty or Dharma and to act against one's duty is *adharma* or irreligion. Dharma is that which leads one towards glory, celebrity, progress and salvation if one follows it truly. Dharma is the root of pleasure and prosperity. It is the path shown by religious scriptures which takes one to the goal of perfection. Those who relinquish the path shown by scriptures, follow their own indecently, never attain perfection, pleasure and salvation.[28] Though the Religion of Works – as a means of attaining prosperity, is enjoined on the several castes and religious orders – leads the devotee to the region of the *devas* and the alike, still, when practised in a spirit, complete with devotion to the Lord and without regard to the results, it conduces to the purity of the mind. The man whose mind is pure is competed to tread the path of knowledge, and to him comes knowledge; and thus the Religion of Works also is a means to Supreme Bliss.[29]

In Hindu Dharma, religion is related to religious performances where various rites and rituals have been prescribed. The Sanskrit word for religious performance or sacrifice is called '*yajna*' which means Vishnu, the creator and sustainer of the universe. He must be worshipped. The *Bhagavad Gita* prescribes, "Having first created, together with sacrifices, the Prajapati (Creator) said, "By this (*yajna*) shall ye propagate, let this be to you the cow of plenty. With this do ye nourish the gods and the gods shall nourish you; thus, nourishing one another, ye shall attain the Supreme God."[30] God while creating the universe provided actions which bring about fruits. There is no fruit without action. All living-beings are constantly active in the universe with the hope to achieve the desired goal. Thus, the engagement in actions is called *dharma-karma*.

Hindu's Sanatana Dharma

The word '*Sanatana*', which means eternity, is very much meaningful. Sanatana Dharma is one which has neither beginning nor end. It prevails forever, even after dissolution of complete creation. In the real sense, Sanatana Dharma is a reflection of God. It is as pure and pious as God himself. The Sanatana Dharma is eternal, assuming the whole universe. It feeds and protects everything in the universe. Rather it upholds creation as a whole. It is enshrined in each atom of the universe. Without eternal Dharma nothing is possible. If Dharma means duty, the base of creation is duty because the net of creation is enshrined in duties. To remove duties from nature or universe means to disintegrate the universe. So, disappearance of religion means destruction of creation. And to protect established Dharma, the Lord incarnates. That is why *Bhagavad Gita* declares:

> Whenever there is decay of religion, O Partha, and an ascendency of irreligion, then I manifest Myself. For the protection of the good, for the destruction of evil-doers, for the firm establishment of religion, I am born in every age. (*Bhagavad Gita*, IV, 7/8)

Thus, it is very much obvious that it is only in the Hindu Sanatana Dharma where God incarnates Himself to protect religion whenever it is harmed by evil-doers. Entire creation is of God, who had created orders and systems to run the universe. These orders or systems are nothing but right path of duties. Falling in the grip of greed, lust and temptation the egoists and atheists, who deny the existence of God, deviate fearlessly from the established right path of duties with the result that it becomes very difficult and inconvenient for the persons whose faith in God is instant and who are the followers of prescribed as well as bounded duties. In other words, the people of irreligion establishing their dominance and influence over the established order of the world create the circumstances where people of religion find themselves unable to remain religious and worship God. At this juncture, God, the *Ishvara*, the mightiest, seated above all, appears in different forms to kill the people or rulers of demonic nature and re-establish religion (right order) in creation. The basic purpose of incarnation of God is to protect creation by protecting religion. This happens not once, but again and again in every age. In other religions, God hardly incarnates Himself. Rather He sends *Paigambars* (Messengers) and Divine Agents to protect religion by teaching people the path of righteousness.

In the universe, every object has its own Dharma. For instance, the Dharma of the Sun is to illuminate and give light and heat to creatures without any interval; the Dharma of the Moon is to be cool and pour down nectar for survival and evolution of creatures; Fire is bounded to burn and grasp oblations given for various gods; and the air is to flow constantly, and so on. The Sanatana Dharma leads a man towards performance of his duties and avail opportunities to obtain salvation in the end. Spirituality is India's distinguished feature. India's music, arts and crafts literature, in fact, the whole of

Indian culture is saturated with spirituality, and spirituality is itself related to religion. For this reason, Indian culture cannot be understood apart from her religion that is Sanatana Dharma. It is the seat or mother of all the philosophies and metaphysics of the world. To be religious means to be fearless and to be irreligious means to invite fear and troubles.

Morality and Religion

The origin of morality may be traced out in the Hindu religious concepts of Dharma, the duty or right conduct towards rational and divine order. If religion means to have absolute faith in absolute goodness and perform the duty assigned by one's own nature, it is the moral philosophy or moral theology. The basic objective of a religion is to obtain perfection (salvation) by following the divine path which is nothing, but right order and good conduct. On the other hand, ethics enables one to distinguish between right and wrong and virtues and vices, and prepares man to follow the life of virtues. Thus, both religion and morality emanates from the belief that there exists absolute goodness and moral order devoid of all sorts of evils. Both teach the people to achieve high moral standard of life by controlling irrational or animalistic conduct or behaviour. The religious sermons or precepts mentioned in the religious scriptures like the *Mahabharata, Bhagavad Gita, Quran Sharif, Bible*, etc, are the prescribed conducts of good behaviour of man which mould him towards perfection. Both religion and morality are not alien to each other. These are internal qualities of the human heart related to the voice of the inner-conscience. Both are products of the soul. That is why religion and morality are immortal, bright and pure. Theologians, philosophers of religions and men of faith regard religion as the determining factor in a culture. According to Errol E Fay, "Religion is the main instrument for expression of values; it is the carrier of ethics, the moulder of personal and social behaviours. It supplies the ethos, the prevalent tone or sentiment of a given culture."[31]

Religion and morality are not something which can be learnt from books or be bought from markets. These reflect in pure hearts. The purity of heart depends upon good moral or religious conduct. Religion is the subject of faith where doubt or suspicion has no room at all. In the words of Swami Vivekananda, "Those who come to seek truth in such a spirit of love and veneration, to them the Lord of Truth, goodness and beauty come."[32] Swami Vivekananda recognized that reason has its limits and that religion commences precisely where reason stops. He also holds that super-conscious experiences can never contradict in the working of the intellect. He maintains that, "Real inspiration never contradicts reason, but fulfils it.... We must take up the study of the super-conscious step just as any other science.... We must follow reason, so far as it leads our foundation, and when reason fails, religion itself will show us the way to the highest plan."[33]

According to Aurobindo Ghosh, men fall largely into one of the four types of *varnas* (Brahmin, Kshatriya, Vaishya and Shudra). The *varnas* are the stages in the self-development of the individual. He begins with a load of ignorance and inertia and, despite his animal indolence; he is impelled by his needs to perform forms of mundane labour. Such men are of Shudra type, who have little knowledge about God and purity. They are generally guided by lust and satisfaction, not by reason and knowledge. They are either ignorant of divinity or they hardly care for divinity. They are dominated by *Tamas guna* of Nature, which is dark and has little reason. The second category of *varna* is of Vaishyas whose interest is in production, fulfilment of needs, accumulation of wealth, etc. They are dominated by *Rajas guna* which is the sovereign of activities and ambition.

The ambition of the Vaishyas is at a lower level, related to wealth and money, not to power and immortality. Kshatriyas belong to the third category of *varnas*. They are more ambitious, courageous and bold. They are under the influence of Rajasic Nature which produces a man "with a more dominant will, with bolder ambitions, with the instant to act in battle and enforce his will, at the strongest to lead, command, rule and carry masses of men in his orbit, the fighter, leader, ruler, prince, king, Kshatriya."[34]

Next in the development of the Individual's quality is the role of *Sattva guna* that predominates and behaves like the *Brahman* type. Here man, with a turn for knowledge, who brings through, reflection, the seeding for truth and an intelligence or the highest spiritual rule into life, and illumines by it his conception and mode of existence."[35] Talking about the three *gunas* of nature, Lord Krishna says to Arjuna, "*Sattva, Rajas, Tamas* – these *gunas*, O mighty-armed, born of *Prakriti*, bind fast in the body the embodied, the indestructible."[36] Describing the qualities of three *gunas*, the Lord further says:

> "Of these, *Sattva*, which, from its stainlessness, is lucid and healthy, binds by attachment to knowledge, O sinless one. Known thou *Rajas* of the nature of passion, the source of thirst and attachment; it binds fast, O son of Kunti, the embodied one by attachment to action. But know the *Tamas*, to be born of unwisdom deluding all embodied beings, it binds fast, O Bharata."[37]

He further says:

> "*Sattva* attaches to happiness, *Rajas* to action, O Bharata, while *Tamas*, enshrouding wisdom, attaches, on the contrary, to heedlessness."[38]

The person who follows *Sattva guna* goes towards God and remains happy forever. But those who follow *Rajas guna* remain in the middle. The worst position in life is of one who is *Tamasic* by nature. Due to absence of wisdom, he is indulged in impious as well as forbidden *karmas* with the result that he has to harvest the worst and stays the perpetual circle of birth and death.

Aurobindo here, as elsewhere, mentions this in his voluminous writings, and accepts *karma* and rebirth. He calls *karma* the ignorance, ignorance of the true nature of man's spirit. Through experience in the world are successive rebirths. One rises from the Shudra type of existence to the *Brahman* type by performing good duties. Religion plays a vital role in transforming the *samskara* of mankind and leads him from the lower life to the higher. It is religion in the true sense that brings for man salvation or *moksha*. The way to *moksha*, as advocated by Aurobindo, is in the integral or *'purna yoga'*. The integral yoga integrates the three main paths to *moksha* – the *Karma Yoga*, the *Bhakti Yoga* and the *Jnana Yoga*, or the paths of work, love and knowledge, respectively. The spirit, in its ascent to the supernatural level, must work in the world to help liberate others. Man must love others in the world, knowing them as divine beings. A man must have knowledge of the ultimate reality and its relation to man and the world. A perfect religion helps man to realize the truth and gives him wisdom to climb up the aluminous path of the transcendental world where one reaching never falls. The movement towards the Supernatural World is a journey which requires light, purity, courage and wisdom. Religion provides all these, provided it is followed and performed righteously. The journey begins with realization of the three essential truths of existence – God, Freedom and Unity. Realization of God must come first because real freedom can only be founded upon freedom of egoism possessing God as one with the Self and the Self of all.

Vaishnava Religion

Vaishnava sect of religion is also a part of Sanatana Dharma which follows the Bhakti Marga as a way to salvation. It deals with *Saguna Brahman* (Ultimate Reality as a personal God). This sect was founded by Ramanuja. His system of religious philosophy is known as Vishishtadvaita Vedanta (qualified non-dualism). *Brahman*, according to this doctrine, is one and personal and the only independent reality. The other two realities are souls and matter, but these are dependent upon God and are organic parts of His being. God is the soul of souls and the soul of nature (matter) and also transcendent and infinite. He is called Vishnu Narayana, and is the *Brahman* of the Upanishads with the qualities of truth, goodness and bliss. Vishnu is the supporter, controller and goal of all beings. There are three classes of souls – (1) eternal *jivas* who were never in bondage; (2) the freed souls who have attained release (*moksha*); and (3) the bounded souls caught in the wheel of *Samsara* till they attain *moksha*. The way to *moksha* has three steps – (1) *Karma Marga*, the performance of rituals and services to others as an offering to gods without selfish motivation; (2) *Jnana Marga* – meditation of the *jiva* until the knowledge of relationship between *jiva* and God as one of dependence is required. This leads to love and devotion for God; (3) In the Bhakti Marga meditation is also essential, but with involvement of feeling of love for God and yearning for eternal closeness to Him until the soul has a vision of God. There is no *Jiva Mukta* in this philosophy because *moksha* is defined as complete release from the sense organs and body generated by *karma*. Here, *jiva* still exists as a true devotee of God. At the death of the final body the soul goes to Vaikuntha, where Lord Vishnu resides with goddess Lakshmi. Here, the liberated soul lives with Lord Vishnu and enjoys divinity.

In general, Vaishnavas do not observe the traditional caste-rules strictly and have taught the way to *moksha* even to outcasts. Ramanuja himself is said to have greatly revered a Shudra saint. There are many Vaishnava sects. *Bhakti* in general is the path to *moksha*.

Chaitanyas

It is another sect of Hindu religion. The founder of this sect was the leader of Vaishnavism in Bengal, who is popularly known as Chaitanya Mahaprabhu. This sect has a large number of followers in Assam and in Odisha as well. In these areas and now around the world, wherever International Society for Krishna Consciousness flourishes, Chaitanya is treated as an incarnation of Krishna. He was born in 1485, and began his mission in life when he was about 23 years old. He denounced the ritualistic system of Hindu Dharma. He propagated that faith in Krishna, love for Him and the singing of His name are the things that leads one to the path of *moksha*. In 1510 Chaitanya became a *sanyasi*. After his initiation under his guru Keshav Bharti, he wandered about the country for six years proclaiming the way of salvation. At the last phase of his life he returned to Jagannath Puri where he lived for the last eighteen years. He gave up his body in 1533.

Philosophical doctrine of Chaitanya is known as *Achintya Bhedavada* (incomprehensive difference and non-difference). In this sect of religion the ultimate reality is called Radha-Krishna. It is the *sat-chit-ananda Brahman* of the Upanishads, but not a *Nirguna* reality. The God-head has an infinite number of powers (*Shakti*). These three main *Shaktis* are *Swarupa Shakti, Maya Shakti* and *Jiva Shakti*. *Swarupa Shakti* is God's eternal power. It is described as the three aspects of God's powers, by which He supports, knows and enjoys His own, and all the souls' existence, consciousness and bliss. It corresponds to the three elements in His own nature – *Sat* (being), *Chit* (consciousness) and *Ananda* (bliss). God is also *antaryamin* (having the strength to know the inner-self), and is also pervasive. *Maya Shakti* of God is inconscient of power of God that gives rise to the material universe. It has two aspects – *Guna Maya* and *Jiva Maya*. Through the former the universe is created out of the *Gunas* – *Sattva*, *Rajas* and *Tamas* – that constitute the material world and involves creatures to act. *Jiva Maya* conceals from the soul its true nature so that its desires cause *jiva* to revolve on the wheel of birth and death until *moksha* is attained. *Jiva Shakti* is the essence of all finite souls.

In this sect of religion, God is significantly characterized as *rasa* (sentiment) and *rasika* (enjoyer of sentiment). Krishna is *rasika* and Radha symbolizes *rasa*. Both are one, but for the sake of creation they are divided. Here, the erotic (*sringara*) is of outmost importance because a *rasika* is found indulged in *rasa* that erotizes or emotionalize *bhavanas* (emotions). Krishna's *shakti* is Radha with whom He is always united in love. Radha represents the sum total of God's *shakti* described above which are the universe, but He is not exhausted by this manifestation. He is also transcendent and infinite. Chaitanya sect condemned Varnashrama Dharma and caste distinctions. It stands against ritualistic approach to religion. It pleads equality and treats everyone as equal for attainment of *moksha* through *Bhakti*.

Thus, it is quite obvious that in the Hindu Dharma, path of devotion (*Bhakti*) to God has been given too much priority by various Hindu saints during the post-Vedic as well as post-Upanishadic period. Though the *Bhagavad Gita* talks much about the path of *Bhakti Yoga*, the saints and poets like Ramanuja, Chaitanya, Kabira, Tulasi, Surdas, Muhammad Jayasi, etc, enlarged the *Bhakti* cult of religion, inviting the common people to join the stream discarding caste-divisions and feeling of superior and inferior birth. They taught people that what God needs is devotion and surrender, not rituals and sacrifices. *Moksha* is not restricted; rather it is open to all. God recognizes devotion and love, not rites and rituals.

Religion and Science

There is no fundamental relationship between science and religion. The former tries to discover outward physical truth of the world while the latter penetrating into the internal aspect of the world, tries to realize ultimate truth. Those atheists who know neither completely science nor religion have created illusion that science and religion are opposite to each other. The greatest scientist, Albert Einstein, who had faith in religion was of the view that science and religion are complementary to each other. He said that science without religion is lame and religion without science is blind. Ultimate goal of both is to search the ultimate reality, but they apply different methods. In fact, science is the greatest testimony of the existence of God because it is science which rationally reveals existence of godly externa! order in matter. It was the ancient Indian rishis who had declared that there are various planets in the universe and the universe is elliptical. Today science has proved the hypothesis. Similarly, science, applying rational method, is revealing various such statements of the Vedas and Upanishads through its discoveries and inventions. It is a fact that reason deals with metaphysical world while science is still busy with the physical world. Its scope has not yet crossed the natural boundaries of the world. Science moves with reason and confirms no truth until it is scientifically verified, analysed, observed and tested. On the other hand, religion uses intuition and establishes relations with unseen and unverified worlds. The energies and powers of nature, that have been recognized and are being used by science today, were discovered by the Indian rishis and saints thousands of years back.

The progress of science is based on research which is further based on causal-effect relations. Science moves a step ahead by establishing scientific truth, but religion goes straight on the basis of intuition and jumps into limitless region. What religion establishes by faith and intuition, science confirms them. It appears that science, at its highly developed status, will merge with religion. The discoveries and inventions of science about universe and its objects had been forecast long ago by ancient Indian seers. Science, in the process of knowing physical construction and discovering energy in the atoms, have succeeded in breaking up atoms, and the results found out through this process confirms that there is God's particles in the entire universe that are the base of creation and source of energy. Thus, it is evident that science and religion differ in methods and approaches, but their aims and objectives are the same.

Both science and religion want to find out the ultimate cause of the universe. However, religion believes in a world of metaphysics while science is silent in this regard because it speaks nothing about the subject unless its existence is scientifically tested and proved. The scope of science is limited and finite while the scope of religion is unlimited and infinite. Science has no faith in any ultimate supreme power because it has not yet been confirmed. However, it does not deny the existence of such power. To the scientist, energy is the source of creation and all activities. Religions believe that the energy which is established by science is a reflection of the supreme power who is the primal cause of all causes. Science, in fact, wants to know what the universe is and what the root cause of creation is. Through scientific methods, scientists have been trying to discover the hidden physical order and analysing their effects which have already been discovered and established by religious philosophers. It seems that science will eliminate the root of agnosticism and nihilism.

True Religion in the Grip of Misconception

To be religious means not only to perform rituals and talk about religion or God, but to follow the ethical conducts and perform the right duties. In the words of Aurobindo, "The Gita's injunction is to worship the divine by our own work; our offering must be the works determined by pure law of being and nature.... Our works should be according to the truth within us; it should be an accommodation with outward and artificial standards; it should must be a living and sincere expression of the soul and its inborn powers."[39] Today, true meaning of religion is disappearing, paving the way for growth of religious fundamentalism and religious misconceptions. A lot of misconceptions about religion have been spread by so-called religious preachers, fundamentalist religious leaders and those who have established undue hold over religious groups. Religion, in the classical sense, stands for good qualities and goodness where reason along with devotion prevailed. In ancient period religious people were those who knew the true meaning of religion and followed the life of sanctity and sagacity. To them, religion was the way to attain salvation, following the right conducts established by religious scriptures. They knew well what God and religion was. Such understanding about religion and God began to decline with the growth of various religious sects. Their preceptors borrowing religious philosophies and precepts from the original religious texts established the way which suited to them. The interpretations what they presented to classical religion or religious scriptures are dissimilar to the original one because their primary goals have been to organize followers to serve the vested purpose or interests.

Such growth in the field of religion has not only created confusion among various communities but also intensified communal riots in the name of religion. There are many who think that to be more religious means to convert more people in their particular sect of religion by hook and crook. This is all because they do not know the real meaning of religion and they are victims of religious misconceptions. Hence, there is immediate need to understand religion in the right perspective and apply effective control over the growth and practice of religious misconceptions. Religion has universal implications. It cannot be confined to a particular class, community or sect. It is unfortunate for people and country both that religion has been divided into several sects and each sect, claiming supremacy, tries to impose its supremacy over others. This is a dangerous trend. It has rightly been said that a true religion never teach division, hatred and ill-will against others. Rather it teaches universal brotherhood, love, affection, morality, kindness, compassion and non-violence. But the religious fundamentalists, putting aside all these good qualities of religion, and establishing their monopoly over their respective religious sects, have captured true religion.

Root of Hindu Religious Rites and Rituals

The religious rites and rituals of the Hindus are rooted in the Sutra period that began at the end of the Vedic period when Hindu civilization had taken deep roots based on Vedic wisdom and belief. By that time, the *varna* and caste system had come into being where the class of Brahmins, having the knowledge of Vedas had developed religious procedures to perform *yajna*. The class of Brahmins who came to be known as *purohit* (priest) assumed the responsibility to interpret Vedic Mantras and perform religious programmes. The priesthood comprising of Brahmins had entered into social as well religious aspects of the people belonging to all *varnas* except the Shudras. The secular views and divine concept of the Vedas had been overwhelmed by religious faith and performances, paving the way for the growth of Brahminism, ritualism and *karmakandas*. Sanskrit literature that developed after the Vedic period summarized the Vedas, providing new interpretations and explanations. Among such post-Vedic literature, the Sutras, which claimed to be Vedic in their nature and significance, prepared rites and rituals that influenced Hindu society in such a manner that ritualism prevailed in all aspects of human life. In the beginning, the rites and rituals remained related to reason, but as the years rolled by, the scope of ritual practices not only expanded its scope but also adopted a number of superstitions and blind faith which kept people away from the light of reason.

Since the root of religious rites and rituals is found in the Sutras, it would be convenient to have a glance over the Sutras. It appears that the Sutra period existed during the 6th century BC. Due to lack of printing facilities, all the Vedas were summarized in a very convincing form, giving a sort description. The Sutras are the technical name given to aphoristic rules that sliding down from the Vedic version came to the common people. The Sutras are also known as Vedangas. The Sutras, on the whole, in the words of Ramachandra, "rest, though not entirely, upon the Brahmanas. The importance of the fact may be conceived from the fact, that the groundwork of the whole ritual, grammatical, metrical and philosophical literature of India is indicted in the aphoristic style."[40] What does he mean by aphoristic style in the wise statements? The Sutras developed, perhaps, to facilitate the pupils in ancient India to grasp the Vedic meanings in the forms of wise statements or maxims. The Vedic materials for the purpose of schooling, perhaps, needed abridgement of vast Vedic literature. So, the Sutras were developed in an abridged form, to enable students to learn the gist of the Vedas and their appendages easily. These came to be known as Sutras (threads) that provided a proper link among various Vedas and their Appendages. There are a number of Sutras, but the most important of them are – *Sankhya* of Kapila, *Yoga* of Patanjali, *Nyaya* of Gotma, *Vaisheshika* of Kanada, *Mimamsa* of Jaimini, Vedants or *Brahmanas* of Badarayana. To explain and elucidate these Sutras, Bhashyas or commentaries were written, and again to explain and elucidate the Bhashyas sub-commentaries were written.

What we mean by Vedic period is a period where the Vedas, Brahmanas, Aranyakas, Upanishads, Puranas, *Dharma Shastras* or Smritis, various Sutras, Bhashyas, etc were produced in Sanskrit language which contain the highest degree of philosophical wisdom and prescribe the religious rites and social norms. During the Vedic period society was propounded abounding in the knowledge of pedantry, metaphysics, Sanskrit as a language, grammar, etc. The rites and traditions established in India during the Vedic period served as a strong base of Hindu society. During the period of the Vedas, where no literature existed except them, the Vedas were treated as the final authority. There was no school to oppose the Vedic statements. The Vedas stood at the apex of wisdom. There did not exist any other doctrines to oppose Vedas or counter them. The teachings of the Vedas were uncontroversial. At the time to speak against the Vedas meant to deny existence of God and be an atheist. Time came when the study of the Vedas became extinct because to understand the Vedas in the right perspective and explain the Vedic hymns correctly became a hard task. It has rightly been said that "the aims and objectives of the *yajnas*, enjoined in them, were lost; and all religious works came to be encrusted with external ceremonies."

The Sutra works are all brief, systematic and enigmatical. Every doctrine, thus, propounded in them is so strained and twisted in every possible manner that it is almost reduced to mere algebraic symbols. They became too vast to understand without consulting keys. Ramachandra has rightly remarked that, "They (Sutras) are certainly one of the most curious sorts of literary compositions that the human mind has ever produced; and if altogether worthless in an artistic point of view, it is remarkable that the Indo-Aryans should have fabricated this most difficult form, and adopted it as the most convenient vehicle of expression of every branch of learning."[41] The Sutras work contains the quintessence of all the knowledge which was then floating in the Parishads, and which the Brahmanas themselves had accumulated during many centuries of study and reflection. The Sutras or the Vedangas are not the part of Vedas, but supplementary to them. The Sutras, what are preserved today, are not treated wholly genuine. They are auxiliary books for understanding the Vedas. Their authors were not inspired, but they produced them for practical purposes. A clear statement as to the rational character of the Vedangas is given in the *Brihadaranyaka* and in its commentary.

Vedanga Shiksha

The first Vedanga is called *Shiksha* which comprises the rules regarding letters, accents, quantity, organs, enumerations, delivery and euphonic combinations. It was prepared by Panini, the great Sanskrit scholar of ancient India. It professes to give only the rules for the correct pronunciation and proper recitation of the Vedic texts. It is said that the *Shiksha* does not belong to the original Vedanga work. There is another tract of *Shiksha* known as *Manduki Shiksha*, which is probably a later production of the Sutra period. The rules of the *Shiksha* had formerly a place in the seventh book of the *Taittiriya Aranyaka*.

Dr Burnell holds the view that the *Shiksha* or at any rate their teachings, to a school of grammarians which is believed to have preceded that of Panini.[42] Kielhorn says that the *Shikshas* are the compilation of modern period.[43] Despite all these controversies, it is a fact that the *Shikshas* were in existence when Patanjali composed his great commentary on Katyayana's *Varttikas*.

Chhanda Sutra

The second is called *Chhandas* which treat metre. Knowledge of *Chhandas* was considered most essential to the right application and correct recitation of the Vedic Mantras. It is believed that Pingala was the author of this Vedanga. But some are of the view that Pingala and Patanjali were the same. The view also prevail that Pingala was the younger brother of Patanjali or he at least belonged to the Patanjali dynasty. The *Chhandas* take their origin from the *Sakala Pratisakhya* which is more valuable. There were also *Nidana Sutra* and *Srutabodha* that contributed to *Chhandas* prior to the *Chhanda Sutra*. Some suppose Pingala was the same as Patanjali, the author of the *Mahabhashya*. However, the identity of Pingala and Patanjali is far from being probable. It is interesting to note that Pingala did not confine himself exclusively to the meters of Sanskrit. He also gave rules bearing on the meters of *Prakrita*; and even *Katyayana-varuchi*, the author of the *Varttikas* on Panini, the great father of Sanskrit Grammar. It is admitted that the treatises of Pingala on *Chhandas* was one of the last books that were included in the Sutra period.

Vedanga/Sutra Vyakarana

The third Vedanga is called *Vyakarana*. The Indo-Aryans cultivated the science of grammar from the earliest times. Eight different schools of grammar prevailed in ancient India. Panini's grammar is very much famous. It is called *Ashtad* and sometimes

Ashtakam Paniniyam. Panini is the only representative of this *Vedanga*. His grammar may be called natural history of the Sanskrit language. The fourth Vedanga is the *Nirukta* of *Yaska*, the oldest glossator of the Vedas. The *Nirukta* is older than Panini. The *Nirukta* is sort of a commentary and frequently, it is found to refer to the Brahmanas. It contains various legends. *Yaska* alludes to virtuous schools of the Vedic expositions which prevailed long before his age. The explanations of the Vedas, which prevailed earlier, conflict with one another. However, it was the very high antiquity. It belongs to the oldest part of the Sanskrit literature excepting the Vedic writings.

The *Mahabhashya* of Patanjali is not a full commentary to Panini, but with some exceptions, only a commentary on the *Varttikas* or critical remarks of Katyayana on Panini. It may be noted that the name Patanjali referred here is not the Patanjali who wrote Yoga philosophy. He probably lived in the second century before Christ. Katyayana belonged to the time of the Nandas during first half of the 4th century BC. Patanjali lived in the reign of Pushpamitra.

Vedanga or Sutra Kalpa

The fifth Vedanga is the *Kalpa* or the Ceremonial. The Brahmanas are the source of the Vedic rituals. In the *Kalpa Sutra* the rituals developed completely and obtained systemization of performances in sacrificial performances. This helped the priests a lot to give practical shape of the sacrifices and *yajnas*. The *Kalpa Sutra* is connected with the *Rigveda* and the *Samaveda*. The *Vaitana Sutra* related to the *Yajurveda* does not belong to the 'remote ancient'. The *Kalpa Sutra* is divided into three classes – *Shrauta, Grihya* and *Samayacharika*. The first prescribes the special Vedic ceremonials such as those which are to be celebrated on the days of full and new moon. The second enjoins the domestic rites to be performed by various stages of life from birth to death. The *Grihya Sutra* prescribes general rules which are to be observed at marriages, at the birth of a child on the day of naming the child and after the death of a person. The *Grihya Sutra* embodies rules for the five daily acts of domestic devotion named *Mahayajna* as well as for those principal and purifying ceremonies which are included under the *samskara* or certain ceremonial rites. There are precise directions in regard to investiture with the sacred thread. The ceremony is of the great importance, and is supposed to confer a second spiritual birth. This is enjoined for a Brahmin in his eight years, for a Kshatriya in eleven years, and for a Vaishya in his twelfth. The time may be extended in each case.

The *Grihya Sutra* prescribes a number of rituals related to human life. It is full of rites and rituals. Even today these rites and rituals are performed in Hindu society. In fact, the traditions related to rites and rituals have complete relevance with *Grihya Sutra*. It specifies the eight forms of marriages, called Brahma, Daiva, Prajapatya, A'rsha, Gandharva, Asura, Paisacha and Rakshasa.[44] They also prescribe the funeral rites to be performed at the cremation and burial of dead bodies. They prescribe four kinds of *Sraddha*, such as *Parvana* (monthly), *Kamya* (voluntary), *Abhyudayika* (performed as thanksgiving on occasions of family rejoicing), and *Ekoddishta* (special).[45] Rites and ceremonies, according to the *Grihya Sutra* are called *Paka Yajna* or sacrifices with food. A *Paka Yajna* consists in a piece of wood being placed in the fire in a hearth, oblations made to the gods, and gifts bestowed on Brahmins. They prescribe what food can be allowed. They also prescribe rules for students emphasizing on maintenance of *Brahmacharya*. Rules regulate the proper diet of a Brahman. They prescribe what food is allowable and what not; what days should be allotted for fasting; and what penances ought to be performed for not observing duties. They decide, in a great measure, the duties and rights of kings and magistrates, the civil rights of the people at large, and even rules of social politeness.

The composition of the *Kalpa Sutra* has great significance in the development of ritual performances in India among the Hindus. *Kalpa* works do not claim to be Smritis. However, they are enumerated amongst the *Svadhyayas*. The *Kalpa Sutra* must have been drawn up for the easy reference of the priests, "who would otherwise have to grope in the dark through the liturgical Samhitas and Brahmanas for the *disjecta membra* of the sacrificial and other rites."[46] Thus, the *Kalpa Sutras* are connected with the *Rigveda* by Ashvalayana, Sankhyayana, and Shaunaka. They are also connected with the other Vedas by various Sutras like *Masaka, Latyayana, Gobhila, Drshayayana, Baudhayana, Satyasadha, Hiranyakeshin, Manava, Bharadwaja, Katyayana, Kusika*, etc.

The sixth and the last of the Vedangas is *Jyotisha*. Though it did not go in depth of the science of astronomy, but it embraces some of the most ancient astronomical ideas. Its main object was to offer only such information about the heavenly bodies as were useful in fixing the days and hours of the Vedic sacrifices. Its purpose was not to teach astronomy as a science.

Among the Sutras the mention of the *Shrauta* and the *Smarta Sutra* is a must to demarcate their differences. Both the *Grihya* and the *Samayacharika Sutras* are included under the common title of *Smarta Sutra*. The *Smarta Sutra* derives their authority from the Smriti and the *Shrauta* from the Sruti. That is why the former is called *Smarta* while the latter is named as *Shrauta*. The *Shrauta Sutra* means the whole body of the Sutras which are closely related to the Brahmanas, Mantra and revelation. The *Smarta Sutra* can have no such claim. The *Shrauta Sutra* latter treats of the grand and public religious ceremonies, rites and sacrifices, while the *Smarta Sutra* is mostly related to individual performances. The *Samayacharika Sutra* is also called *Dharma Sutra*, and it seems to have been the source of the *Dharma Shastra*.

The *Kalpa Sutra* is a complete system of ritualism, and gives the whole method sacred ceremonial with great precision. It has not yet proved whether the *Kalpa Sutra* is a part of the Vedas; and, in fact, it is not possible to decide. During the period of the composition of various Sutras, the whole systems of social organizations were developed, and the distinction of caste was fully established.

The *Kalpa* works brought about a turning point in the literary and religious history of India. The works contributed to the total extinction of the numerous Brahmanas establishing a new meaning of Vedic versions and giving new direction to social and religious faith as well the behaviour of the people. The Brahmanas talk of the divine forces not in an elaborated manner whereas the Sutras (specially the *Kalpa Sutra*) provided enlarged interpretation of the Divine power and its divinity. They developed elaborated manner of the entire system of divine worship. The systems of divine worship which they developed were not uniform, but different to each other. In the words of Ramachandra, "The *Kalpa* books established the whole course of the rites of worship. They direct which of the priests have to take part at each of the stages of the sacred rites. What hymns are to be recited, and further define the time and place for the celebration of these rites."[47] On the other hand the Brahmanas' main objects had been to define *Brahma*, the Supreme Power and the sources of all energies. The rites what they developed were highly sacred related to the conceptions on divine matters.[48] Their vision was related to the divine power spreading from sky to the earth, pervading over each atom. On the other hand, the Sutras viewed God as the Supreme Power, no doubt, but they provided the means to approach and please Him for blessings. The means and ways what they prescribed came to be known as rites and rituals. Thus, the introduction of the *Kalpa Sutra* was the introduction of a new book of liturgy.

There is another class of Sutra named *Anakramani* related to the *Rigveda* and perfect in every respect. It is called the *Sarvanukraman* which gives the first word of each hymn, the number of the verses, the names and families of the authors, the names of the deities to whom hymns are addressed. It was composed by Katyayana. He wrote in prose much after the fashion of the later Sutras. The relation between Shaunaka and Katyayana was very intimate and both of them belonged to the same *Shakha* (Branch). However Shaunaka was superior to Katyayana. There is a class of works commonly designated *Parishishtas*. They have Vedic rituals and sacrifices for their subject matter. It is said that most of the *Parishishtas* are the productions of the Shaunaka and his associates. The *Parishishtas* represent a distinct period of Indian literature, and they are evidently later than the Sutras. However, they are taken in the realm of the Vedic character. There are a number of *Parishishtas* for each of the Vedas. The object of the *Parishishtas* is to supply the deficiencies in the Sutras. They treat everything in a popular and superficial manner. None of them was composed probably before the middle of the third century BC. They throw light on the progress and decay of the Hindu thought.

Declining Influence of the Vedas and Emergence of Blind Religious Faith

As the years rolled by and other Vedic literature except the Vedas and its appendages came into being, the direct influences of the Vedas began to disappear. The new creations which explained and interpreted the Vedic hymns and substances in a new manner, enabled more people to know and understand the Vedas on the one hand, and develop interest of the people in religious performances on the other. In the beginning, the Vedas were the only source of knowledge and truth to the Hindu people. At that time the Vedas stood beyond any controversy. It was universally assumed that all doctrines must be based on, and all controversies must end in, what was taught by the Vedas. The Vedas were considered the highest height of knowledge, and to speak anything against them meant to be an atheist. Thus, the Vedas had assumed unchallenged authority among the Indo-Aryans. It was believed that the words of the Vedas are infallible because of its revelation and divine relevance. But a time came when "the study of the Vedas became gradually extinct, the understanding and explaining of their meanings became a hard task; theism and objectives of the *yajnas*, enjoined in them were lost; and all religious works came to be encrusted with external ceremonies."[49] At the same time the rites and rituals developed by different the Sutras for worshipping of different gods and following a religious life paved the way for the growth of extreme Brahminism where blind orthodox traditions as well as conventions shadowed Hindu society. The priests belonging to the class of Brahmins prevailed and taught people how to live, how to sleep, how to get up, how to behave, what to eat and what to speak, and what should not be done. They also developed the concepts of *pap* and *punya*, hell and heaven, curse and blessing, etc. They prescribed the religious ways to earn *punya* and reserve the place in the heaven by performing worship and *yajnas*. They developed the religious methods to please gods/goddesses and obtain their blessing in this life. It appeared that the Brahmins had searched out the ways of heaven and hell. People having blind faith in them followed in the ways and manners prescribed blindly to avail the benefits or material as well as spiritual gains. The words of the learned Brahmins or priests were taken as final, thinking that they knew the Vedas, and they would never be wrong. It was this blind faith of the people about the statements of the Brahmins and their teachings that made the common mass irrational as well as traditional.

At such circumstance the Vedas were interpreted as per the convenience and usefulness of the scholars especially of Brahmanas who assumed the responsibility to represent Vedic knowledge and be religious teachers. The performances of various rites which they had developed, became the recurring source of income of the priests. These orthodox priests or Brahmins while performing *yajnas* became violent in the sense that they permitted to sacrifice various animals on the altar of the *yajnas*. Even the rulers of the period became so religious minded that they began to perform various *yajnas* like Rajsuya, Ashvamedha, etc where the role of the priests were dominant.

When religion, traditions and conventions overshadowed the rational faculty of mind, there is no way left to discuss, analyse, investigate and search new truth. The path of rational development was blocked with the result that darkness prevail over the human thinking. Religion is not bad, but to follow religious rites blindly is not good. There is too much difference between to become rational and be religious. Rationalism in the study of religion keeps the scholars on right track because it beholds light, but religion without rationalism is not only dark but harmful, too. In ancient Greece, so long as the rational philosophers like Socrates, Plato, Pythagoras, Aristotle, etc, remained and contributed rational thoughts; Greek society was rational and people possessed the capacity or quality to distinguish between right and wrong. Their mental faculty was sharp because superstition or blind faith did hardly block their progressive way of life. It was theological truth of ancient Greek thinkers which provided rational light all over the world and helped the people of Europe to come out of the Dark Age which prevailed there due to spread of religious superstitions and unreasonable customs. In Rome and the European countries Christianity fell into the hands of orthodox religious leaders and became based on blind faith, interpreted and explained by so-called Papal authorities, encrusted entire light of rationalism with the result that the whole of Europe passed through a dark phase. Christianity had become so strong in the name of religion that one could hardly dare to oppose blind religious practices and establish customs. It is another fact that when Martin Luther King strongly protested the practices of Orthodox Christianity and rational thinkers like Bodin, Hobbes, Locke and Montesquieu, etc, broadened the path of rationalism, the whole of Europe was rescued from being swallowed by irrational darkness.

Impact of Irrational Religion on Indian Society

In case of India, with the advent of ritualism supported by the class of Brahmins on the logic of following of rites and rituals, Hindu society began to lose the significance it had achieved during the early period of the Vedas. The theosophy, philosophy and vision of the Vedas changed into performances of rites and rituals. There was no originality in the liturgical creation of post-Vedic period. Though they claimed to be as true as to the Vedas, yet the Vedic vision and philosophy were not available. Rather faith prevailed either blind or true. Gradually, traditions developed which could not allow reason to interfere in its domains and affairs. A period of theology appeared which began to talk about various doctrines related to existence of God and gods. Not only that, even a number of saints, preachers, *sanyasis* took the lead to provide new meaning of religion and abode of Supreme God. All these created dire confusions and controversies. But no one dared to condemn the blind Hindu ritual practices. At that very critical movement, Gautam, popularly known as the Buddha, getting enlightenment, dared to challenge and condemn the blind faith of Hindu religion and the ritual practices. Since the clash between Buddhism and Hinduism have been discussed separately in the succeeding chapter here it is enough to say that advent of Buddhism gave a big jerk to the so-called Brahminism and Hinduism that changed the direction of Indian history.

The practice of *varna* and caste system during the period of Brahminism in India, divided Indian society into various hostile classes. The privileged class comprising of the Brahmins and Kshatriyas took better benefits of the existing circumstances while the people of the lower castes and classes remained totally deprived of the benefits of the changing situation. Rather they remained victims of exploitation and suppression. The Shudras were debarred from study of the Vedas and religious scripture, and were excluded from the performance of any religious acts. Doctrine was developed that they suffered due to their past bad *karmas* and the only way of their release was to endure what ill fate came to them. Women remained suppressed, assuming a second grade in the society. The conditions of the widows became so pathetic due to prescribed rites related to them that they were left to suffer the whole of their remaining life. Education was reserved for the people of the upper classes. However, blind religious faiths kept all these people together despite their different status.

Notes and References

1. *Encyclopedic Dictionary of Society*, Vol 4, Sharma, BB (ed) New Delhi, p 786.
2. Ibid.
3. Ibid.
4. Ibid, pp 786-77.
5. Ibid.

6. Mandelbaum, "Religion in Modern India", in Griraj Gupta (ed), *Main Currents in Indian Society*, New Delhi, 1983, Introduction p VIII.
7. *Oxford English Dictionary*, 1991, Vol XIII (2nd edition), RW Burchfield (ed), New York, pp 568-69
8. Ibid, p 569
9. Ibid.
10. RP Sharma, 1995. *Women in Hindu Literature*, New Delhi, p 5.
11. Sarat Jhingrau, 1996. "Religious Communalism", in B Bidawai, H Mukhia and A Vanaik (eds) *Religion, Religiosity and Communalism*, New Delhi, p 62.
12. Quoted in DV Anthalyes, *Swami Vivekananda: A Study*, New Delhi, 1975, p 62.
13. BB Sharma (Ed) 1994. *Encyclopedia of Society*, Vol IV, New Delhi, p 786.
14. Ibid.
15. Mandelbaum, quoted in Griraj Gupta (ed), *Main Currents in Indian Society*, Vol V, *Religion in Modern India*, New Delhi, 1983 Introduction, p VIII.
16. Mandelbaum, "Transcendental and Pragmatic Aspects of Religion", in *American Anthropologists*.
17. Ibid.
18. Ibid.
19. Griraj Gupta (ed), *Main Currents in Indian Society*, Vol V, *Religion in Modern India*, New Delhi, 1983 Introduction, p IX.
20. Ibid.
21. Speech of Swami Vivekananda at Flora Hall of Colombo on 16th January 1897,
22. *Swamiji's Return to India*, A Booklet published by Ramakrishna Mission Institute of Centre, Calcutta, 2009, p 14.
23. Ibid.
24. Ibid, p 26.
25. Ibid.
26. *Bhagavad Gita*, III/5.
27. *Manu Smriti*, 2/6.
28. *Bhagavad Gita*, 6/1/40.

29. Commentary of Sri Shankaracharya on the *Bhagavad Gita*, translated by Alladi Mahadeva Sastry, Samta Books, Madras, 2007, p 5.
30. *Bhagavad Gita*, III, 10/11.
31. Quoted in D Smith's, 1963. *India as a Secular State*, Princeton University Press, p 373.
32. Quoted in DV Anthalye's *Swami Vivekananda: A Study*, op cit, p 62
33. Ibid.
34. Aurobindo, Sir, 1949, *Essays on the Gita*, Calcutta, p 326.
35. Ibid.
36. *Bhagavad Gita*, XIV/5.
37. Ibid, XIV, 6/7/8.
38. Ibid, XIV, 9.
39. Aurobindo, Sir, 1949, *Essays on the Gita*, Calcutta, p 326.
40. Ramachandra Ghosh, 1988, *History of Hindu Civilization*, Kaushal Prakashan, Delhi, p 77.
41. Ibid, p 78.
42. Dr Burnell, *Aindra School of Sanskrit Grammarians*, p 47.
43. Kielhorn, *Remarks on the Sikshas*, p 9.
44. *Manu*, III, 21; *Yajnavalkya*, I, 58, 62.
45. *Manu*, III, 123, 286.
46. Ramachandra, op cit, p 92.
47. Roth, *Introduction to the Nirukta*, p XXIV ff.
48. Morley, *Digest of Indian Caste*, p CXCVI.
49. Ramachandra, op cit, p 100.

8

Conflicts Between Hindu Dharma and Buddhism

Buddhism as a religion or a cult of scientific philosophical thinking emerged in India during the 6th century BC. Its basic philosophies were propounded by Gautam, the son of the king Shuddhodana who ruled Lichhavi Ganarajya whose capital was at Vaishali, a district of Bihar. His mother, Mahamaya who belonged to the clan of the Shakya dynasty, died after seven days of giving birth to Gautam. Regarding the exact year of the birth of Gautam, scholars differ. It is generally believed that Gautam was born in 563 BC at Lumbini that was situated in the forest of Kapilavastu in the Himalayas. However, Smith is of the view that he was born in 563 BC and got *parinirvana* in 543 BC.[1] He was called Bodhisattva because all aims of his father were accomplished after his birth. Before his renunciation, he was known as Prince Siddhartha. The word Buddha or the 'enlightened one' was often used for Gautam only after he obtained enlightenment at Bodhgaya under the Bodhi Tree. Prior to that period, he was simply called Bodhisattva (in Pali Boddhista) which means a being destined ror enlightenment. The Buddha was often addressed by his disciples as 'Bhagavat' or 'Bhagava', meaning Lord. He was also called as Tathagata which means 'perfect one'. Similarly, the term 'Shakyamuni' (the sage of Shakyas) was common and frequently used in the Sanskrit works. Sometimes, he was referred as 'Gautam' (Pali Gotma) after his clan name, or 'Mahasramana' or the 'Great Ascetic'. However, his personal name was Siddhartha (Pali Siddhattha) which means one who has achieved all his aims. He renounced his body in BC 477 at Kushinagar in the district of Gorakhpur in Uttar Pradesh. It is believed that the Buddha was born in the full moonlit night (Purnima) of Vaishakha and he left his body on the same day. That is why Buddha Purnima is a central holiday in the Indian gazette and it is celebrated all over the country even today.

What is Buddhism?

Buddhism did not start as a new and independent religion. It was an offshoot of the more ancient faith of the Hindus. Perhaps schism or a heresy that occurred in Buddhism after the death of the Buddha and where the school of Mahayana (Theravada) appeared, and it inclined much more to the ancient Indian philosophy. He protested against certain practices which were in vogue at the time. He refused to acquiesce in Vedic ceremonialism. His main object was to bring about a reformation in religious practices and a return to the basic principles. His humanism crossed the racial and national barrier. The Buddha revolted against the ignorance and superstition, the dread and the horror, which accompanied popular religion. Theistic views generally fill men's minds with dogmatism and their hearts with intolerance. Doctrinal orthodoxy has filled the world unhappiness, injustice, strife, crime and hatred. The way established by the Buddha had no room at all for social injustice, strife and crime.

Buddhism is not a metaphysical speculation. Rather it is a practice. Truly speaking, it is a *sadhana* which encompasses various methods. The Buddha was a Bibhajyavadi which means this world is not real. It is a conglomeration. The world where we live, according to Buddhism, is Pancha Skandhatmaka – Rupa, Vedana, Sanjya, Samskara, and Tijuana. All these elements are not real entities. Like the philosophy of Vedanta, Buddhism believes in the transitory phase of the material world that is in constant change. What one sees and observes through his sense organs is not true, but an illusion. Truth that is ultimate is different and it can be grasped through *sadhana* (meditation) which leads one to the goal of ultimate reality. God or so-called Supernatural Power has no place in Buddhist philosophy. The concept of God is too vague to present a picture to be grasped by the human mind.

Protest Against Orthodox Brahminism

The sixth century BC was an age of great spiritual upsurge. Ascetics and hermits roamed about from place to place throughout the Gangetic valley of India, advocating mental discipline and asceticism as means of salvation. As the ceremonial acts and sacrificial rites prescribed in the Vedic texts could not satisfy the urge of the philosophers, it became necessary to go to deeper depths to reach the ultimate truth. The neo-philosophers who appeared in the sixth century BC denied the authority of the Vedas as having superhuman origin and rejected the usefulness of sacrificial rites enunciated by the priestly class. They denied the existence of an intelligent first cause of the universe. They did not believe in efficacy of caste, but enunciated the thesis that it is not through birth but through one's own deeds, a person either an untouchable or a Brahmin should be counted. At the same time the philosophy of Charvakas which taught non-existence of God or soul, prevailed. He denied the existence of any supernatural power. Rather, he advocated the philosophy of materialism. They held that consciousness was not the quality of any unperceived non-material or spiritual entity, but a by-product of material elements such as earth, fire, water, air and ether. Charvaka's philosophy also denied concepts like next transcendental world, rebirth of soul and salvation. Thus, numerous philosophical schools outside the pale of Brahmanism in the days of the Buddha and Mahavira prevailed that created more confusion and caused more conflicts among the people. Need was felt to develop a religious as well as spiritual knowledge without complicacy. The Buddha appeared here to fill in the gap and correct Hinduism.

Upendra Thakur is of the view that "Like other great teachers and reformers of the age, the Buddha, too, utilized the Hindu inheritance in order to bring about some improvement in it."[2] Though the Buddha went against the teaching of Brahminism, the Vedantic philosophy served as the fundamental base for the development of his doctrines. The extremely rigid forms of religious sacrifices of the Brahminical period evoked a great spiritual unrest and revolt against the 'formalism and Brahminical system' in the Upanishadic age.[3] Expensive sacrifices and ritualism were denounced as 'irreligious and foolish by intellectual stalwarts like Yajnavalkya, Janaka Videha, Ajatashatru of Kashi, etc. The reaction and protest against this worn-out system invoked Gautam to protest it. This Brahminical cult overlooked the philosophy of Upanishads which emphasized on the significance of Brahma and Atman. But a close analysis of the Buddha's teachings and ways of life prescribed by him has some direct or indirect association with Hindu philosophy.

Brahminism and Ritual Superstitions

The Indo-Aryans had not obtained a clear and logical comprehension of the characteristics which they themselves ascribed to the objects of their worship. The concept of the

Godhead, indicated in the hymns, is of a fluctuating and undecided character. The remarkable representations of a host of subordinate objects of worship, exhibited to the people a conception of the universe by the Indian rishis which was mythical, sacramental, polytheistic and even pantheistic. The idea of faith is found in the *Rigveda*, and it is that faith which gives the place for emergence of, sometimes, scepticism. Basing on that faith a number of rites and rituals appeared which falling in the hands of the priests left enough scope for emergence of blind faith in practice of rituals in sacrifices and *yajnas*. It has already been discussed that the primitive Aryan religion and their mode of worship changed with the advancement of time and development in the understanding of the people, and became more and more elaborate and complicated. In a history of ancient Sanskrit literature the Mantra period is the most interesting and most important from philosophical point of view. In the Mantra period the state of society being simple and religious worship had become necessary. Each family had its own priest who imparted religious instructions, which were treated too sacrament to avoid or neglect them. In the words of Ramachandra Ghosh, "In the process of time, such a religious worship underwent a gradual, but marked change. And as soon as we step into the Brahmana period, we observe the gross superstitious character which that primitive religion and worship gradually assumed. In this period priesthood was systematically created; and nothing could be done without a priest.[4] Various kinds of priesthood appeared that engaged in various religious performances.

Buddha's Attack Upon Brahminism

The Buddha confronted with such conflicting philosophies. He had fully realized the futility of orthodox Brahminism in the life of mankind. He took no time to understand that rise and growth of Hinduism was on shaky foundation of blind faith which prepared the fertile ground for appearance of superstitions. He also realised that the superstitions developed under the shadow of Brahminism were not only useless but harmful also to the general mass. So his first attack was on excessiveness of Brahminism and secondly, he too, denied the existence of any supreme power like God as a creator of the universe, and soul as an integral particle of God. However, the path which he developed was not on the line of Charvaka, nor it accepted the view of nihilism. Rather he preferred a middle way. He neither approved the doctrine of perpetual eternality (Shashvatavada) nor of those nihilists who believe consciousness to be a product of material elements, which is destroyed along with the destruction of the Body. Though he condemned ritualism of Brahminism, he did not reject the doctrines of *karma* and rebirth as well as *nirvana* which existed in the Hindu religion prior to the advent of Buddhism. Main concern of the Buddha was not the metaphysics, but the mundane world and the people. He emphasised on pragmatic aspect of philosophy preferring psychology and morality. He thought that the mankind had been caught in the whirlpool of ignorance resulting in pains and suffering. So he devoted his efforts to get the man realise the reality of life and adopt the ways searched by him to get rid of pains and suffering. He was either unknown to the idealist and speculative theory of Ultimate Reality or he knowingly avoided it thinking its non-usefulness in the practical life of mankind.

Upanishads, too, were not clear about the concept of Absolute Truth. Its Dogma related to God, '*Na iti, Na iti…*' (this is not, this is not…) created more confusion. The Buddha had to find out the reality not for him but for all common people. The scholars are of the view that Buddhism was but a natural reaction to this obscure and difficult philosophy of the Upanishads which was quite unintelligible to the ordinary mind. So the knowledge related to absolute truth reflected in the Upanishads had become the property of a few who could understand it. Popular discontent began to grow and seek some outlet elsewhere. According to GC Pande, the leaders of Hinduism had themselves prepared the ground which proved very fertile for the new religion – Buddhism – to thrive on. Buddhism originated in the same region as the *Shatapatha Brahmana*, for instance, the country of Videhas, the Koslas and the Shakyas. Moreover, the doctrine promulgated by Yajnavalkya in the *Brihadaranyaka Upanishad* is, in fact, more or less Buddhistic.[5] The Buddha vehemently denounced the heretical views of the time 'fruitless'. The Buddha was not alone to criticize Brahminism, but attack was made from other scholars also. Brahminism had by now become "an island in a sea."[6] The majority of the people followed the new order till the rise of Shankaracharya.[7]

Ritualism and Superstitions

In practising Hinduism, based on blind faith, a number of rites and rituals appeared which falling in the hands of priests left enough scope for emergence of blind faith in practice of rituals in sacrifices and *yajnas*. The complicated nature of the ceremonial practices necessitated the distribution of sacrificial duties among several distinct classes of priests. They had popular duties to perform, which are prescribed in the Brahmanas. The Adhvaryus had to recite the verses of the *Yajurveda*, to measure the ground, to build the *vedi*, or altar, to make the sacrificial vessels, to fetch wood and water, to light the fire, to bring the animal and immolate it. There was also the lowest class of priests who had to chant songs of the *Samaveda*, and to act as the chorus. The peculiar duty of the *Hotris* (kind of priest) was to recite in a distinct and loud voice certain verses of the *Rigveda* in praise of the deities during the time of sacrifices. There was Brahma priest who was supposed to know the whole ceremonial rites and all the three Vedas used by the Hotris, Adhavaryus and Udagatris. The Adhavaryus was the chief priest whose role was to organize the *yajna*, control the ritual processes, and direct other priests and conduct the sacrifices.

Under such circumstances Brahminism that covered the mind and practice of people, played a dominant role in showing and obtaining people heaven (*Swarga*). The belief prevailed among the common masses that if gods are pleased, they may fulfil worshippers' desires including the desire to dwell in heaven and enjoy the divine status. The prescribed ways and means to please gods were to offer him oblations in sacrifices. As a result, ritualism and formalism became dominant everywhere in the life of people because it was said that ritualism was the viable base to attain heaven. Belief spread that by performing *yajna* one could achieve the things in this world which he desired. It was also believed that there are a number of gods upholding creation, who are capable of blessing the desired things, provided they are pleased; and the way of pleasing them was prescribed through performing *yajna*. It is the day-to-day observation that common people are desirous of worldly pleasures and they can go to any extent to achieve the material gains. So, people indulged in practice of ritualism propagated by learned Brahmins, and they followed what was said to them by their priests.

The most ancient name of a professional priest was *purohita*. He was, in fact, the councillor of a chief, and minister of a king. A king could not do a thing of importance, including war and peace, without the suggestion of the *Rajpurohita*. He used to occupy prominent rank among ministers of the king. According to Ramachandra, "The chief occupation of the *Purohita* was simply to perform the ordinary sacrifices; but his office also partook of a political character."[8] Throwing light on the appearance of priesthood as a class, Ramachandra writes: "The term *Brahmana* originally denoted a devout worshipper of a contemplative sage or poet, who composed hymns in praises of gods, But after the ceremonial of worship became highly developed and complicated; and the sacred functions became quite distinct from other occupations; the epithet gradually came to be employed for a minister of religion, and at last it came to signify one particular class of priests with certain special duties. Then the hierarchy of Brahmanas was completely organized."[9] Weber is also of the view that "priesthood formed an exclusive caste, which for the most part became a hereditary order."[10] Among them all were not equally qualified and wise. Some of them were mere followers having little Vedic knowledge. The system of worship that appeared later on where most of Brahmins availed the opportunity to get employment, brought both wealth and fortune to the class of Brahmanas. Their honour and respect increased among right from the king to common people. They became entitled to receive salute from the people of any class or caste.

Worshipping Procedures Among Hindus

It has already been described that religion is nothing without worship and without a cult. Religion in early history of mankind played great roles to subjugate people and make them civilized. Religion is both a faith and a fear towards unseen power. Man who is greedy and ambitious by nature wants to obtain more and more wealth and prosperity. The faith that the natural unseen powers may bless them with anything makes man blind follower of religion and worshipper of deities. Man does not like to be in trouble. The faith that the unseen natural forces may cause injuries or losses if not pleased, forced man to keep the gods constantly pleased; and for that he adopted the method of worship. Mankind remained attached to the system of worship from very beginning of the human civilization. Man worshipped the unseen power when he was passing through different period of civilization. During the pastoral and agricultural period of civilization a sacrifice was a reality. The Vedic poets and thinkers, too, used various symbols to express their emotional thought. These symbols have been collected from the sources like name of various gods, world of vegetation and world of animals. The gods established by Vedas are symbols of different deities who represent different fields of our universe. They play various roles in the creation and governance of human life. Shri Aurobindo is of the view that if these gods are worshipped with faith and honour, they may fulfil the aims and ambitions of worshippers. Indian religious literature puts emphasis on *yajnas* which is performed with certain pious materials like water, ghee, milk, sweet, *durva, kusha*, betel nut, coconut, betel leaves, leaves of trees like mango etc. Through *yajnas* various gods who are engaged in holding the universe and controlling its activities are pleased by offering different things of their choice. It is believed that being pleased they not only bless people with wealth and prosperity but also tightly uphold the systems of creation.

The system of Vedic sacrifices throws light on many a dark point in the history of the Indo-Aryans. Sacrifices had deep impact upon social and religious life of people. The sacrificial system had penetrated so deep into the social life of the people that no one could dare to challenge or avoid religious customs. In the performance of sacrifices philosophy, literature and different branches of knowledge, trade and commerce, military valour, and tilling of the soil were all brought into requisition. There was no part of life which was unaffected from sacrificial norms. It governed social, religious, economic, political, physical, and spiritual way of life. Priests had become guides and philosophers who taught people how to live, how to talk, how to sleep, how to get up, what to eat and what should not be eaten, and how to behave. People were asked to participate in sacrifices or any ritual performance with faith. They were also asked to honour the established order of worshipping. The rites which were simple in the beginning became more rigid and complicated as the years rolled down. Under the developed system of worship and *yajnas* various kinds of animals were sacrificed on the altar. Various kinds of beasts and birds were also sacrificed. The rites, offerings, oblations, sacrifices were all performed with the distinct purpose either to avert an evil or to secure a coveted object by divine intercession, or to prohibit the gods themselves. They were offered to obtain the goodwill of some offended deities, or through the dread of others.

Srutis say that worship without water, performance of *yajna* without *kush* (a kind of grass) and pouring of *ahuti* (oblation) in fire without ghee is fruitless. It is believed that *kush* is the most pious grass, capable of destroying all sins of a worshipper. The mat made of *kush* is taken as the most pious and it is still used by Hindus during *yajnas*. It is still believed that in the root of the *kush* Brahma resides, in the middle sun and at the top Mahashiva lives. The *Rigveda* mentions *darbha* or *durva* [a kind of grass which is considered very pious and to be used in *yajnas*]. (*Rigveda*, 7.142.1)

Inhumane Practices of Rituals

At the celebration of the Darsapurnamasa sacrifice the *Adhvaryus* (priests) had to place two cows and calves together. The sacrifice was celebrated at new and full moon. There were various types of sacrifices, namely, Rajsuya, Agnihotra, Ashvamedha, Somayaga and Purushamedha, etc. The Ashvamedha or horse-sacrifice was probably adopted by the

Indians from the Scythians, before they crossed the Indus. It is said that at this sacrifice six hundred nine animals of various descriptions, domestic and wild, were tied to twenty-one posts. After the completion of customary prayers they were three times led around the sacrificial fire prior to the actual sacrifice. Elephants, camels, buffalos, birds, tortoises, crocodiles, snakes and even mosquitoes were included among the animals. It was all done in accordance with the hymns of the *Rigveda*. The *Rigveda* and other religious scriptures permitted animal sacrifices.[11] Some sacrifices like *Sulgava*, was ceremonized at a proper isolated place, in the midnight, where no human being was allowed to witness. Some of the practices were barbaric; and over time such barbaric animal sacrifices lost their significance and appeal.[12] The sacrifice known as Ashvayuji properly belonged to the pastoral age of civilization. The Gomedha was not certainly typical as many are disposed to believe. The Gavamanayana was held for four days. The religious scriptures like Aranyakas, Brahmanas, etc, have traces of these sacrifices.

It is also said that human sacrifices were in practice, but for some special purposes. In reality, it was entirely of an expiatory nature. It required full forty days for its celebration. A hundred and forty-five men of various tribes, characters and professions were essentially required to be bound to eleven posts and consecrated to various deities. Thus, the 'holocaust' of human victims formed part of the ancient cults of India, and there is strong presumptive evidence that Sunassepa was intended for an actual immolation.[13] It is evident that the Indo-Aryans were familiar with the notion of human sacrifice.[14] Even the serpent-sacrifice was in practice. Though the practice of such wild sacrifices gradually declined later on, yet its impact upon the people could easily be discerned even today. The faith and belief that one can achieve desired goals by worshipping gods with prescribed rites made people blind followers of religion.

Since it all was done by the Hindus, such practices became a part of Hinduism. Hinduism became a religion comprising of philosophical, spiritual, religious, social, economic and ritualistic faith. It became more orthodox by nature. Reason began to disappear from the religion leaving the place for growth of superstitions and customary laws which needed modification in the interest of the common people as a whole. At such critical juncture the Buddha with charismatic character appeared and adopted the lead to oppose Brahminism based on blind faith and orthodoxy.

Buddha Wanted to Replace Brahminism

The advent of Buddhism was indeed an expression of revolt against ritualism and formalism practised by the cult of Brahminism and an aversion to scholarship. The sixth century BC when the Buddha was born, was known as the age of great spiritual upsurge. Ascetics and hermits roamed about from place to place throughout the Gangetic Valley, advocating mental discipline and asceticism as means of salvation. As the ceremonial acts and sacrificial rites prescribed in the Vedic texts could not satisfy the urge of the contemporary philosophers, it became essential to go deeper to fathom of the ultimate truth. Here comes the period of the Upanishads (700 BC-600 BC). The need was felt to research ultimate truth going beyond the limit of Veda's versions related to Supreme God. The questions which perplexed the mind of the philosophers or seers were: What is Brahman? Wherefrom do we come? How should we live? Who controls happiness and misery? What is this Universe like? How did it start and who created it? When will it end and so on? Gautam Buddha's effort to find the ultimate truth provides the right answer. His goal was to find out the ultimate cause of sufferings and search the ways to get rid of such sufferings and pains.

The region of Magadha (south Bihar) situated east of Kashi on the right bank of the Ganga, was the centre of intellectual and spiritual activities. Among those who fostered the ferment were the Buddha, Mahavira and others. The Brahminical scriptures did not regard Bihar as a pious land. Rather it was regarded as a land of sin where the performance of sacrificial rites was prohibited. The inhabitants of this region were considered as 'aliens and infectious fever'. In comparison with the sacred Kashi, Magadha was considered unholy. It is evident from the statement of a Jain pilgrim of 18th century who referred to a common belief that if a cow died in Kashi, it attained salvation, whereas a man dying in Magadha was reborn just a donkey.

There appeared various philosophers who began to interpret absolute reality in different ways, creating more confusion. There were also philosophers who denied the existence of God and believed in the theory of non-existence of any Absolute power. It has already been discussed that among them the school of Charvaka appeared more dominant. Charvaka denied the authority of Vedas as having supreme origin and rejected the usefulness of sacrificial rites, enunciated by the priestly class. They denied the existence of an intelligent first cause of this universe. They did not believe in efficacy of caste and enunciated the thesis that it is not through birth but through one's own deeds. A person either an untouchable or a Brahmin, should be recognized on the basis of their performances, not birth. A philosopher like Charvaka, who believed in the philosophy of materialism, attacked Vedantic knowledge. He did not believe in the existence of soul apart from the body. The school of Charvaka held that consciousness was not the quality of any unperceived non-material or spiritual entity, but a by-product of material elements such as the fire, earth, water air and ether. To substantiate his fact Charvaka quoted a passage from *Chhandogya Upanishad* which stated that "If there is no separate existence of soul, it is useless to believe in the next world, rebirth, good or bad deeds and merits and demerits." Therefore, in the opinion of Charvaka, as long as we live, we should live happily because there is no life after death. He totally denied the theory or philosophy related to existence of God and soul. They have quoted Brihaspati, the propounder of their philosophy, saying: "Oblation to fire, the three Vedas, the three staves and be smearing ashes to the body – all are nothing but the means of livelihood for those who are devoid of intelligence. They are more sarcastic about the priestly class." They further pointed out: "If killing of animals for sacrificial purposes, leads to heaven, why does not a sacrificer kill his own parents. And, if the *shraddha* ceremony observed in honour and benefit of dead relatives causes them satisfaction, then is provision for those who undertake a journey not necessary?" Furthermore, "If the same colour of blood flows in the vein of a Brahmin and a Chandala (Shudra), and both look alike, where lies the question of their being either high or low?[15]

Buddha's Emphasis on Scientific Empirical Approach

It is the matter of great pride and honour first for Bihar and then the people of whole India that fruitful tree of Buddhism originated on the most pious, religious and spiritual land of Bodhgaya situated in Bihar. The prosperous branches of the tree of Buddhism spread not only inside the country but also in a number of foreign countries. The light of divinity and spiritualism that Buddhism reflected spread far and wide leading millions of people to the right path of knowledge. Buddhism, in fact, appeared at the time when wisdom in India had been enveloped by blind faith and superstitions falling in the hands of orthodox Brahmins who were badly engaged in Brahminical cult of religious ceremonies performing *karmakandas*.

They hardly paid any heed to evil consequences of the religious performances practised by them. At the time, the ancient Indian Hindu philosophy that had reached to the climax of philosophical knowledge had become either out of catch to common mass or a slave of so-called orthodox Brahmins who were actively and whole-heartedly busy with practice of *karmakandas*. It was the practice of *karmakandas* widely prevailed in India that taught people *yajnas* and sacrifices which has already been discussed above. Rituals and formalities had superseded reason. Sacrifices of innocent animals during *yajnas* had made people merciless towards all sorts of animal and birds. So, their survival was in constant danger. Such historic period of India may be capered with the 'Dark Age' of Europe during the middle period where reason had been swallowed by blind religious faith and hollow conventions.

In Europe, it was Martin Luther King who first challenged the practice of Orthodox Christianity, and in India it was the Buddha who uncovering reason from the veil of ignorance taught peoples that philosophy and religion both needed scientific understanding. People need faith, but not the blind faith. Superstitions or superstitious beliefs must be verified with the logical eyes of reason. While accepting religion and philosophy and performing religious norms one must consider its evil consequences in the society. The Buddha also emphasized that philosophy and religion are not meant for a particular high as well as developed classes, but it must be applicable to all without the barrier of caste and *varna*-system. Religion is meant for all. Salvation is open to all. Lord Buddha taught that each amoeba has inner quality as well capacity to evolve to the level of Buddha (supreme consciousness). Universality of religion depends upon its applicability to each one at every door. Buddhism achieved the status of universalism due to its scientific and liberal approach.

Buddha's Scientific Approach

Scientific is an approach where a hypothesis is tested, verified, analysed, and examined on the basis of reason. Before coming to the conclusion various methods are applied to confirm the truth. Science is practical, not dogmatic. It needs reason and logic. So scientific truth once established becomes universal because there is no variation. Gautam Buddha was a thinker, a monk, a saint and a scientist. He did not believe in blind faith and superstition. Rather he preferred reason. He had the reason to distinguish between right and wrong, good and bad, acceptable and non-acceptable, etc. So, his thoughts and actions all had been reasonable. He believed in the knowledge that is gained through logical experience. He observed reality and ultimate truth applying reason from the deepest levels of insight and enlightenment of his mind-body. What he discovered was the fruit of his great endeavour and pain. Though his followers observing his qualities and achievements regarded him God, he never claimed himself as God or incarnation of God. Regarding existence of God he preferred to be silent because the concept of God is so vast and vague that human mind cannot even rightly apprehend about it. He neither approved God's existence nor denied it. It is all because he was not able to say scientifically whether there is God or not. So, he preferred to remain silent on this issue.

His outlook was broader, balanced, analytical and observational. His vision was based on his inner-insight. He did not accept any truth until it was reasonably verified. It is true that what he said or taught was not new. It was said and taught before his advent. But the way and the method of his teaching of the truth was very much different because of its reliability on scientific attitude. The philosophical truth that he established related to existence or denial of God, soul, circle of birth and death, salvation, the way of attainment of truth etc, are all scientific. His various doctrines like *sunyata, anatmavada*, theory of *karma*, death and rebirth etc are scientific. His every attitude and angle is scientific. The truth which he talked about is not new, but the method and style to establish truth are new. The philosophies which he carried were based on scientific understanding. His teaching became popular because it was simple and understandable even to common mass. Moreover, his teaching helped number of people to come out of the captivity of *karmakandas* and ritualism. That is why the orthodox Brahmins became bitter critics of the Buddha and Buddhism both. However, it did not dampen the courage and block the way of the Buddha. He remained firm in his postulates and hard in endeavour.

Buddhism as a Religion

The Buddha did not teach a sectarian religion. He used the word Dhamma in Pali which means truth and law. Dhamma, according to him is the way to liberation and to the end of suffering. His teachings are universal and applicable to all religions and people from all backgrounds. He put emphasis on *vipassana* which means insight. It is *vipassana* that leads to the inner calm of relaxation and also to the insight or wisdom of reality. He emphasized that the truth would be realized through the practice and not by the sermon or preaching of some individuals. The answer to life and the end to suffering are found by oneself as one own teacher and discoverer. Truth is achieved through the practice of insight meditation, not by hearing sermons and performing *yajnas*.

Buddhism is a religion of kindness, humanity and equality. The Buddha aimed at a new spiritual existence attained through *jnana* or *Bodhi* or absolute illumination. The Buddha deemed "the highest goal of a man to the stage in which there is neither old age nor fear, nor disease, nor birth nor death, nor anxieties, and in which there is no continuous renewal of activity."[16]

Each religion contains certain, tenets, precepts and doctrines. It establishes moral and ethical values and attempts to interpret metaphysic and speculate about transcendental world. Buddhism, too, has precepts, doctrines and golden path to get rid of worldly sufferings and obtain *nirvana*. Though the Buddha's intention was not to set up any particular religion, with growing strength of his followers both inside and outside the country, and also coming of new interpretation of Buddhism, gradually it assumed the status of a religion. It became Buddha Dhamma. The basic purpose of the Buddha was to oppose excessiveness in the practice of Hindu Dharma by orthodox Brahmins who had developed the cult of *karmakanda* based on ritualism and formalism. The Buddha wanted to set a new philosophy devoid of blind faith and superstition. However, Buddhism became a religion.

Buddha's Views about God, Universe and Religion

Traditionally in most Dhamma books, Buddhism generally the Buddha has often been described as atheistic. But this does not state the whole picture on the issue for many reasons. The Buddha was not so much atheistic as he was opposed to discussing metaphysical questions in general. He described his teachings using the analogy of a physician who treats the patient without keeping in mind who he is or what caste and community does he belong to. The doctor's only mission is to cure the ailment of the patient. The Buddha without going into depth of the metaphysics simply adopted that it is the human mind that creates the world. So there is no creator, except for what one mentally wishes to create. The Buddha adopted the middle way whereby his emphasis was on the reality, not the abstract idealism. He had no faith in abstraction. Some Buddhists tend to be him atheistic because of the measurable silence of the

Buddha on such issue. The Buddha was, in fact, opposed to a concept of an all-powerful God who exists somewhere. He rejected the idea of a first beginning or creation or that there is a creator sitting somewhere. It is his adoption that some people take him as an atheist. In other religion existence of God, His mercifulness and benevolence are described in such a manner that He is listening to the prayers of mankind and He grants blessing being pleased. The Buddha discarded such faith. God has been taken as a personal entity in other religions, but in Buddhism there is no place for personal god.

The term *nirvana* that is very much popular in Buddhism means to enter into Divine Ocean or the ocean of complete tranquillity where there is no noise, no movement, no activity, no pain, no birth or death. There is eternity. According to the Buddha one may enter into the ocean of *nirvana* through enlightenment that is to be achieved by oneself. Since the Buddha believed in the cycle of birth and death based on *karmas* and *samskara*, and also in *nirvana*, it appears that there is something beyond our universe. It is this something which seems that the Buddha was not an atheist. Rather he was theist or pantheist. Even the Buddha, after getting enlightenment, became something as a symbol of worshipping in heavenly realms. The Western thinkers while analysing the Buddha's concept of theism and atheism advance the logic that how can there be a religion without a belief in a personal God figure. The Buddha's God is not like the God of other traditional religions. His God is different about whom nothing definitely may be said anything. So, it is better to remain silent. Notable fact is that he neither approved the issue of God nor rejected it.

Imprint of Hinduism on Buddhism

Guru Nanak, the founder of Sikhism once told that a religion is without its moorings till it joins the life current of humanity and socially and spiritually insulates itself into them.[17] According to the Buddha, development of morality, truth, concentration and purification of the mind are the important aspects of a religious life for salvation.[18] The Buddha, in fact, was a realist, an empiricist. His entire concern was related to the present life that is shrouded in miseries and pains. The Buddha talked much about the universe, the world of ours and the people living in this world. His purpose was to release mankind from the captivity of sufferings and pains. He found that despite the presence of various sects of religion man had been suffering from different kinds of pains both mental and physical. He had realized the root cause of pain and sufferings. So what he contributed religiously or philosophically is mostly related to this world where we live. While setting his doctrines, he explained birth, death, oldness, disease, *nirvana* etc prescribing certain right ways to get rid of these worldly affairs. Buddhism from analytical point of view is, in fact, not a religion like Hinduism, Islamism or Christianity, but a way of the life of sanctity, sagacity, purity, simplicity and what not. His faith in existence of soul does not stand. His explanation is mostly psychological where status of mind and consciousness is largely discussed and explained. The Buddha did not write any scripture. It is his followers who being divided into various schools, developed written scriptures that present fluctuating details of Buddhism. So, Buddhism is a religious way having its own texts, meanings, costumes and the method to perform worshipping. While doing so a lot has been borrowed by the Buddhists from the Indian religion (Hinduism). While observing Buddhism the imprint of Hinduism may easily be discerned. However, it stands differently and differs much from the metaphysical Hindu's philosophy.

He travelled from place to place, touched the life of hundreds high and low, princes and peasants. They all came under the spell of his great personality. He taught for forty five years the beauty of charity and the joy of renunciation. There are two sides of the Buddha – individual and social. Individual Buddha is a sage, yogi, absorbed and withdrawn to the joy of his inner meditation. Another Buddha is concerned with sorrow of men, eager to enter their lives, heal their troubles and spread his message for the good of the many.[19] To the Theravadins, the Buddha is a man not God, a teacher and not a saviour. However, all of Buddhism agree that the Buddha was the founder, that he strove and attained transcendental wisdom as he sat under the Bodhi Tree, that he pointed a way from the world of suffering to a beyond, the undying, and those who follow the path for liberation may also cross to the wisdom beyond.[20] In the words of Dr Radhakrishnan, "The Buddha did not feel that he was announcing a new religion. He was born, grew up and died a Hindu. He was restating with a new emphasis the ancient ideals of the Indo-Aryan civilization."[21] He aimed at a new spiritual existence attained through *jnana* or Bodhi, absolute illumination.

Thus, it is evident that the Buddha did not found a new religion. Rather he collected some evidential elements of other religions especially from Hinduism and branded them in the form of Buddhism. He accepted metaphysics of Hinduism, no doubt, but did not go into depth because his basic concern was to the world where humanity lives and suffers. Due to his inclination towards Vedic philosophy and acceptance of the theory of birth and death, theory of *karma* and *samskara*, he was, later on, regarded as incarnation of the Hindu god Lord Vishnu. He utilized the Hindu inheritance to correct some of its expressions. He came to fulfil, not to destroy. He left his footprints on the soil of India and his mark on the soul of the country with the habits and convictions. Slowly Buddhism became an integral part of Indian culture. Dr Radhakrishnan is right when he says that, "In a sense the Buddha is a maker of modern Hinduism."

God, Religion and Devotion

Before we have a detailed discussion about Buddhist's religious philosophies, it would be better to have a cursory glance over religion, God and devotion. Each religion is related to the concept of God who is supreme, transcendental, invisible, omnipotent, omnipresent, all powerful, capable of doing anything, creator, sustainer and destroyer of entire creation, etc. He is Eternal, Imperishable, Indestructible, Ultimate Truth, source of power and qualities, etc. These all are the faith which cannot be proved scientifically. A devotee has to believe in existence and supremacy of God. A number of views, opinions and doctrines have been developed to understand God by various metaphysical schools, thinkers, philosophers, seers, poets, etc. Their views and opinions are different and conflicting. There is also a school that has no faith at all in existence of God. The school of Charvaka denied the existence of God. To this school the creation is not the result of God's power, but it is eternal and there is automation in the creation. Even the Indian Vedas though believe in God's supreme power, say nothing definitely about God's existence. It says: '*Na iti, Na iti* (that is not, that is not). The school of agnosticism is doubtful about existence of God. It maintains to keep silence in this regard because the concept of God is beyond the catch of human senses and understanding. To the Nihilists there is no God at all. They have no faith in a concept related to God. To them the ultimate reality is material world. Various religions, like Hinduism, Islamism, Jainism, Judaism, Jewish, and Christianity etc, talk much about God, soul and world, but they come to different conclusion and prescribe different ways as well as methods to apprehend God and visualize Him. However, they are unanimous about God's supremacy and transcendency. Once the existence of God is accepted or belief in God's supremacy is established, it requires devotion to obtain

His blessing and kindness. So, devotion to God in a religion is a must. Devotion is complete faith and absolute surrender to God. Here there is no scope for any logic or argument. It comes out of heart, not mind. The base of devotion is complete faith and total dependence on God's mercy and kindness. It is believed that once the devotee devotes to God, it is God who takes care of him. The devotee totally relies upon God's mercy and remains in peace and pleasure forever. It is also said that with devotional force anything at any moment can be achieved. One may even personify God.

According to Shankaracharya's *parmarthika* standpoint, Brahman alone is real. There is no creation, no creator like God or *Ishvara*, no created effect like *Jiva-Jagata*. Creation is illusion (*maya*). So, there cannot be any question of religion at all. No question of sweet relation between God and soul because the soul or *jiva* itself is Brahman. So there cannot be a worshipper of *Ishvara*. The proposition of Shankara is related to the Vedas. It is *Sankhya Darshana* where emphasis is on pure knowledge. This doctrine believes in monistic theory of God. Except God there is nothing. What we see or feel is reflection of that absolute power which alone exists. There is rope only, no serpent. The serpent is imagination only. It is nothing more than illusion. The world is reflection of Brahman. Brahman is only truth, not the world. The reflection is like shadow and it is not permanent. Its nature is temporary and illusory. According to Shankara, religion is possible and has value only from the *vyavaharika* (empirical) standpoint. *Ishvara* and *Saguna* Brahman is creator, the object of the worshipped, while the *jiva* is the created effect and the worshipper. The relation between *Ishvara* and devotee is not real, but adopted. Since there is nothing except Absolute *Brahman*, the question of existence of *jiva*'s soul does not arise. However, this doctrine of Shankara has been criticized by many others that have been described in detail in the succeeding chapter of this book.

Doctrine of Soul According to Indian Vedanta

Soul, according to the philosophy of Indian Vedanta, is permanent universal element that has consciousness, light, energy and that is the base of everything in material world and light of the spiritual world. According to the *Bhagavad Gita*, the soul is immortal and eternal like God because it is the integral particle of God. The *Bhagavad Gita* says:

> For the soul there is neither birth nor death at any time. He has not come into being, does not come into being, and will not come into being. He is unborn, eternal, ever-existing and primeval. He is not slain when the body is slain. (*Bhagavad Gita*, 2/20).

Talking about immorality of soul, text 22 of the Chapter 2 of the *Bhagavad Gita* says:

> As a person puts on new garments, giving up old ones, the soul similarly accepts new material bodies, giving up the old and useless one.

It is further said:

> The soul can never be cut to pieces by any weapon, nor burned by fire, nor, moistened by water, nor withered by the wind. This individual soul is unbreakable and insoluble, and can be neither burned nor dried. He is everlasting present everywhere, unchangeable, Immovable and eternally the same. It is invisible inconceivable and immutable. Knowing this you (Arjuna) should not grieve for the body. (*Bhagavad Gita*, Text-23/24/25 Chapter 2).

Thus, it is evident that soul is as pure as God; it is as bright as God; it is as immortal as God. Being the integral part of God, soul is deathless and eternal. God is the primary cause of creation. So in the human life it is soul that upholds everything. Soul is wisdom, light, illumination and what not. The relationship between God and soul is not only integral but indivisible also. The individual soul in a body is the captive of material world. Since the material world is subject to decay, body meets to the fate of destruction, but not the soul due to its immortality. It changes body in the form of rebirth where soul remains as it is. The human body has two aspects mental and physical. Mental aspect is made of mind. Mind is related to the *chit* that upholds consciousness (awareness), ego (I) wisdom and activity through sense as well as physical organs. Except soul all these elements are impermanent. The *chit* that is very near to soul is the upholder of the essence of all *karmas* that results in rebirth of a *jiva*. According to the Upanishads, soul and *jiva* are two different aspects. *Jiva* is the living being having effects of *karma* and enjoys the fruits of *karma* while soul is upholder, witness of every activity of *jiva* and illumination of the heart. According to Vedanta it is *chittakash* which is the holder of numerous imprints of *jiva*'s activities. It serves as the bedrock of the *jiva* from where all aspirations, emotions and imaginations of a *jiva* take place and gradually became strong in the form of activities.

Buddha's Conflicting Theory of Soul

The denial of the Buddhist philosophy of soul is fully based on the universal principle of impermanence. When the doctrine of universal permanence is accepted, then in that case the acceptance of eternality, absolute unity or supreme authority in any case becomes meaningless. As a result of it, an existence like the above cannot have *Atman*. However the Buddha accepted the provisional existence of personal ego. This is evidence from the statement mentioned below:

> The Tathagata sometimes taught that the *Atman* exists and at other times he taught that the *Atman* does not exist. When he preached the *Atman* exists and said to be the receiver of misery of happiness in the successive life as the reward of its *karma*, his object was to save man from falling into the heresy of nihilism. When he taught

> that there is no *Atman* in a sense of creator or perceiver or an absolute free agent, apart from conventional name given to the aggregate of the five *skandhas*, his object was to save man from falling into the opposite heresy of externalism or *shashvatvada*.[22]

The question is which of these two views are correct? It creates more conflict and the conflict is very much difficult to be resolved. Nagarjuna further says:

> This doctrine is so difficult to understand. It was not intended by the Buddha for the ears of those whose intellect is dull and in whom the root of goodness has not thriven. And why? Because such man by hearing the doctrine of *anatman* would have been sure to fall into the heresy of nihilism. The two doctrines were preached by the Buddha for two different objects. He taught the doctrine of *atman* when he wanted to impart to his listeners the conventional doctrine. He taught the doctrine of *anatman* when he wanted to impart to them the transcendental doctrine.[23]

Thus, it is very much evident that the Buddha followed the middle path where he neither rejected the theory of absolutism nor he accepted the theory of nihilism. He did not approve the existence of an independent supra-soul as it has been presented in the *Bhagavad Gita* or other religious books of Hinduism, However, he does not deny the existence of intellect, though that is not immortal. Immortality is *nirvana* which can be achieved through individual personal effort. His basic purpose was to teach people how to get liberation from pains and sufferings of this world. The fact is that he accepted an identity that does not die even after death of the individual and it carries the imprint of past *karmas* and causes rebirth accordingly. He talks of *Hinatma* and *Mahatma*. The former is cause of suffering having resemblance with the egoism of *Sankhya* philosophy, while *Mahatman* can be attained by the practice of the highest motive. This motive is Buddhahood. *Mahatman* means Tathagatagarabha which means the womb of Tathagata. To be more explicit, it is the treasurer or store in which the essence of Buddhahood remains concealed under the veil of *avidya*. It is also the womb of the universe. In the terms of psychology Tathagatagarbha means "the transcendental court of man coming under the bondage of *karmic* causation." Some scholars are of the view that Tathagatagarabha has correspondence to the *Paramatma* or the universal soul of the Vedantins. Despite that there is a great difference between the meaning of the *Paramatman* of the Buddhists and the *Paramatman* of the Vedantins. In the case of the former the *Paramatman* is complete tranquillity, without any form and shape. It is ocean of complete peace that has no concern to the universe at all. In the case of the latter, the *Paramatman* is creator, sustainer and destroyer of the universe.

The Buddha who had learnt the theory of soul prescribed in the Indian religious scriptures denied the existence of soul as it has been stated by the scriptures. However, he accepted consciousness instead of soul that follows one even after death. It means it is not mortal. It exists and causes the rebirth. Denial of soul of the Buddhist philosophy is fully based on the universal principle of impermanence. Once this doctrine is adopted, there is no case of the acceptance of eternality, absolute unity or supreme authority. So, there is nothing like 'Ego' or *Atman* that exists and governs. Like Shankaracharya, the Buddha believed in one Absolutism about which nothing definitely or determinately can be said. However, it is the only reality and there is nothing except it. The Buddha believed in universality of universal nature, but he denied that there is any supreme power that governs the nature. It means there is no God or supreme commander. The world is as it is. There is automation and everything is moving by losing its original shape in this continuous or endless automation. Man is the captive of his own nature that is full of *trishna*, lust, desire, etc, and he suffers because he is in ignorance. He is wrapped in the thick cover of *Avidya*.[24]

Vedantism in Buddhism

The question is whether the Buddha discovered that there is no soul. Most of his philosophical thoughts and principles are very much related to the Vedantic philosophy such as theory of *karma*, theory of death and theory of rebirth, theory of salvation, etc. An investigation made into the thoughts of the Buddha, it reveals the truth that he was not much confirmed about non-existence of soul. He, sometimes, thought that the *atman* exists and at other time he taught that *atman* does not exist. Prabhakar Mishra has rightly observed that the Buddha was of the view that *atman* exists and as "to be the receiver of misery or happiness in the successive life as the reward of his *karma*."[25] The Buddha mentioned about the existence of soul with the marked object to save man from falling into nihilism. When he taught that there is no *atman*, in the sense of a creator or perceiver or absolutely free agent, apart from conventional name given to the aggregate of the five *skandhas*, "his object was to save man from falling into the opposite heresy of externalism or Shashvatavada."[26] The Buddha knew well that common man whose intellect and understanding about God, universe and soul is vague, not sharp, would definitely fall into the category of nihilism if the doctrine of *atman* is not propagated. Perhaps under this understanding he supported the view of *atman*, but in different form. Once it is accepted that one has to go through the process of rebirth due to one's past *karmas*, then there must be something immortal like the soul being the upholder of the essence of *karmas*. Otherwise who dies and who gets birth? Who carries the essence of *karma* and who eats the fruits of *karma*? Consciousness about which the Buddha talks is a psychological term and it may dismantle with the dismantling of the body.

The existence of *atman* and Dharma of the Ego and the phenomenal world is affirmed in the sacred canon provisionally and hypothetically and never in the sense of possessing a real and permanent nature.[27] The similar views are also recorded in the *Samyutta Nikaya* of the Pali canon and Vasubandhu's own commentary on his *Abhidharmakosha Shastra*.[28] Thus, it is evident that Buddha, with a view to maintaining the middle way, preached sometimes the principles of *atman* and sometimes *anatman*. If there is salvation, who gets salvation? Who is in the body that suffers? Salvation is freedom from the material world and it is related to one who is in the captivity of the material world. It is soul that is the captive of the material world which is governed by *Maya* or *Kalchakra*. So long as the soul is not liberated, it shall have to suffer.

The Buddha followed the theory of *Sarvam Anatmam* which means 'All is Egoless' and there is no such element that is subtle and upholds individual's will, desire, his account of action and other things. There are no such things that inspire the individual to act and obtain. It is lust and desire, entanglement with the worldly affairs for pleasure that activate him and binds him to remain confined to the circle of birth and death. Buddhist philosophy has always spoken of the denial of existence of an everlasting individual soul which is reflected in numerous earlier Buddhist writings. In other religious theories soul is regarded as the most subtle non-visible element and it is difficult to differentiate it from nominal and phenomenal concept. But reality is that if existence of soul is denied, entire Mansion of Buddha Dhamma would collapse then and there.

Transmigration of Soul

In the Indian philosophy the theory of *karma* and transmigration of soul is very common. The individual gets another body in the next birth according to his *karma* and *samskara*. The supreme reality is the law of change and that is causality. The universe is governed by causality. There is no chaotic anarchy or capricious interference. According to the Buddha, carving or lust felt in the previous life causes the birth of new individual who was to inherit the *karma* of the former one. Immortality of soul is one of the cardinal principles of all theistic religions. However, the teaching of the Buddha in this regard is unique. The Buddha denied the existence of soul in the narrow sense of the word. According to him, the narrow self-related to the individual is not the real self. The narrow self needs to be subdued and spiritualized. Transmigration posits continuity from one life-span to another. The Buddha believed in rebirth. The question is if there is no soul who takes rebirth or how rebirth is possible. The Buddha resolves this problem by the analogy of fire which maintains itself unchanged appearance yet is different at every moment. The Buddhists admit the continuity of an ever-changing identity. The seeming identity from moment to moment consists in a continuity of an ever changing identity. The individual is only a bundle of changing *skandhas*, changing from moment to moment, and from life to life, and it was only *nirvana* which could bring about their final dissolution.

Observing the transient nature of things, Buddhists reduced things and soul to forces and functions and move events and processes and adopted kinetic conception of reality. Life to them is nothing but a series of manifestations of becoming and extinctions. The Buddha repudiated the popular delusion of the individual ego. The objects with which one identifies oneself are not true self. Even body and mind are not true self. The Buddhists adopted the 'theory of non-self' which means anything perceived is not the self. Accordingly, body, feeling, perception, dispositions and consciousness, all these are not-self because nothing of them is substantial. They are appearances, empty of substance or reality. Buddhism is not a metaphysical conception, but it is a practical aspect of religion. So it does not believe in spirituality of soul.

Buddha□s View of Self-Enlightenment

The Buddha, like Shankaracharya, believed that the world is *mithya* (futile) having no permanent existence. It is made of *pancha skandhatmaka* (*rupa, vedana, sanjya, samskara, vijnana*). They are not real entities because they are ceaselessly changing. Change is there, no doubt, but continuity remains intact. Things come and go, appear and disappear, but the process of coming and going or appearing and disappearing in different form remains static. *Chit* (inner-consciousness) of common man governs human activities and behaviours either good or bad. Theravada tradition believes that *chit* is full of *cetasikas* as quality of *chit* due to which it is considered *kushala* or *akushala*. To observe *chit*'s qualities and human activities one stand above it being pure neutral. Question is who stands above it? The Hindu philosophy states that it is soul that stands above all in human body. Soul is the base or rather upholder of consciousness, mind and other organs of the body. Consciousness is the quality of soul. It is soul that supplies energy to all and give light to wisdom. Until one reaches to soul or realizes it closely, he cannot understand reality nor may he obtain salvation. In Buddhism, it is consciousness that is upholding essence of human *karma* and until it is destroyed because it is not permanent, liberation is not possible. It contains the seed of rebirth because the *samskara* is there having the essence of past *karmas*. Action ends, not the imprint of action which is printed on consciousness in the form of *samskara*. Thus, *samskara* is the nature of a being. It is formed out of actions or behaviours. Good *karma* means good *samskara* and bad *karma* means bad *samskara*. The individual falling prey to the lust and *trishna* indulges in prohibited *karmas* with the result that he gathers bad *samskaras* which not only causes rebirth but also brings about miseries and troubles in the present birth. On the other hand, Vedanta, too, takes the *samskara* into the account, but it talks of soul that stands above it, and it cannot be destroyed.

According to the Vedantic philosophy, self-consciousness of the Self is integrally related to the Absolute. So Self and Absolute is one. They are united, but it does not mean that heterogeneous factors are brought or bonded together. It means that there is the need to know the two which are originally one. Separation is due to ignorance. Once the *avidya* that has covered Self (*atman*), is removed, its union with the Absolute that is already there, will soon be visualized. There is also the need to know that these two elements that are basically one, is not different or separate. It seems separate due to effect of continuous *samskara* gathered in different births. To think that the self dies with the death of body is *avidya*. So once it is firmly realized that soul is without death and eternal, the ignorance disappears. There is no Absolute outside, but it exists within the soul. That is called self-realization. All animate and inanimate things between heaven and earth are nothing, but shadow of Self. This is the fact that the Buddha found within the Self. When emphasis is laid down on the self, the whole universe is self and when emphasis is shifted to the universe, the self will be submerged into the universe and there will be no such thing as the self. This is the merger of self into the Absolute. That is called salvation or *nirvana*. *Nibbana* in Buddhism is complete merger of individual identity into the fathomless ocean of eternity where there is nothing.

To attain this enlightenment is the vital concern of the seeker of the self-conscious or seeker of the truth. This stage can be achieved through meditation. What the Buddha achieved through meditation is self-enlightenment. The difference between the religion of prayer and the religion of self-enlightenment lies in the fact that the former finds it outside the self while the latter finds it within the self. The Buddha found it within the self without prayer and ritual of *karmakanda*. He applied the method of meditation and went deep into the ocean of knowledge. So he became Buddha, which means the embodiment of absolute reality. The first man that ever found the absolute within himself was Shakyamuni, the Buddha. Therefore, Shakyamuni was at once a man and the Buddha.

Absolute Truth According to Buddha and Vedanta

The Buddha saw two aspects of Absolute Truth – the first, universal, non-manifested, all pervasive, free, independent and untouched by anything, and the second manifested through creation, dependent, and concealed. It is dependent on material world not for its energy, but for its reflection. It is concealed in the cover of ignorance due to lack of real wisdom. Describing about the nature of the Absolute Truth the *Bhagavad Gita* states that it is *nirankara* (shapeless) that lies beyond the perception of the senses, all pervading, inconceivable unchanging, fixed and unmovable.[29] Every living being from the amoeba to Brahma is endowed with such light of absolute truth in the centre of the heart. This is another matter that unenlightened one is ignorant about it. Once ignorance is removed, the reflection of the light is clearly visible. To remove ignorance means to apply the prescribed methods. The cover of ignorance is too hard to penetrate into and too difficult to overcome. In the *Bhagavad Gita* the way prescribed is either to pray God with full devotion or to know the Absolute Truth through meditation. The truth that is manifested or unmanifested is one and indivisible. It appears different due to ignorance. Once ignorance is away, both aspects of truth unites together as the sky surrounded in a jar merges into the sky after destruction of the jar and becomes one. After getting full realization, the self residing in the body merges into Absolute Truth forever since there is neither ego nor individuality. The individual becomes universal and universal becomes individual. Individual's thoughts, actions and behaviours all become universal. He is now for everyone because he sees himself in everyone. The

Buddha obtaining self-enlightenment became Buddha and the only purpose of his life was to release ignorant people from darkness and worldly miseries, and lead them towards the light of absolute wisdom. Visualizing the absolute Truth the individual Gautam became the universal Buddha.

Shrikant is also of the view that in the religion of prayer, man seeks to be emancipated from the suffering of the world and enjoy a beautiful life through reliance on the Absolute Being termed as God. But in the religion of self-enlightenment man strive to realize the Absolute within his individual self. Both in the religion of prayer and the religion of self-enlightenment the central idea is the Absolute (God in Christianity, Islamism and Hinduism and Buddha in Buddhism). Describing the difficulty to be faced in the self-realisation, Shrikant says; "But in the world of ours, we cannot expect this aspiration to be gratified. Consequently, man tries to seek a solution by conjuring the Absolute (Buddha or God). That which cannot be realized in the world of ours must then be realized in the realms of God or Buddha. Thus, we prostrate ourselves before the Absolute."[30]

The method that the Buddha prescribed to achieve *nirvana* through meditation, not prayer, is not easy for everyone. It is a difficult path. It is the path of *sanyasis* or yogis who devote the whole life in penance and meditation living aside the family and renouncing the world. For common man who lacks understanding, the path that is the easiest is either the path of *Karma Yoga* or the path of *Bhakti Yoga* (devotion). One can reach to Absolute Truth or God by performing right duties in the name of Almighty or one may also attain salvation by devoting his life in the service of God. Great Vaishnavas like Ramanujam and Chaitanya Mahaprabhu recommended the easiest path of *Bhakti* wherein salvation may be achieved through chanting and singing Harinam like 'Hare Krishna

Hare Ram'. But the Buddha who did not believe in any concept of super-being that governs the universe, taught that man has to attain the stage through his own self effort. He has to learn the way and be determined to achieve salvation. The ways suggested by the Buddha are Four Noble Truths and Eight-fold Nobel Ways.

Thus, the Buddha's enlightenment is the acquisition of right universal wisdom capable of seeing things as they are. He reached to the spiritual stage which was open and free world where everything was embraced and the distinction of self and non-self had been done away with. "The shell of egoistic self had been smashed. His eyes (divine) saws things as they are. The opposition which hitherto had stood between the self and non-self disappeared. He was the only being in the whole universe who became one with the whole universe. He attained such a conscious and became Buddha."[31]

Concept of *Nirvana* in Buddhism

The primary postulate on which the entire ethical system of Buddhism rests is the fundamental premise that there is a supreme end in human life, and that all rational and intelligent persons ought to aim at achieving *nirvana*. This goal, the *summum bonum* of Buddhism, is referred to the Pali sutras as *Nibbana* (*nirvana*). It is the goal which is aimed at, either remotely or immediately, by both lay man and recluse (*bhikhu*). The religious or holy life is said to be lived to achieve this goal. The goal of *nirvana* is the guiding principle for moral action in Buddhism. *Nibbana* itself is conceived as a state of moral perfection and purification. It is defined in the *suttas* as the elimination of lust and greed, the elimination of hatred and the elimination of delusion. It is characterized as the highest *kushala* which means goodness. Since goodness is the base of

Nibbana, in Buddhism emphasis has been laid to be good in the life forever. Later on, the term *Nibbana* was interpreted in metaphysical term. It has been interpreted as a transcendental reality, beyond any form of conceptualization or logical thinking. This has been largely the result of the influence of the absolutistic and transcendental views stemming from the Vedic tradition. Dr Radhakrishnan, observing the fact in this regard rightly says:

> *Nirvana* is an eternal condition of being, for it is not *samskara*, or what is made or put together, which is impermanent. It continues, while its expressions change. This is what lies behind the *skandhas*, which are subject to birth and decay. The illusion of becoming is founded on the reality of *nirvana*. Buddha does not attempt to define it, since it is the root principle of all so it is indefinable.[32]

The Buddha never spoke of *Nibbana* as the metaphysical ground that explains the empirical universe. Metaphysical concepts such as God, Barman, Alman, Purusha, presenting ultimate metaphysical grounds as explanations, are discouraged in Buddhism. Dr Radhakrishnan furthers states:

> *Nirvana* is timeless existence, and so Buddha must admit the reality of timelessness. There is a being at the back of all life which is unconditioned, above all empirical categories, something which does not give rise to any effect and is not the effect of anything else.[33]

Thus, such concepts at describing the nature of Buddhist *Nibbana* have transformed its character from being a concept having ethical and psychological significance to being a concept having metaphysical and ontological significance, and this seems to be contrary to what was intended by the Buddha. This view has resulted in the interpretation of Buddha's *Nibbana* as an escapist and life denying ideal which involves the most radical form of salvation doctrine. Some have gone to the extent of saying that the highest spiritual attainment in Buddhism transcends morality together. For instance, Tachibana says that one who attains *Nibbana* is free from such distinctions such as good and evil, pleasantness and unpleasantness, purity and impurity on so on. When one reaches this stage of culture, distinctive ideas will be absolutely abolished. In his own words:

> He (Buddha) has reached the mental condition where there is not consciousness of moral, aesthetical, or logical distinction; the relative ideas therefore of good and evil, pleasure and pain, agreeableness and disagreeableness, right and wrong are all annihilated for him.[34]

However, there is the Buddhist scholars who deny that in Buddhist culture of *nirvana* transcendency has preceded or finished morality. Morality is still the base of Buddhism. The scheme of moral evaluation in Buddhism can be clearly seen to be relative to the goal of *Nibbana*. In the moral evaluation of persons, one who has attained *Nibbana* is judged to be the most praiseworthy person. A disciple who has confidence in the Buddha and who has his ultimate aim in attainment of *Nibbana* is described as a noble disciple. The *Dhammapada* describes the *arahantas* the highest being extend, as far as the end of the realm of becoming, the *arahantas* are the highest, the supreme being in the universe.

Buddhist Doctrine of *Sunyata*

The Buddhist Doctrine of *Sunyata* is related to the doctrine of nothingness. Entire edifice of Buddhism is built on the doctrine of *Sunyata*. *Sunyata* or emptiness means no form, nor feeling, nor perception, nor impulse, nor consciousness, no eyes, ears, nose tongue, body, mind; no form, sounds, smells, tastes, touches or object of mind; no sight element, and so forth. There is no ignorance, no extinction of ignorance. There is neither decay nor death. There is no extinction of decay and death. There is no suffering, nor origination, no stopping, no path. There is no cognition, no attainment and non-attainment. In *sunyata* a Bodhisattva resides there because of his non-attainment through having relied on the perfection of wisdom. He dwells there without coverings. In the absence of thought coverings he has not been made to tremble; he has overcome what can upset; and in the end he attains to *nirvana*. Thus, it is clear that a Bodhisattva, while reaching to the stage of *sunyata* is not affected by any thought, any action, any thinking, any worldly essences and anything. He stands or lives without attachment. Things are around him, but to him it seems that there is nothing except himself. This is in the Buddhist term, in fact, a state of *nirvana* which means go above the attraction of the mundane world and its influences. *Nirvana* means to remain in absolute emptiness where there is nothing except all pervasive tranquillity. All those who appear as Buddhas in the three periods of time, are fully awaken to the outmost, right and perfect enlightenment because they have relied on the Perfection of Wisdom. Therefore one should know the *prajnaparamita* as the great spell, the spell of great knowledge the outmost spell, allayer of all suffering, in truth for what could go wrong. By the *prajnaparamita* has this spell been delivered.

Emptiness and Nihilism

The Western scholars who developed deep interest in the Buddhist philosophies regarded that the Buddhist concept of Emptiness is equivalent to the concept of nihilism, but it is not so. Both Emptiness and nihilism are different and they differ in their basic conception. What is nihilism? Nihilism is the branch of philosophy dealing with the transcendental concept of absolute reality, and it concludes that there is no such absolute truth that exists somewhere. Since nothing definitely and confirmly can be said about transcendental truth or absolute truth, it is futile to talk about it. According to it, reality is unknowable, that nothing exists, that nothing meaningful can be communicated about the world. Since the senses of human faculty is unable to comprehend such absolute truth (if it exists), it is all meaningless to talk about it and derive conclusion related to it. It is convenient to accept that there is nothing. So, nothingness is the basic concept of the Nihilist's philosophy regarding existence of God or ultimate truth. They are sceptical about this truth. On the other hand, the Buddhist philosophical concept of ultimate truth is quite opposite to that of nihilism. It thinks that ultimate reality is there and it is knowable. There is a clear-cut ontological basis for phenomena and that we can communicate and drive useful knowledge from it about the world. So emptiness of Buddhism cannot be confused with nihilism. Emptiness is not non-existence and it is not non-reality.

Inherent Existence

The Maḥayana school of Buddhism developed 'dependent ordination' which means nothing is absolute alone. Existence either in physic or without physic is not alone. Something exists in combination of several elements. It may be inferred that mental experience requires sensory experience or respectively memory of sensory experience. Sensory experience in turn requires the body. If one carries through a thought experiment and examined whether each of the *skandhas* is able to exist without the other four, one finds that this is not possible. The latter four aggregates all depend upon the body. Without the brain and the nervous system there is no consciousness, no sensation, nor perception and no mental formulations. On the other hand, we cannot imagine the body to function without the mind. The body and the mind depend upon each other. So the five *skandhas* depend upon each other. That is congregation. It may be concluded that none of the *skandhas* is absolute or may stand alone. Body, sensations, perceptions, mental formation and consciousness are interrelated. Experiences emerge after the interaction of five *skandhas*. Just as object, experience are conditioned by the inter play of multiple phenomena. Experience has no inherent existence either. The percept is the mental expression; the subject is the owner of it, the thinker; and the object is that which causes the mental impression. This threefold divisions seem so natural to us that it reflected in the grammar of most human language. We perceive the separation of subject, percept and object as real, because mind attributes an owner to experience and thought. This owner is 'self', the subject, the centre of consciousness, the supposed psychological entity. Surprisingly, this identity remains completely undetectable. Body, feeling, precipitation and mental formation are not the self. Consciousness is not the self either, otherwise it would follow that the self temporarily ceases to existence during unconsciousness, for instance during the deep sleep.

Is it true that self is independent of supporting the surrounding world? According to Buddhism, obviously it is not. The self cannot exist in mental vacuum, a world devoid of sense impressions, thought and mental images. It seems there is no basis of an independent entity. It seems more that the self is an emergent phenomenon arising from the application of complex interpretative schemes to perception. In particular; it arises from the conceptual division between subject, object and percept. Through introspection it is possible to realize that the 'self' is not fundamental. It is created by the mind through identification and discernment. The 'self is itself a mental formation – a product of mind. It is therefore, empty of inherent existence.

Concept of *Moksha* in Hinduism

The concept of *nirvana* originated in Hinduism and is similar to the Buddhist concept, meaning to blow out, extinguishing the flame. Conflict in understanding this term has lead to divergent views of Buddha and Buddhism. Some Buddhists worship the Buddha as a divine being; others Buddhists view him as an ordinary man. Tibetan Buddhists, see the Dalai Lama as the reincarnated Buddha, who was not annihilated into *nirvana* but chose to come back and help those still here. *Encyclopaedia Britannica* states:

> The living process is linked to a fine burning. Its remedy is the extinction of the fire of illusion, passion and cravings. The Buddha, the enlightened one, is one who is no longer kindled or enflamed. Many poetic terms are used to describe the state of the enlightened human beings – the harbour of refuge, the cool cave, the place of bliss, the further shore. The term that has become famous in the West is *nirvana*, translated as dying out-that is, dying out in the hit of the fierce fire of lust, anger, and delusion. But *nirvana* is not extinction, and indeed the craving for annihilation or known existence was expressly repudiated by the Buddha. Buddhists search not for mere cessation but for salvation. Though *nirvana* is often presented negatively as 'release from suffering,' it is more accurate to describe it in a more positive fashion: as an ultimate goal to be sought and cherished.[35]

The view of *nirvana* contrasts with the Brahman Hindu views those teach that *nirvana* means to be united with the universal soul. The Buddha believed according to some, that the soul elements along with individual identity are extinguished at *nirvana*.

The philosophies of Hinduism related to *nirvana* or *moksha* is different. It is soul, the integral particle of Almighty God and surrounded in mysteries as well as ignorance, is released. *Moksha* that is complete merger of individual soul into the Absolute *Brahman* is a process that is achieved through various ways, such as having complete faith in God and absolute surrender to God's mercy, realizing God fully, controlling actions and performing pious duties in the interest of the society as a whole etc.[36] Individuals living in the world are in constant ignorance. They are far away from reality with the result that their activities are impure that cause circle of birth and death. The *Bhagavad Gita* stating the fact says: "all living entities are born into delusion, bewildered by dualities arisen from desire and hate." Regarding liberation of the soul it further says:

> Persons who have acted piously in previous lives and in this life and whose sinful actions are completely eradicated, are freed from the dualities and delusion, and they engage themselves in My service with determination.[37]

Performing pious duties and knowing God fully, the person never comes back to this world. It is evident from the statement of the Gita. It says:

> After attaining Me, the great souls, who are yogis in devotion, never return to this temporary world, which is full of miseries, because they have attained the highest perfection.[38]

It further says:

> From the highest planet in the material world down to the lowest, all are places of misery wherein repeated birth and death take place. But one who attains to My abode, never takes birth again.[39]

Regarding the God's supreme abode the *Bhagavad Gita* says:

> That which the Vedantists describe as unmanifested and infallible, that which is known as the supreme destination, that place from which, having attained it, one never returns – that is My supreme abode.[40]

Thus, it is quite obvious that in the Hindu religious philosophy *moksha* means rising above the worldly desires, lusts, affections and having everlasting association with noble principles set by Almighty. Those who have complete faith in God and have totally devoted to God's principles, later or sooner avail *moksha*. A divine consciousness is needed that leads one to *nirvana*. It is said:

> By virtue of the divine consciousness of the previous life, he automatically becomes attracted to the yogic principles – even without seeking them. Such an inquisitive transcendentalist stands always above the ritualistic principles of the scripture.[41]

To avail *moksha* is a continuous process that continues even after death of the individual. The efforts applied in this direction never ends. In the next birth, consciousness having religious performances or devotional acts remains intact. *moksha* needs purity of life. It is an understanding. It is the final goal of mankind. It releases one from the shackle of death and birth forever. It releases man from all types of worldly sufferings forever. *Moksha* means to avail the status where is complete peace, no quos, no repentance, no birth, no death, no fear, no worry, no scarcity etc. It is a status of reaching to the point where there is no variation in thought and action. In the *Bhagavad Gita* such status is known as *Sthitaprajna:*

> Whose happiness is within, who is active and rejoices within, and whose aim in inward is actually the perfect mystic. He is liberated in the Supreme, and ultimately he attains the Supreme.[42]

Again:

> Those who are beyond the dualities that arise from doubts, whose minds are engaged within, who are always busy for the welfare of living beings, and who are free.[43]

Thus, it is evident that the concept of *nirvana* of Buddhism has too much similarity with that of Hinduism. In Hinduism the concept has largely been explained. Both the concepts related to *nirvana* are similar in the sense that both talk of freedom from this life or to get rid of the circle of birth and death forever. Both emphasize on the renunciation and the life of purification where there is no lust, no desire, no worldly willingness, no attachment, no greed and no falsification. Both believe that there is continuity of life even after death and one has to harvest the fruits of actions what one does. To attain *nirvana* wisdom is required that comes out of meditation. *Nirvana* is a status of complete peace where there is neither any upheaval, nor any noise, neither beginning nor end. To both the Dharma the mundane world is illusion having no permanent essence. According to the Buddha Dhamma there is no any Supreme God whose mercy or kindness is needed to avail *nirvana*. Rather it is attained with the self-help of the individual through the path of meditation. While the Hindu Dharma believes that *nirvana* cannot be achieved without God's mercy. Hence not only faith in God is needed but blessing of God is also essential.

Conclusion

India has been the land of metaphysical prosperity, philosophical insight, religious as well as ritual performances and a place for divine incarnation. It has produced a number of renowned rishis, maharishis, munis, seers, saints, philosophers, thinkers, social reformers and poets of eminent significance who provided new expanding base of Indian

Vedantic philosophy. No doubt, Hinduism, in course of time, inclined towards Brahminical cult of ritualism and formalism paving the way for the growth of blind religious faith and superstitions, but it has been the most prosperous and dominant religion of the country. However, it never remained inimical to other religions. That is why religions like Buddhism, Jainism, Islamism, Sikhism, Christianity, etc, availed the supportive circumstances to grow and prosper in India. India is known as Deva Bhumi (land of gods) because big divine personalities like Lord Shri Krishna, Rama, Mahavira, Gautam Buddha, etc, were born who taught the world the lesson of humanity, new way of life leading towards happiness and eternal bliss.

The highest philosophy of Vedanta related to transcendentalism and Absolute Truth emerged in India and it is still the founding base of eternal Hindu Dharma. Various religious scriptures like Vedas, Srutis, Smritis, Brahmanas, Puranas, Upanishads, *Bhagavad Gita, Ramayana, Mahabharata*, etc, emanated from the philosophy of Vedanta and are the expansion of the Vedantic philosophies. The philosophy of Vedanta, in the nutshell, talks the Absolute Reality that is eternal, *nirankara, nirvese*, omnipotent, omnipresent, all pervasive, all powerful and final abode of origin and demolition of everything in the creation of mundane world of ours. Vedanta basically is related to the concept of God, Soul and World. The creation (world), according to Vedantic philosophy, is nothing but reflection of the supreme energy of the all-pervasive Absolute *Brahman*. So, the mundane world is not real, but momentary, illusive, being the subject of decay and disappearance. What one talks of soul is an integral particle of God that is immortal, illuminative, energetic, stable, and as pure as God and base as well as primary cause of creation. It neither gets birth nor does it die because it is eternal.

The teachings of the Buddha went against the grain of Hindu psychology and it failed to take an abiding root in India. Hinduism was based on *Shabdabramana* (the Vedas) where the Buddha repudiated all authority and traditions. The Hindus were prone to metaphysics while the Buddhists showed indifference towards it. The existence or non-existence of God did not at all interest the Buddha as, according to him, man was the architect of his own future. There is no place for ritualism in Buddhism. Ritualism was deep rooted in the Hindu's mind that is still prevailing in each and every Hindu household. The Buddha's conception of Dhamma was not sufficiently concrete for practical purposes. The result was obvious. The Buddha gradually came to be defied and Buddhism was very much influenced by Hindu thought. On the other hand, Buddhism, too, exercised, almost great overwhelming influence on Hinduism. It gave birth to neo-Hinduism which absorbed the best elements of Buddhism. It was the result of that influence that the Shaivas borrowed the monastic and contemplative elements of Mahayana *Sramanas* and the Buddha was given a place in Hindu pantheon as the Tenth Avatara (incarnation) of Lord Vishnu. Mahayana was built on wholesale borrowing from Hinduism, and this process of intermingling went on until in the sixth century AD. In the words of Upendra Thakur, "Buddhism was borrowing even from *Saktism*, the most esoteric form of Hinduism. It ultimately gave rise to Tantricism and Vajrayana with the result that the feminine divinities now found their way into the Buddhist pantheon."[44] The Hindu society did not adopt Buddhism as a separate religion from Hinduism, but it borrowed a lot of things from the former to make Hinduism more effective. Adoption of the Buddha as an incarnation of the Lord Vishnu reveal the fact that the Hindus refused to practice Buddhism, but agreed to worship the Buddha.

Notes and References

1. Smith, BA, 1924, *Early History of India*, Oxford, pp 49-50.
2. Upendra Thakur, "Buddhism in Bihar: Past and Present", in PN Ojha (ed), *Homage to Bhikhu Jagadish Kashyap*, published by Nava Nalanda Mahavihara, Bihar, 1986, p 2.
3. Rapson, *Ancient India*, p 63. Also see, Upendra Thakur, *History of Mithila*, p 97. GC Pande, *The Origin of Buddhism*, p 309.
4. Ramachandra Ghosh, 1988, *History of Hindu Civilization*, op cit, p 210.
5. GC Pande, *The Origin of Buddhism*, Chapter- II.
6. *Buddhist India*, pp 155-56.
7. Ibid.
8. Ramachandra Ghosh, 1988, *History of Hindu Civilization*, op cit, 212.
9. Ibid, 213.
10. Weber, von A, *Indische Studien*, I, p 296.
11. *Rigveda* (I, 162,163); *Shatapatha Brahmana*, XIII, *Katyayana Shastra*, XX, 6, 78.
12. *Katyayana Shastra*, I. 102, 11.
13. Ramachandra Ghosh, 1988, op cit, p 220. Also see, *Ashvalayana Grihya Sutra*, IV, 9.
14. Weber, von A, *Indische Studien*, III, p 111.
15. *Prachina Tirthamala Samgraha*, I, p 4.
16. *A History of Indian Philosophy*, III, p 537 *also see* p 528ff.
17. Ashvaghosha, *Buddhacharita*, XI, 59.
18. Maheep Singh, "Guru Nanak: Bridge Across all Paths", *The Times of India* 14th November, 2000.
19. Maha Thera, Narada, *Buddhism in a Nutshell*, pp 35-57.
20. Quoted in Sarvapalli Radhakrishnan's Foreword in *2500 Years of Buddhism*, Bapat, PY (ed), Publications Division, Ministry of Information and Broadcasting, Government of India, New Delhi (sixth reprint), 1959, p vii.
21. Ibid, p viii.
22. Ibid, p ix.

23. Nagarjuna in the Commentary on the *Prajnaparamita Sutra*.
24. Ibid.
25. Prabhakar Mishra, "The Doctrine of Selflessness (*Sarvam Anataman*)" in Rabindra Pant (ed), *Buddhism in Universal Perspective,* 2001, Nava Nalanda Mahavihara, Bihar, p 61.
26. Ibid.
27. Dharmapalacarya, in his commentary on *Vijnanamatra Shastra*.
28. *Bhagavad Gita*, 12/ 3-4.
29. Ibid.
30. Shrikant Singh, "Zen Buddhism", in Pant, RB (ed), *Buddhism in Universal Perspective*, Nava Nalanda Mahavihara, Bihar, 2001, pp 203-04.
31. Shrikant Singh, "Zen Buddhism", in Pant, RB (ed), *Buddhism in Universal Perspective*, op cit, p 204.
32. S Radhakrishnan, *Indian Philosophy*, London, George Allen & Unwin, 1929, Vol I, p 449.
33. Ibid, p 452.
34. Shundo Tachibana, *The Ethics of Buddhism*, Colombo: The Buddha Sahitya Sabha, 1943, pp 37-38.
35. *Encyclopaedia Britannica*, 2004, Nirvana.
36. *Bhagavad Gita*, Chapter 7, Verse- 27.
37. *Bhagavad Gita*, Chapter 7, Verse- 27.
38. *Bhagavad Gita*, Chapter 7, Verse- 27.
39. Ibid, Chapter 6, Verse-44. Ibid, Chapter 5, Verse- 25.
40. Ibid, Verse- 25.
41. Ibid, Chapter II, Verse- 71.
42. Ibid, Verse- 25.
43. Ibid, Verse- 25.
44. Upendra Thakur, "Buddhism in Bihar, Past and Present", in PN Ojha (ed) *Homage to Bhikhu Jagadish Kashyap*, op cit, p 16.

9

Conclusion

Veda means knowledge. The Vedas which have been handed down by the early Indo-Aryans carry a vast treasury of knowledge related to the wonder of universe, its origin, its expansion, its infinity, its forces, its powers comprising of various gods, goddesses and supernatural beings, their nature, mechanism of the universe as a whole. The Vedas talk of laws, order and thought of Divine Beings. The Vedas contain the thread which links the present with the past. It mentions about the most convincing religion of antiquity that throws sufficient light on the rise and growth of various religions in human world. In the words of Ramachandra Ghosh, "To the Vedas must be attached an undying interest and an ever increasing value not only for their greatest antiquity, but also for the immense flood of light which they throw on the primitive state of Indo-Aryan society, Indo-Aryan speech and general mythology."[1] The Vedas are the primeval sources of Indo-Aryans' theological, philosophical, moral, ethical, social, religious and political understanding. They abound in the knowledge of theology, philosophy, astronomy, geometry, etc. Ramachandra agrees that "In process of time, the Vedic religion, whatever it was, has become through the corruptions and prejudices, of a most revolving type, of successive ages a heterogeneous medley of theology, philosophy and science."[2] The age in which the Vedas and their appendages were produced, has exercised the blandest influence upon all succeeding periods of Indian history. Every later branch of literature is closely connected with the Vedic traditions. The religious and moral ideas have been derived from them, and the Indo-Aryan life, in all its aspects, has been moulded by traditionally precepts. Even today, the influence of the Vedas and religious scriptures related to them has tremendous impact upon the mind and heart of the most of the Hindu community. In fact, Vedas, Vedic religion and Vedic civilization are in their blood.

The rishis and munis of Indo-Aryans were sensitive, inquisitive and penetrative in their approach. From the beginning, they were interested in searching and knowing the nature if the universe, primal cause of its origin, the systems of its working and the power and energy enshrined in each atom of the universe. They devoted their whole of the life in penance and mediation sitting in the dense forests or in the mountains to quench their curiosities to find out the answer of the questions that agitated and astonished their mind. In that course of search and research, they produced Vedas and other Vedic literature which talk of God, soul and universe. Finding out the divine truth related to our mundane world as well as vast universe, they presented the picture that help one to know about the origin of the universe and working of its various systems. They also prescribed certain ways and means to follow for the betterment of human life. The culture and civilization founded by ancient Indo-Aryans were full of highly developed cultural ethos, moral values and social behaviours. The social structure based on four *varna* systems was established discovering the human qualities and their usefulness in social orders. They discovered the ultimate truth and its role in creation of the universe. Their deep thoughts and thinking in the form of Vedas lay down the foundation of Vedic religion and Hindu Dharma. It is Vedic religion that came to be known as Sanatana Dharma which means it is eternal. Since it emerged among the Indo-Aryans who were called Hindus, the Sanatana Dharma is called Hindu Dharma also. The Hindu Dharma is rooted in Vedic philosophy that mostly talks of God, soul and universe. According to Vedic rishis, God is the concept that can be felt, not described. It is omnipotent and omnipresent supreme energy spread in the most subtle form all over the universe being the primary cause of creation. It is that eternal energy known as God about whom whatsoever is said is not final and complete because of His vastness and vagueness. However, that unseen power is the sole base of creation. What one talks of soul is spiritual energy being the integral part of God. Like God soul is immortal. Soul is divine subtle presentation in entire universe that is the base of universal actions and activities in the manifested world. Soul is the base of living beings.

So far the creation of universe is concerned, nothing definitely can be said when and how it came into existence. Creation is a mystery. According to the Vedanta, it is manifestation of Supreme *Brahman*. In other words, universe is reflection of supreme energy of the Absolute *Brahman* that is unlimited ocean of energy, light and consciousness. That, being unmanifested, serves as the primal cause of manifestation of the universe. Creation is called as *lila* of great Supreme *Brahman* who desired to be many (*akoham bahushyam*). First of all, He created *para-prakriti* (Superior nature) and *apara-prakriti* (inferior nature). The former is subtle and the latter is physical. Creation of the universe came out of these two set of *prakriti*. The *apara-prakriti* is inferior, impure, productive of evils and cause of the bondage of the *Maya*. It is evident in the statement of the *Bhagavad Gita* that says, "Know that all beings have their birth in these (two *prakriti*). So I am the source and dissolution of the whole universe."[3] It is further said that,"Know Me, O Partha, as the eternal seed of all beings; I am the intelligence of the intelligent, the bravery of the brave."[4] Regarding the status of creation Lord Krishna says that "In Me all this (creation) is woven as clusters of gems on a string."[5] Creation is in *Maya* (Illusion, ignorance) which itself is God's production. It is *Maya* which has covered divine eyes of living being. All the living-beings of creation are in bondage of *Maya*. They cannot get liberation without especial mercy of God that can be achieved through devotion and prayer.

Universe that is the creation of *Para-Brahma* is infinite, mysterious and the indicator of God's endlessness, infinity, wisdom, astonishment, wonderment and greatness. Creation has its origin, existence and destruction. Creation is in time and space. At the time of total annihilation (*Mahapralaya*) entire creation along with its objects disappears. At the desire of God new creation takes place. Describing about the status after total annihilation of creation *Matsya Purana* says that after disappearance of entire creation entire movable and immovable objects of the universe disappeared into vast and dense cover of darkness where nothing could be viewed except blank and dark sky. Neither its objects could be speculated nor could anything be known. There was no sign of anything. All elements had disappeared with their objects. New creation began after long time when God desired to be many. With a view to bringing about new creation, God in the form of great divine light penetrating through darkness emerged. The darkness disappeared soon with the appearance of God alone.[6] Describing the same fact, *Shiva Purana* says that at the time when entire world (creation) along with its movable and immovable objects had disappeared, there was nothing except complete darkness. Neither the sun was seen nor the moon. There was no sign of any planate and celestial body. Day and night were traceless. No essence of water, earth, air and fire was available. Except sky covered with darkness nothing was available. Even words had disappeared. All elements of creation including *Panchamahabhuta* and *Panch-Tanmatra*, mind, wisdom, consciousness and ego had gone away from the sight. There was no indication of any direction in the space. Dense darkness had spread all over the sky where nothing could be seen or imagined. At this moment great imperishable God, the primal cause of creation and dissolution, appeared with the desire to be many in the form of divine light from which new creation took place. The energy that appeared automatically came to be known as *para-prakriti*, and from *para-prakriti apara-prakriti* came into existence along with its three *gunas – Sattva, Rajas* and *Tamas*. The *para-prakriti* being the symbol of first reflected energy was called as *Adi Shakti* (first energy) which served as the root cause of creation comprising of *Trimurti* (Brahma, Vishnu and Mahesh) who began the process of creation.[7]

Brahma, Vishnu and Mahesh are three different shapes of same God. They appear different for the sake of creation, but in reality they are expanded force of one Almighty God. In the *Bhagavata Purana* God says "I am the first and prime cause of creation of the universe. I am *Paramatma*, witness of everything, soul of all, self-illuminated and without name. Accepting my three-fold *gunas* (*Sattva, Rajas* and *Tamas*)…. I use to create the world, protect it and destroy…. I have adopted the names like Brahma, Vishnu and Mahesh for the sake of creation. We Brahma, Vishnu and Mahesh are the same."[8] According to the *Vishnu Purana*, the whole universe is His incarnation.[9] When the universe had totally disappeared along with its all objects and there was nothing except complete darkness, Lord Vishnu appeared in the form of splendid divine light that soon spread over the sky removing darkness. Thereafter, several spheres of *mandalas* (layers) including heaven and earth came into being.

The Vedic philosophy is not only the oldest human thought on the earth but it is also the scientific and convincing philosophical accounts related to the mundane and transcendental world. It talks of both manifested and non-manifested *Brahma* (*Nirguna-Nirakara* and *Saguna-Sakara* Brahma). The Vedas are religion in the sense that it claims to have discovered the ultimate power (God). The Vedas also present the accounts related to appearance of different gods and goddesses and their role in the universe. The Vedic civilization is the oldest one which teaches people how to live, what to do and what not to do. The Vedic religion and civilization are universally applicable to all human beings since they bring people near to God on the one hand, and assist people to make their life meaningful and prosperous on the other. Vedic religion is secular in the sense that it is based on absolute truth. The social system established by Vedanta is reality whether one accepts it or not. That is why the truth mentioned in the Vedas have been highly appreciated and highlighted by several modern thinkers and philosophers of the West. For instance, Max Muller, a great German scholar, highlighting the significance of Vedic philosophies said that except in Vedas there was no culture and civilization on the earth which could produce such a dignified richest philosophy. Herbert Spencer said that Even those migrating Aryans had by then developed such a high state of civilization and culture that they were able to face and conquer the other races in course of time to establish their sway over the whole of Asia and Europe.[10]

This is another fact that, the Vedic religion falling in the hands of fundamentalist Hindu Brahmins who later developed the doctrines of *karmakandas* based on blind ritualism as well as formalism got perverted and became the sole property of the Hindu Brahmins. The practice of *karmakandas* brought about number of social evils that damaged and maligned the purity of Vedic religion. However, the originality of Vedic religion is still fresh, and Vedic philosophy, if it is understood in the right perspective, there is no literature on this planet of ours that can supersede metaphysics.

Religion in the spiritual sense is an intuitional or philosophical vision which stands above the personified religion. If a religion is a faith in God, it is only one, but its essence and rebuts reflect through various religious sects carrying the same message of love and benevolence. A religion is not the property of a particular group or a community or a sect. It is universal, uniformed, comprehensive and applicable to all in the similar degree of goodness. A religion in the real sense is the highest spiritual knowledge which "cannot be bought nor can it be acquired from books." A religion is a way to God as well as man's relations with his fellow beings. In the opinion of Swami Vivekananda "religion cannot be found anywhere except in the core of the human heart. It is not a monopolistic dominance of a particular religious community or a group. Rather it is a system of belief, practice and philosophical values concerned with definition of the sacred, the comprehension of the life and salvation from the problems of human existence.... Religious traditions are the results of man's attempt to capture and enshrine his philosophical and spiritual insights so that they are available to the individual as well as he faces life and its stresses, confusion and complexities.[11] Today, with the appearance of various sects of religion real meaning of religion is being overlooked. So-called prophets or messengers of God who have founded religions where a number of their disciples and followers with a view to expanding religious scope and influencing other joined the bracketed religion providing it sectarian base. They have provided various ways and means to adopt religion and personify God. As a result, religion has become sectarian in its character, where creed and dogmas whose primary aim is to dominate other religious sects, play vital role to polarise the society.

Hindu's Sanatana Dharma is a "people's belief and practice towards their concepts of all that is beyond man's own power and mundane knowledge."[12] Hindu Dharma is transcendental which is ultimate supernal derived from the Sanskrit text and elates to system maintenance, long term welfare and ultimate goals; universal gods and annual cyclical rites; and is derived from the knowledge of higher priests who are acknowledged to be the reservoirs of religious wisdom and learning. Another aspect of Hindu's Dharma "is pragmatic, complex, compassed of lesser, regional or local deities of various types, including the spirits of dead, the regulators of diseases, epidemic, natural disasters and community guardians."[13] Hinduism is generally believed as an amorphous body of beliefs, philosophies, worship practices and codes of conducts. It is all because Hinduism has not been studied thoroughly and carefully. The root of Hindu religion and religious philosophy is rooted in the depths of mystery which needs both patience and wisdom to penetrate into the depth and know reality. Those who have fully investigated the Hindu's doctrines of religion know better that Hinduism is not only a religion but it is also highly civilized way of living and unparallel to any other civilization of the world. The base of Hindu Dharma is not in speculation and imagination, but it is rooted in both manifested and unmanifested concept of *Brahman*, the Ultimate God, and the Primal Cause of creation, sustainer and destroyer. The scope of Hinduism is broader; the concept is larger; and the benevolence towards others is greater. Griraj Gupta rightly remarks that the very nature of Hinduism leads to a greater tolerance of other religious thoughts among its adherents as they tend to believe that the highest divine power complement each other for the well-being of the mankind.[14] He further says that the quality of reliance, absorption and respect for other alternative ways of reaching the same goals, perhaps, are the characteristics which have vitality generally in Hinduism from millennium.[15]

Religion is a faith related to the power that is ultimate and the super most. It is that supreme power that has no comparison, no limit and no dependence. It is absolute and independent. It can do anything at anytime and anywhere. This faith is found in any religion of the world. This power has been called by different names in different religions. It is called God, Allah, Akbar, Parmatma, Akal Purusha, Rama, Rahim, Krishna, Hari, etc. He is also called as Kripasindhu (ocean of kindness), Dinbandhu (brother of the poor and suppressed), and Dindayal (kindly to the poor). He is known as all powerful, all pervasive, *antrayamin* (knower of inner-soul), eternal, imperishable (*Aksharam*), omnipresent, and what not. He is the creator and sustainer of the universe. This is all people's faith who believe in God. It is also believed that God is rescuer, protector, supporter, and giver. He is the friend of those who abide by the established religion and foes of those who avoiding the path of religion, moves towards irreligion. So, He is the balancer and supreme judge who do justice according to the performances of living beings. He sends heaven to those who are true religious by faith and action and pushes down to the hell who are indulged in misdeeds falling victims to the insatiable lust and *trishna*. Being invisible, He is visible to His devotees. He is farthest and the nearest also. He is capable of doing anything. He hears without ears, sees without eyes, speaks and eats without mouth, moves without feet, and accepts without hands.

Vedanta philosophy of India is of the voice of the Indian image, philosophical base and social behaviour. The Vedas are base of Indian culture, philosophy, religion, ethical views, spiritual visions, ultimate human aims, objectives, dreams and desires. Ancient Indian religious thoughts and views are the products of Vedic philosophy which itself is based on deep meditation, logical speculation and rational interpretation. The major part of Vedic literature consists mainly of the Vedas, Brahmanas, Aranyakas, Smritis, Puranas, Upanishads, *Dharma Shastras* like *Mahabharata, Ramayana, Grihya Sutra* and the *Itihasa*. The Vedas which are four in number are the oldest Sanskrit literature of the world.

The Aryans who migrated to western-northern part of India carried with them not only rich as well as prosperous philosophical speculation but also certain religious procedures how to worship and please unseen forces. They had discovered the forces of divinity enshrined in the universe. However, their concept related to God or Ultimate Supreme Power developed gradually and slowly. While discovering such power they came across various gods and goddesses whom they recognised as different aspects of God. They came to know that these forces are in the universe to uphold creation sustaining various divine systems which keep the universe active and intact. The Vedas do not talk of worshipping procedure of God or gods. The Vedic hymns applaud them and their energies. The Vedas never classify or define the objects of worship. The objects of worship came into being when the commentators of the Vedas expressed their views. While producing the objects of worship they differed from the original Vedic concept of gods. Every object in the universe awed our earliest forefathers, and roused them from stolid wonderment to think and ponder on the greatest problems of life. In the early period of the Indo-Aryans their faith looked for the infinite in the moon, in the sun, in the sky, in the storm, and in the flash of lightening. So, they first called it the builder of the thunderbolt, the giver of the rain, the bringer of light, the bestower of food and life. At last they took them the creator, the king, the father and the God of gods. Concept of gods developed along with the development of religious thought. Hence the relationship between gods and religion is indispensable. In the words of Ramachandra, "All that we see is that they (early Aryans) felt the presence of God in every object in the universe; and that they tried to rise from nature up to nature's God. Indeed, we see a real transition from the known to the unknown, from the visible to the Invisible, from the finite to the infinite. In fact, the infinite underlies the finite."[16]

The rishis and sages of the early Indo-Aryans had fully realised that the universe is full of mysteries that tell the tale of the ultimate supreme power that stands above all beings and that is the primal cause of everything. They also visualised that the creation of the universe is not at random, but it has meaning and purpose. There are cosmic laws and systems which are constantly at work. There is cause and effect in creation. Though things of creation are not imperishable, but the process of happenings works without any pause. Things appear and disappear, but there is something that remains constantly static because there is no force of time and speed that can devour it up. It is that which is the base of creation. It remains as it is even after dissolution of whole creation. Perhaps, this is God. So God is permanent, imperishable, and indestructible.

The rishis of the Indo-Aryans penetrated into mysteries and complex innumerable systems of the universe, and discovered the Sole and Ultimate Power (God) from Whom the entire creation emanates, in Whom it resides and prospers and lastly it dissolves into the unfathomable ocean of eternity. God resides above creation. They came to know that God being involved in creation is yet far away from creation. Creation is in God, but He is not in creation as cloud is in the sky, but not the sky in the cloud. Everything is in God, but He is not in anything in the sense that He stands aloof from the creational activities. So, God is completely pure (*nirmal*), pious (*shuddham*), and without dirt (*nirvikar*). Impurities (*vikaras*) and demerits are in *prakriti* (creation), not in God. They also knew that God is infinite and limitless. It is beyond definition because mind and language have no approach to such power. People may think and talk about God, but living within their own limit. What so ever is talked about God is not final. There is something more and more which cannot be produced in any human language. So, the Vedas even call God '*na-iti... na iti...*' (this is not...this is not).

The early Indo-Aryans also discovered that from that Ultimate Source of Power intelligence, wisdom, non-illusion, patience, self-restraint, calmness, pleasure, pain, birth, death, fear, and security appears. He is the beholder of equanimity, contentment, austerity, beneficence, fame, shame etc. Everything evolves from Him. They recognised Him as the Supreme *Brahman*, the Supreme Light, Purifier Eternal, Divine *Purusha*, the Primal God, Unborn, and Omnipresent. They found Him as the Ultimate source of all glories both heavenly and unevenly. The *Bhagavad Gita* attributes *Paramatma* as *aksharam* (imperishable), *Anirdeshyam* (neither be directed nor pointed), *avyaktam* (unmanifested), *achintyam* (beyond thought and thinking), *achalam* (immovable), *sarvatragam* (all pervasive), *kutstham* (always remain as it is), and *dhurvam* (permanent). Different gods and goddesses are nothing but extension and expansion of divine glories. They all emanate from God and remain active for the sake of God only. The entire cosmic manifestations, moving and unmoving, are manifested by different activities of Supreme Godhead. What energy we witness in the universe including the sun and the moon is manifested attributes of God. Except God no one is independent. All depend upon Him.

According to the *Rigveda*, various gods like Indra, Varuna, Agni, Mitra, and others are manifested divine glories of one

God Who is alone. All the prayers and eulogies being done to *Paramatma* in different names and *rupas* (faces) by different people, gods goddesses, Gandhravas, Apsaras, etc, are being done to one God Who is alone. There is only one God who has been reflecting in the forms of gods, goddesses, Gandhrvas, Yakshas, Asuras, human beings, animals, birds and insects. According to the Vedas it is God Who being desirous of *akoham bahushyam* (Let I be expand in various forms) appeared in different forms and shapes. According to the Srutis, the great ocean of energy from that all the beings emerge, and in that they live and lastly in that they are dissolved is called God. In the *Bhagavad Gita* Lord Krishna says that "Of the Adityas I am Vishnu; of the radiances, the respondent Sun; I am Marichi of the Maruts; of the asterism, the Moon.[17] He further declares: "Of the Vedas I am the *Samaveda*, I am Vasva of Gods, and of the senses, I am the mind, I am the intelligence in living beings. And of the Rudras I am Shankara, of the Yakshas and Rakshasa the lord of wealth, and of the Vasus I am Agni, of the mountains I am the Meru."[18]

Sankhya Darshana propounded by Shankracharya talks of only one absolute God. There is nothing except the *Brahman*. To him creation or universe is not a reality, but an illusion which is *mithya* (nothing). It is *Maya* which has no existence in reality. It is mere an illusion like hallucination. The image of creation or mundane world appears as real, but it is illusion because in reality it does not exist. There is only one *Brahma* that is real because it never perishes. Except *Brahma* whatsoever appears like existence is not existence because their appearance is not permanent. It is all due to *Maya* of the *Brahma*. The creatures from the beginning have been trapped in this vast net of *Maya*. The Vedas teach people how to liberate from such bondage of *Maya* and return back to the immortal place reaching that no one comes down to the mundane world. That is called salvation. In other words, Vedas describes not only the nature of *Brahman*, but also presents the ways to the mankind for revival and liberation. *Karmakandas* prescribed in the Vedas or Vedic literature are the means to please various gods and goddesses to satisfy the longings of man. While practicing *karmakandas* a man comes to realise the divine significance and ultimately he inclines towards the power of ultimate resource. His desires are satisfied gradually by performing sacrifices and his knowledge as well as wisdom develops to such an extent that he gradually lands into the land of God where there is neither ignorance nor bondage. He learns from the Vedas and its appendages like Sruti, Smriti, Puranas and Upanishads, etc, the glories of God. That makes him pure and fit for grasping divine knowledge that results in devotion to God. He realizes his true nature (soul) and establishes close link with God and obtains His blessing. At such stage of his spiritual development his illusion disappears; and he develops the qualities that put him in the divine land that is immortal, perfect, pure, free from all types of pains like birth, death, diseases, scarcity, old age, etc. This is the place that stands above the land of destruction. Here, there is neither *Maya* nor ignorance. If there is anything, that is divine rays of non-manifested *Brahman* that never ends. It is *Sanatana* (without beginning and end), full of divine bliss, illuminated without suns and moons, and beyond the approach of *Maya*. Thus, the Vedas and their appendages help one to realize his soul and its nature and its relationship with God and adopt the devices to emancipate himself from the bondage of *Maya* and ignorance. The Vedas present nature of God and explains advent of creation of the world, its qualities and nature and also relationship between spiritual as well as material worlds.

Religion, in fact, is related to divine knowledge. A religion is divine reflection that is established by God's messengers,

God's incarnation, saints, sages, sheers, prophets, viewers, etc, who penetrates into the inner depth of reality, and lay down the right order for betterment of human life. According to *Encyclopedic Dictionary of Society*, religion "is a system of belief, practice and philosophical values concerned with definition of the sacred, the comprehension of life, and salvation from the problem of human existence."[19] Man from beginning has been curious to answer the questions like, what is universe?, who created it?, what is the purpose of human life? How to get rid of worldly pains and miseries? In that course of research religion that tries to understand the root cause of creation and its systems of working people established religious traditions expressing firm as well as unshakable faith in Supreme Power. Religious traditions are the results of man's attempt to capture and enshrine his philosophical and spiritual insights so that they are available to individuals who face life and its stresses, confusion and complexities.

Again, "religion is a social phenomenon because it necessarily stresses fellowship in the development, teaching and perpetuation of religious insights and Knowledge."[20] Religion deals with concept of supernatural or path of salvation. Observing the transitory life circle of beings and non-beings on the earth and also uncertainty of life, propounders of religion searched out the ways and means to get rid of circle of birth and death. It is religion that helps mankind to obtain salvation. The Hindu religion that is called Sanatana Dharma (having neither beginning nor end) is a people's belief and practice towards their concepts of all that is beyond man's own power and mundane knowledge. Mandelbaum, an American anthropologist, talks of two aspects of religion – transcendental which is ultimate and universal gods and annual cyclical rites known by priests who are acknowledged to be the reservoirs of religious wisdom and learning. In India religion that is also known as Dharma is a concept developed out of the notion of *Rita* in the *Rigveda* which means right order and harmony in the cosmos and in the human world. In the human world it includes moral order. The Dharma that is duty is needed in the life of an individual and also in the society so that no one may deviate from the duty that has been endowed upon him according to his nature.

According to *Shrimad Bhagavatam* (6/11/40) religion means to obey duties prescribed in Vedas. According to *Vishwamitra Smriti*, the duties which are appraised and approved by the self-enlightened Aryans are Dharmas, and condemned as well as rejected duties are *Adharmas*. In the Hindu religion the world synonymous to Dharma is *punya* (pious duty and justice) which are mentioned in the Vedas and other religious scriptures. The inspiration and commands mentioned in these scriptures are religious, to be performed and followed without suspicion. According to Manu (*Manu Smriti* 2/6) and *Yajnavalkya Smriti* (11/13), Vedas, Puranas, religious scriptures, Mimamsas and code of conducts established by learned saints who are specialists of Vedas are sources of religion. Again, the Shanti Parva of the *Mahabharata* says that the authority, according to which the whole of creation is active and protected, is religion. According to the *Narayana Upanishad*, Dharma is the base of whole of the world's existence. Dharma, in fact, is the root of pleasure and happiness. According to the *Bhagavad Gita*, "He who relinquishing path shown by scriptures, follow his own independently, never attains perfection, pleasure and salvation." Since Dharma upholds the universe and keeps it constantly active, it is the divine force that has its root in *Brahmajyoti* (divine light) which never perishes or disappear. So, Santantan Dharma is eternal. It is Dharma that is the base of creation. It is a godly force. Dharma keeps one object separate from another on the one hand, and leads the objects towards progress and ultimately to perfection (salvation) on the other.

Religious faith in God generates mental and moral attitude in the individual or in a community devoted to religion. Religion affects human conducts and behaviours to make the people generous, noble, complacent, pure, kind and benevolent. Though a religion has been criticized by many observing the evil forces that emerged through a religion, its sanctity and sagacity cannot be denied. If a religion is followed in right perspective, it is still the viable means to make man morally high, spiritually developed and behaviourally better. The people, having complete faith in religion, follow the path of the life which is linked to the goal of perfection and salvation. The base of a religion is strict discipline, control of wild emotion and sentiments suppress unquenchable desires and uproot egoist tendencies. It leads one towards the path of sacrifice, satisfaction with minimum, universal brotherhood and compassion for the poor, troubled, disabled and week creatures. Violence has no place at all in a religion. Self-restraint, self-sacrifice and life of simplicity are the basic criteria of a true religion. Religion has been playing the role from the beginning to make man civilized teaching him the significance of non-violence and universal brotherhood. It calls upon its followers to devoid all sorts of deceits, violent acts and their evils. In short, religion does not permit dual personality. Rather it shows man the mirror of self in which one recognizes his real personality that has been covered by countless layers of ignorance (*avidya*) and selfishness. Every religion of the world puts emphasis on honesty, sincerity, simplicity, kindness, non-violence, love for humanity, sympathy for poor and sufferers, and universal brotherhood. Religion, in fact, teaches man to follow the life of sanctity and sagacity. It is the subject of inner-consciousness and property of each individual. The Vedic religion is the richest having all the attributes said above. It makes man pure, kind, merciful, benevolent, self-controlled, self-disciplined, truthful, and honest.

Advent and growth of Indian culture and civilization is not at random. Rather it is rooted in Vedic knowledge. The early Indo-Aryans lived and moved in groups like tribal people, no doubt, but their understanding and ways of living were very much different from other early peoples. The culture and civilization founded and developed by early Indo-Aryans were unique and imitable because of the reasonable ethos and values of civilization. In general parlance, culture is adopted habits and traditions that help people to grow and prosper in right direction preparing the fertile ground for emergence of powerful state or nation based on the habit of well-established administrative system along with justice. It also comprise of education, economic system, judicial provision and social stratification. The early Aryan civilization was based on Sanskritisation where religious as well as philosophical literature played greater role to establish cultural values. The root of ancient cultural civilization of the Aryans was so strong that even the arrival of westernisation along with the imperial rule in India could hardly erode Hindu civilization. Cultural change means changes in customs, cultural ethos, social relationship, social structure, religious faith, habits, traditions etc. In India with powerful flow of Muslim invasions and Western civilization along with Christian faith, Sanatana Dharma stood firm like a rock because of its strong base. Nothing could deter the Hindu faith from their Vedic religion, culture and civilization. It is true that the flow of Western culture influenced Indian old culture to a considerable amount of changes especially in the field of education, dress, living style, code of laws and justice, administrative system, etc, but so far the case of the Hindu's traditional habits and religious faith is concerned, it remained little affected. It is all because the faith and love of people of India in Vedic knowledge and Vedic religious philosophy were so affectionate and great that they thought it wise to remain committed to their own religion, culture and civilization rejecting new changes.

According to Max Weber, emphasis on formal rationality, experimentation, codification, verification and rational utilitarian orientation in behaviour and thought are some of the unique qualities of Western cultural tradition. India adopted Western cultural traits, tools and changes in the habit of life styles. Cultural structures are education, law, science, technology, new form of politicization, urbanization, industrialization, etc. India, coming in close contact with Western culture and civilization could not remain uninfluenced in these directions, no doubt, but the faith of the Indian people especially of Hindus could not be changed in the field of social stratification, caste system, religious belief and philosophical knowledge.

Social structure of an indigenous culture deeply rooted in traditional values changes when a form of cultural response involves attributes which are basically universalistic and evolutionary. They are pan-humanistic trans-ethnic and non-ideological. An indigenous tradition of faith is affected by a powerful higher order of culture and civilization. Since Indian ancient culture and civilization were universalistic in nature and superior in status, the current of Westernization failed to impose Western civilization on the people of India. The faith of people in their ancient Sanskrit literature could not be removed despite the external efforts to destroy it. Social structure based on *varna* system which put emphasis on quality, not birth, as the base of the four *varnas*, could not change. Faith and in the procedures of worshipping them are still in practice among each Hindu household. The faith of the Hindus in the doctrine of birth, rebirth, death, salvation, etc, is yet unchanged. Ethical conducts of the people have deteriorated, no doubt, but it has not been uprooted.

Notes and References

1. Ramachandra Ghosh, 1988, *History of Hindu Civilization*, Kaúshal Prakashan, New Delhi, p 2.
2. Ibid.
3. *Bhagavad Gita*, 7/6.
4. Ibid, 7/10.
5. Ibid, 7/7.
6. *Matsya Purana*, 2-3/25-26.
7. *Shiva Purana, Rudra Samhita*.
8. *Shrimad Bhagvad Purana*, 4-7/50-54.
9. *Vishnu Purana*, 1/17/84.
10. Spencer, HS, 1965, *The Aryan Ecliptic Cycle*, Poona, pp 15-16.
11. *Encyclopedia of Society*, Sharma, BB (ed), Vol IV, New Delhi, p 786.
12. Mandelbaum, quoted in Giriraj Gupta (ed), *Main Currents of Indian Society*, Vol V, *Religion in Modern India*, New Delhi, 1983, Introduction p VIII.
13. Mandelbaum, "Transcendental and Pragmatic Aspects of Religion", IV, *American Anthropology*.
14. Giriraj Gupta, *Main Currents in Indian Society*, Vol V, *Religion in Modern India*, Introduction p IX.
15. Ibid.
16. Ramachandra Ghosh, op cit, p 2.
17. *Bhagavad Gita*, 10/21.
18. Ibid, 10/22-23.
19. *Encyclopedia of Society*, Sharma, BB (ed), Vol IV, New Delhi, pp 786-87.
20. Ibid, p 786.

Bibliography

Original Sources

Rigveda
Yajurveda
Samaveda
Atharvaveda
Matsya Purana
Visnu Purana
Chhandogya Upanishad
Brihadarnyaka Upanishad
Bhagavad Gita
Shatapatha Brahmana, XI
Shvetashvatara Upanishad
Shiva Purana
Vayu Purana
Kathopanishad
Taittiriya Upanishad
Mandukya Upanishad
Shrimad Bhagavad Purana
Smritis, Srutis, Puranas and *Upanishads*.

Books

Agrawal, BS, 1953, *India as Known to Panini*, Lucknow.

Allchin, R, 1955, *The Birth of Indian Civilization*, Hrmondsworth.

Ambedkar, BR, 1938, *Who are Non-Touchable?*, Delhi.

_______, 1916, *Who are Shudras?* Bombay.

Anderson, B, 1983, *Imagined Communities*, Verso.

Anthalyes, DV, *Swami Vivekananda: A Study*, New Delhi, 1975.

Aurobindo, Sir, 1949, *Essays on the Gita*, Calcutta, p 326.

Balaram Srivastava, 1968, *Trade and Commerce in Ancient Times* (from earliest time to 300 AD) Varanasi.

Banerjee, *Dialogue on Hindu Philosophy*.

Bapat, PY (ed), 1959 in *2500 Years of Buddhism*, Publications Division, Ministry of Information and Broadcasting, Government of India, New Delhi (sixth reprint).

Basham, AL, 1954, *The Wonder That was India*, London.

Bougle, C, 1971, *Essays on the Caste System*, Cambridge.

Chakravarty, HP, 1966, *Trade and Commerce of Ancient India* (200-650 BC), Calcutta.

Chandrika Singh, 2008, *Paramatma ka Sachha Swarup aur Mukti ke Marga* (Hindi), Janki Prakashan, Patna.

Chanana, Deoraj, 1960, *Slavery in Ancient India*, Delhi.

Chattopadhyaya, DP, 1964, *Indian Philosophy*, New Delhi.

Das Gupta, SN, 1947, *A History of Sanskrit Literature*, Calcutta.

Desai, PB, 1957, *Jainism in South India*, Sholapur.

Deussen, P, 1906, *The Philosophy of the Upanishads*, Edinburgh.

Dutt, BN, 1944, *Studies in Indian Social Polity*, Calcutta.

Dutt, RCA, 1989-90, *History of Civilization in Ancient India* (based on Sanskrit Literature), 3 volumes, Calcutta.

Elphinston, M, 1941, *The History of India*, London.

Encyclopaedia Britannica, 2004, Nirvana.

Ghosh, JC, 1902, *Brahminism and Shudra*, Calcutta

Gordon, DH, 1958, *The Prehistoric Background of Indian Culture*, Bombay

Ghurye, GS, 1950, *Caste and Class in India*, Bombay.

Giriraj Gupta (ed), 1983. *Main Currents in Indian Society*, Vol V, *Religion in Modern India*, New Delhi.

Mandelbaum, D, 1970, *Society in India*, Bombay.

Havel, 1975, *The History of Aryan Race in India*, New Delhi

Hegel, F, 1974, *Lectures on the Philosophy of History*, London.

Held, GI, 1935, *The Mahabharata: An Ethnological Study*, London.

'Hindus', in *Encyclopaedia Britannica*, Vol 8, pp 888.

Hille, Brandt A, 1986, "Brahmana and Shudras", Festschrift Karl Weinhold, Breslau.

Hopkins, EW, 1981, *Mutual Relations of the four Castes in Manu*.

_______, EW, 1901, *India Old and New*, New York.

Iyengar, KBR, 1949, *Aspects of the Social and Political System of Manu Smriti*, Lucknow.

Jayatilleke, KN, 1963, *Early Buddhist Theory of Knowledge*, London.

Jayaswal, KP, 1924, *Hindu Polity*, Calcutta.

_______, 1932, *Some Aspects of the Hindu View of Life according to Dharma Shastra*, Baroda.

Johnson's *Oriental Religions*.

Kane, PY, 1942, *History of Dharma Shastra*, Poona.

Kosambi, DD, 1956, *An Introduction to the Study of Indian History*, Bombay.

_______, 1966, *Culture and Civilization of Ancient India*, London.

Law, BC, 1941, *India as Described in Early Texts of Buddhism and Jainism*, London.

Lyall, A, 1889, *Asiatic Studies*, London.

Majumdar, RC and others, 1978 (4th edition) *An Advanced History of India*, Macmillan, Delhi, p 24.

Majumdar, RC, 1918, *Corporate Life in Ancient India*, Calcutta

_______, 1986, *Ancient India*, Motilal Banarsidass, Delhi.

McCrindle, JW, 1877, *Ancient India as Described by Megasthenes and Arrian*, London.

Max Muller, 1883, *India: What Can It Teach Us?*, London.

Max Muller, *Chips from a German Workshop*, I, p 38.

Max Muller, *Lectures on the Science of Language*, II,

Max Muller, *Hibbert Lectures*.

Mill, J, 1820, *The History of India* (two volumes), London.

———, 1811, *History of British India*, London.

Mitra, SK, 1920 (trans) *The Social Organization in North East India in Buddhist Time*, Calcutta.

Mukherjee, DP, 1645, *On Indian History: History and Method*, Bombay.

Oxford English Dictionary, 1991. Vol XIII (2nd edition), RW Burchfield (ed), New York, pp 568-69.

Pande, GC; *The Origin of Buddhism*.

Pargiter, FE, 1922, *The Ancient Indian Historical Traditions*, London.

Pathak, VS, 1966, *Ancient Historians of India*, London.

Pandey Rajváli, 1986, *Hindu Samskar* (Hindi), Motilal Banarsidass, Delhi.

Poliakov, L, 1974, *The Aryan Myth*, New York.

Pravesh Saxena, 2012, *Bharatiya Darshan Men Kya Hai* (Hindi), Hindulogy Books, New Delhi.

———, *Vedon Men Kya Hai* (Hindi), Hindulogy Books, New Delhi.

Radhakrishnan, S, 1953, *The Principal Upanishads*, London.

Radhakrishnan, 1929, *History of Indian Philosophy*, London, George Allen and Unwin.

Rajaram Patil, DK, 1986, *Cultural History from Vayu Purana*, Motilal Banarsidass, Delhi.

Ramachandra Ghosh, 1988, *The History of Hindu Civilization*, Kaushal Prakashan, Delhi.

Raja Rammohun Roy, *Introduction to the Abridgment of the Vedas*.

Risley, HH, 1908, *The People of India*, London.

Thapar, Romila, 2009 (12th impression), *Interpreting Early India*, Oxford University Press, New Delhi.

Sarkar, SB, 1928, *Some Aspects of Earliest Social History of India*, London.

Sastry, Alladi Mahadeva (trans.), *Commentary of Sri Shankaracharya on the Bhagvat-Gita*, Samta Books, Madras, 2007.

Sharma, BB (ed), *Encyclopedic Dictionary of Society*, Vol 4, New Delhi, p 786.

Sharma, BB (ed), *Encyclopedia of Society*, Vol IV, New Delhi pp 786, 1994.

Smith Vincent, A, 1908, *Early History of India*, Oxford, London.

Sharma, RS, 1959, *Some Economic Aspects of the Caste System in Ancient India*, New Delhi.

———, 1968, *Shudras in Ancient India*, Delhi.

———, 1969, *Changes in Early Medieval India*, Devraj Chanana Memorial Lecture.

Spencer, HS, 1965, *The Aryan Ecliptic Cycle*, Poona.

Sengupta, P, 1974, *The Story of Women in India*, New Delhi.

Speech of Swami Vivekananda at Flora Hall of Colombo on 16th January 1897.

Srinivas, MN, 1952, *Religion and Society Among the Coorgs of South India*, Oxford.

Subbarao, NS, 1911, *Economic and Political Condition in Ancient India*, Madras.

Shundo Tachibana, *Ethics of Buddhism*, Colombo: The Buddha Sahitya Sabha, 1943.

Swamiji's Return to India, booklet published by Ramakrishna Mission Institute of Culture, Calcutta, 2009, p 14.

Thapar, Romila, *Interpreting Early India*, Oxford, New Delhi.

———, 1975, *The Past and Prejudice*, New Delhi.

Tripathi, RS, 1986, *History of Ancient India*, Motilal Banarsidass, Delhi.

Upadhyaya, Bhagvatsharan, 1961, *Guptkal ka Sanskritik Itihas* (Hindi), Lucknow.

Weber, M, 1958, *The Religion of India*, London.

———, 1976, *The Agrarian Sociology of Ancient Civilization*, London.

———, 1965, *The Sociology of Religion*, London

Wittfogel, K, 1957, *Oriental Despotism*, New Haven.

Warder, AK, 1972, *An Introduction to Indian Historiography*, Bombay.

Articles

Bailey, HW, "Iranian Arya and Daha", *Transaction of the Philological Society*, London, 1959, pp 71-91.

Barth, *Religions of India*, p 25.

Bose, NK, 1953, "The Hindu method of tribal absorption," in *Cultural Anthropology and Other Essays*, Calcutta.

Dasgupta, "The Myth of India's Unity", in *The Statesman*, Calcutta, August 15, 1990.

Dales, GF, 1965, "New Investigation at Mohenjo-Daro", *Archaeology*.

Leopold, J, "British Applications of the Aryan Theory of Race to India", 1850-70, *The English Historical Review*, 1874, pp 578-603.

Hopkins, EW, 1899 "Position of Ruling Caste in Ancient India", *Journal of the American Oriental Society*, VIII.

Ketkar, SV, "The Basis of the Indian History", *Journal of the American Oriental Society*, LXXV, New Haven, USA, 1955.

Lambrick, HT, 1967, "The Indus Flood-plain and the Indus Civilization", *Geographical Journal*, pp 483-95.

Mandelbaum, "Religion in Modern India", in Giriraj Gupta (ed), *Main Currents in Indian Society*, New Delhi, 1983, Introduction, p VIII.

Maheep Singh, "Guru Nanak: Bridge Across all Paths", *The Times of India*, 14th November, 2000.

Mandelbaum, "Transcendental and Pragmatic Aspects of Religion", in *American Anthropologists*.

Prabhakar Mishra, "The Doctrine of Selflessness (*Sarvam Anataman*)" in Rabindra Pant (ed), *Buddhism in Universal Perspective*, 2001, Nava Nalanda Mahavihara, Bihar, p 61.

Raikes, RL, "The end of the ancient cities of the Indus", *American Anthropologist*, 1964 66(2), pp 284-99.

Romila Thapar, "Genealogy as a Source of Social History", in *Ancient Indian Social History: Some Interpretations*, New Delhi, 1976, pp 326-60.

Sarat, Jhingrau, 1996, "Religional Communalism", in B Bidawai, H Mukhia and A Vanaik (eds), *Religion, Religiosity and Communalism*, New Delhi, p 62

Sharma, AVN, "Decline of Harappa Culture: A Relook", in KN Shastri's Felicitation Volume, Madras, 1971.

Singh, G, "The Indus Valley Culture", *Archaeology and Physical Anthropology in Oceans*, 1971 6(2), pp 177-89.

Shrikant Singh, "Zen Buddhism", in Pant, RB (ed), *Buddhism in Universal Perspective*, Nava Nalanda Mahavihara, Bihar, 2001, pp 203-04.

Stein, B, 1968, "Social Mobility and Medieval South Indian Hindu Sects", *Comparative Studies in Society and History*, Suppl 3, pp 78-94.

———, "The Study of Society in Ancient India", in *Ancient Indian Social History: Some Interpretations*, 1978, pp 211-39.

Thapar, Romila, "The Study of Society in Ancient India", in *Ancient Indian Social History: Some Interpretations*, 1978, pp 211-39.

———, 1976, "Genealogy as a source of Social History", in *Ancient Indian Social History: Some Interpretations*, pp 326-60.

———, "The Ramayana: Themes and Variations", in Mukherjee, SN (ed), *India: History and Thought*, Calcutta, 1982, pp 221-53.

———, "Renunciation: The Making of a Counter Culture", in *Ancient Indian Social History: Some Interpretations*, Delhi, 1978, pp 63-104.

———, "The Image of the Barbarian in Early India", in *Ancient Indian Social History*, pp 152-92.

Upendra Thakur, 1986, "Buddhism in Bihar: Past and Present", in PN Ojha (ed), *Homage to Bhikhu Jagadish Kashyap*, published by Nava Nalanda Mahavihara, Bihar.

Index